Leadership in 19th Century Africa

Essays from Tarikh

DATE DUE			

Leadership in 19th Century Africa

Essays from Tarikh

Editor:

Professor Obaro Ikime

University of Ibadan, Nigeria

with a Foreword by

Professor J. F. Ade Ajayi

Vice-Chancellor, University of Lagos Nigeria
and President, the Historical Society of Nigeria

and a Preface by

Professor J. B. Webster

Dalhousie University, Nova Scotia, Canada

Published for the
Historical Society of Nigeria

by Longman
and in the United States by Humanities Press

Longman Group Limited
London

Associated companies, branches and
representatives throughout the world.

Distributed in the United States and Canada
by Humanities Press, 171 First Avenue,
Atlantic Highlands, New Jersey 07716 U.S.A.

First published 1974

ISBN 0 582 60893 7

U.S. ISBN 0 391 00357–7

PRINTED AND BOUND IN ENGLAND BY
HAZELL WATSON AND VINEY LTD
AYLESBURY, BUCKS

Contents

Acknowledgements

The publishers are grateful to the following for permission to reproduce photographs:

The Mansell Collection for page 27; Cambridge University Press for page 90; East African Publishing House for pages 93 and 101; Hutchinson Publishing Group Ltd. for page 100; E. C. Tabler: *The Far Interior*, Cape Town, 1955, for page 138; E. Sik: *The History of Black Africa*, Vol. 1, Budapest, 1966, for page 139; Rhodesian National Archives for page 147; T. W. Baxter and R. W. S. Turner: *Rhodesian Epic*, Howard Timmins, Cape Town, 1966, for page 148; E. J. Alogoa: *The Small Brave City States*, Ibadan and Wisconsin, 1965, for page 154; R. Rotberg: *A Political History of Tropical Africa*, Harcourt, Brace, and World, 1915, for page 161; Nigeria Magazine for page 165; Weidenfeld and Nicolson for page 174.

The publishers are unable to trace the Copyright holders of the remaining photographs, and would be grateful for any information enabling them to do so.

Foreword

The Historical Society of Nigeria has always regarded the publication of *Tarikh* as one of its most important services to the study of African history. *Tarikh* is, indeed, an essential complement to the *Journal of the Historical Society of Nigeria*. Whereas the *Journal* is directed mainly to other professional historians and scholars, *Tarikh* is an attempt by professional historians to hold a dialogue with the wider public, and to communicate the results of recent research and the insights gained from ongoing research to a general readership, particularly the upper forms of secondary schools, first year university undergraduates, and teachers in secondary schools and teacher training colleges. In *Tarikh*, scholars are challenged to say exactly what they mean without the use of technical jargon they might otherwise employ in presenting the same information to other scholars and professional colleagues.

The subject of biography, through which this volume approaches the history of the African continent in the nineteenth century, is a rewarding one. It highlights the subtle ways in which the circumstances and events of history shape personalities, and how strong personalities and leaders help to make history. All the leaders treated are, in a real sense, men of their times and societies. At the same time, their character and activities have given the history of nineteenth-century Africa its special flavour and direction. Biography is a particularly fruitful introduction to the study of the history of any society, movement or period. It adds the perspective of the individual to the interest inherent in the confrontation of ideologies and events, and of chance and design. The impersonal forces and factors of history become meaningful in relation to a human being with whom the reader can all the more easily identify.

This volume of biographical studies has the further merit of drawing attention to several African leaders of stature whose life work might have been in danger of being forgotten, underrated or misunderstood. The volume contains a judicious mixture of different types of leadership. Indeed, the variety revealed in this sample of African leaders suggests that in the nineteenth century and, as we believe, in other centuries as well, Africa produced men comparable with leaders in other continents in their capacities and worth relative to their environment and the problems and challenges they faced.

The Historical Society of Nigeria is pleased to offer this work as an extension of the service being rendered by *Tarikh* to the students of African history, and to all who have an interest in the history of human beings and their problems.

University of Lagos,
March 1974.

J. F. Ade Ajayi,
President, Historical Society of Nigeria.

Preface

Leadership may come from a recognised royal house which for centuries has provided the rulers of a people, or less frequently it may come from outstanding commoners. Opportunities for the abilities of commoners arise during times of crisis when traditional rulers fail to inspire confidence among the people. The nineteenth was a crisis century for Africa and many of Africa's greatest leaders were either commoners or men whose claims to legitimacy were in some doubt. Kabalega was the son of a servant woman, Theodore's mother a lowly street seller, Shaka's mother, an outcast, Jaja was of slave origins, and Ali a foreign soldier.

Most of these leaders came to power in times of crisis and through violent opposition to the 'aristocratic establishment'; Ali against the Mameluks, Theodore against the Rases, Jaja and Kabalega against the Pepple and Babito royal establishments respectively. Most of them came to power by appealing directly to the populace over the heads of the traditional king-maker class; many of them fell before an alliance of the traditional aristocracy and the incoming Europeans. It was the traditional aristocracy which stood and cheered when the British marched in and ended the careers of Theodore, Kabalega and Jaja, and the Turkish establishment which egged on the European powers to halt the revolutionary policies of Muhammad Ali.

A commoner must possess something extra to appeal to the populace. He does not enjoy legitimacy. His rise to power must arouse sentiments and groups of people to active support. In modern times there has been much discussion of charisma in leadership. No author in this series has discussed charisma. Nevertheless leaders such as Shaka, Samori and Kabalega possessed it, using their influence over people to create national unity and become a 'living legend' in the traditions of their people.

Most of the leaders discussed here can be considered nationalists in that they tried to create new political unities, new nations. Shaka, Moshesh and Kimweri created new states, Maba, Samori and Abdel Kader sought to do so but were frustrated in their efforts. Muhammad Ali, Menelik and Kabalega sought to revitalise ancient nations. Generally they could be divided into conservative pragmatists and radical idealists, particularly in their dealings with their paramount problem, the alien intrusion and penetration of their societies. The conservatives sought to maintain national sovereignty by all means short of war. In many cases when they discovered that they had few options if war was ruled out, they worked to negotiate the best settlement possible with the Europeans. The Pepples of Bonny, the elite of the Sokoto Caliphate, Moshesh, Lobengula and Ovonramwen were good examples; the latter two kings not being given enough room to negotiate a submission with any degree of dignity. Both Lobengula and Ovonramwen give the impression of having been forced into military action against their own better judgements.

They were caught between intractable Europeans and inflexible domestic political forces.

Both Menelik and Koko found themselves in similar circumstances to Lobengula and Ovonramwen. But Menelik and Koko had shown themselves more accommodating to the European presence than either Lobengula or Ovonramwen. Menelik had offered the European powers many concessions, Koko had adopted Christianity. All four leaders might well have been looked upon as conservatives and collaborators had the Europeans not forced them into military action. They have become heroes because they resisted, but in reality all of them were reluctant resisters.

European armies did not march into the heart of Africa at the invitation of the progressives but rather over the resistance of the innovators. In most cases Europeans came to the support of the conservatives, the 'legitimate' rulers, the powerful families of past decades whose grip on power was rapidly loosening in the late nineteenth century. However, this does not suggest that all resisters were in fact radical innovators. The cases of Menelik, Koko, Lobengula and Ovonramwen have shown that this was not so. Colonial administrators and imperial historians in their concern for Menelik and Lobengula have shown that there was something amiss in European diplomacy which failed to secure collaborative alliances with both of these leaders. It is suggested that these two leaders should have been natural allies, conservative pragmatists predisposed to collaboration.

Apolo Kagwa falls outside this framework. From the external point of view Kagwa was the collaborator *par excellence*, a devout Christian who sought to live in a European style, a man ready to accept British overlordship as long as he and his political faction were installed in power. From a domestic point of view Kagwa in the 1890s was involved in a revolutionary struggle against the autocratic abuses of a despotic establishment. Buganda may then form an exception; a state where imperial forces rode in on the backs of the progressives. However, once the Anglo-Buganda pact was sealed Kagwa rapidly became a conservative and by 1914 he was resisting any further changes in society.

Here lies one of the historian's most intractable problems. How much was the conservative stagnation of colonialism a result of the ideology of African leaders chosen as sub-imperialists at the beginning of the twentieth century and how much was it embedded within the philosophy of colonial rule in general and indirect rule in particular? Even where a Kagwa was the agent, he survived only in so far as he became a pillar of the status quo.

In modern western historiography there has been a tendency to underrate leadership qualities and man's choice. Someone who fails becomes a leader who had to deal with a combination of difficult circumstances. The reader is often left with the feeling that given the context anyone would have failed. On the other hand successful leaders are occasionally given less than their due by the historians' implication that given the trend of events and the climate of opinion of that age, what was necessary for a politician to achieve greatness was merely to ride the tides of public opinion. It tends to a mechanistic interpretation.

Oral tradition in Africa adopts a different approach. Man is the controller of his destiny. Great men are great because they made certain choices and history is moulded by the choices of leaders. Within the last decade no other continent has shown itself as prepared as Africa has been to tear down leadership idols. Africans are less prepared than Europeans to excuse a leader or soften the judgement of history by such phrases as 'he was a victim of circumstances', or 'he accepted unfortunate advice'.

There is, of course, one significant exception and that relates to those African leaders who were unfortunate enough to have to deal with the period of the European conquest. Almost any historian has to admit that the Europeans were determined to conquer Africa and they possessed almost 'supernatural' military superiority. So utterly hopeless was the situation that even should an African army achieve a brilliant military success—as at the Battle of Isandhlwana which one writer has called the most humiliating defeat in the annals of the British army—it was normally the knell of doom. It might be argued that the Zulus are still suffering because they *won* at Isandhlwana. Moshesh has been praised for his understanding of the fact that it was dangerous to defeat the British Empire.

Historians have been almost universally sympathetic with African leaders of the conquest period who had few options, none of them in the least attractive. Those who preferred death or exile to submission have been admired, those who sought to negotiate the least obnoxious terms of surrender have been applauded and those who lifted their hands in hopelessness have been excused. Given the circumstances of the conquest it is difficult to applaud or condemn, to argue that man is an intelligent being in any meaningful manner in control of his destiny.

History as mechanistic forces or history as the rational choice of man has had a larger dimension in Africa. Since the early colonial period and still pervasive in some writing on Africa was the idea that Africans from centuries back did not have the requisite technical achievements to subdue and conquer the natural forces of their continents. Explanations were permeated with geographic or other forms of determinism. It was implied that Europeans to a greater degree than Africans were in control of their destiny.

As long as colonialism was being applauded as a civilising mission, so the Europeans were seen as making moral choices. As colonialism became more universally condemned, then historians began to turn to a more mechanistic interpretation of the conquest. Many historians would now have us believe that the Europeans were impelled into Africa by forces either beyond their understanding or, at least, beyond their control. African historians tend to be sceptical, insisting upon the importance of individual decisions. Do we approach the depressing conclusion that if a nation or leader's policy is adjudged beneficial it is attributed to moral choice, while if it is condemned as oppressive it becomes the working out of economic or other forces beyond his control?

J. B. Webster, Dalhousie University,
Halifax, Nova Scotia, Canada

Introduction

This book, a collection of articles first published in various issues of *Tarikh*, deals with leadership in Africa. Although a few of the figures discussed lived on to the present century, most of them are nineteenth-century figures.

If one were to ask the question, 'What is the significance of the nineteenth century for the history of Africa?' the most likely answer would be that that century witnessed the colonisation of Africa by European powers. Indeed the colonisation of Africa by Europe in the last two decades of the nineteenth century has attained such importance that there are those who see European colonisation of Africa as *the* event of the nineteenth century. Following on that, there are scholars who have argued that the history of Africa in the nineteenth century was essentially a history of African reaction to European penetration. What is more, such scholars regard African reaction as essentially negative. From their viewpoint Africans were no more than passive spectators of the events which shaped the history of their continent in the nineteenth century; it was the Europeans who dictated the pace throughout that period while we Africans did no more than respond to their dictation. This book, it is hoped, will furnish evidence to controvert this assumption. It is important to stress that the idea is not to disprove that African history was influenced by Europe's greater involvement in our affairs in the nineteenth century. All history consists of the interactions of peoples and races and of civilisations and ideas and our history can be no exception. Rather what this book will do, apart from providing different facets of leadership in Africa, is to demonstrate that there were various strands in our history in the nineteenth century and that the issue of African reaction to European pressure was only one strand in a much more complex movement.

The phenomenon of state building

The first part of the book deals with state or empire builders. State building was not a nineteenth-century phenomenon. African history is full of examples of states and empires which rose in response to certain environmental and other stimuli and collapsed when the conditions which brought them into being ceased to exist or proved inadequate to ensure continued existence. The ancient kingdoms and empires of the western and central Sudan owed their existence to control of the trade between North Africa and West Africa. The presence of certain natural resources such as gold, and the facility with which these states obtained slaves for sale to North Africa, Europe and Asia ensured a continuous supply of commodities which could be exchanged for the salt and manufactured goods which came down south from the north. Decline set in whenever trade routes shifted or when the political situation in

North Africa made peaceful trade impossible. The Old Oyo Empire was similarly dependent on trade with her neighbours which enabled her to develop into a strong military power. In the Niger delta in the period before the nineteenth century, long-distance cross-delta trade as well as trade with the hinterland peoples prepared the way for the rise of the famous city-states of the delta. The augmentation of this internal long-distance trade by the overseas trade in slaves merely resulted in the acceleration of the transformation of what started as fishing villages into city-states. A noticeable feature of this transformation was the modification of the political arrangements. Where before the head of each fishing village, the *amaokowei*, was no more than the oldest man in the settlement, now the *Amayanabo* of the city state was deliberately chosen because of his personal qualities, qualities which among other things included the ability to ensure the success of his state in the competition for trade which was a noticeable feature of inter-state relations in the delta. So then, in whichever part of the continent one looks, one finds that states and empires arose in response to certain ascertainable stimuli.

In the nineteenth century, various stimuli led to the rise of various states and empires as had been the case down the ages in Africa as elsewhere. In Southern Africa one of the most decisive factors responsible for the rise of new types of state was population explosion. J. D. Omer-Cooper has stated that 'the eastern coastland of South Africa is' one of the most attractive places for human settlement in the whole of Southern Africa'. Fertile and malaria-free, this area could support a large population. Increasing population led to increased pressure on the land and this produced inter-group conflict for possession and use of available land. Conflict of this type led to the need for a new political system and new military devices that could ensure victory of a lasting nature. New military devices and the need for lasting victory gave a new dimension to warfare in Southern Africa. War became total, requiring that the vanquished be totally wiped out or fully incorporated into the following of the victor. The fear and general insecurity which attended this new concept of war raised a new crop of leaders of men whose primary claim to leadership lay in military prowess which ensured victory. Names like Shaka, Mzilikazi, Moshesh, some of which appear in this collection of essays, were the products of the situation which existed in Southern Africa in the nineteenth century. Although a few misguided scholars have sought to explain the developments which took place in this part of Africa in terms of some European influences, no serious-minded inquirer can fail to see that the states which arose in Southern Africa in the nineteenth century were intrinsically a product of a situation essentially internal to Southern Africa. The chapters on Shaka and the Zulu nation and Moshesh and the Basuto make this conclusion inescapable.

While pressure on available land was resulting in the rise of a new type of leadership and state in southern Africa, other factors were operating in East Africa. There had arisen in that region various states in the period before the nineteenth century. Of these perhaps the best known are the states of the late districts of East Africa. Among other factors, the fertility of the soil of this region played an important part in the rise of states. Agriculture was largely the pursuit of the womenfolk. This left the men free to pursue more active work like hunting for ivory and for slaves. The demand for these commodities in Arabia and other eastern countries stimulated the development of long-distance trade from the lake districts to the coast and this long-distance trade provided the economic base for the states of the lake district. Of these states Bunyoro was the leading one from the late seventeenth century to the eighteenth.

As in the Niger Delta, so in East Africa, the external trade was in fact no more than an intensification of the internal long-distance trade. Perhaps this was best demonstrated in the area which now constitutes Tanzania. There a variety of occupational pursuits—farming, the making of iron weapons and implements and the manufacture of salt—provided the many groups with exchange commodities for long-distance trade among themselves. This long-distance trade was accelerated in the nineteenth century with the increased activities of the Omani Arabs based in Zanzibar. The Arabs were particularly interested in ivory and slaves. The peoples of the Tanzanian mainland responded to the increased demand for ivory and slaves by intensifying their hunting expeditions and slave raids on weaker or hostile neighbours. Inter-group wars became, in the circumstances, one of the noticeable features of East African history in this period. The Arabs by supplying guns and ammunition ensured that these wars took on a new dimension. In addition the new war tactics developed in Southern Africa were exported to these parts. As in Southern Africa, the fact of war threw up a new crop of leaders among whom Mirambo was one of the most famous.

However, increased insecurity was not the only or even main explanation for the rise of new states in East Africa in the nineteenth century. Rather it was the rise of a new elite—big and successful farmers and traders—which began to call for a re-definition of the roles which people played in society. The ritualistic base of authority in earlier years began to give way to authority based on wealth acquired from increased agricultural production and long distance trade. One area in which this produced far-reaching political changes was the Unyanyembe country in present-day Tanzania. The story of Kimweri's rule in the Vuga kingdom which is told in this book is thus no more than a single illustration of a phenomenon that was widespread throughout East Africa not only in the nineteenth century but even earlier.

Nineteenth-century West Africa was deeply affected by two developments. One was the suppression by force of the overseas slave trade. The other was the islamic reformist movements which occurred in the Sudanic belt of West Africa. The first, which had the effect of increasing European activities in West Africa, ultimately led to the collapse of many states in the coastal and forest zones of West Africa. The second had, at least in the period before the new imperialism of the 1880s and 1890s, the very opposite effect, for it saw the rise of various islamic states of which the Sokoto caliphate, the empire of al-Hajj Umar, and Bornu are well known examples. The revival of Islam which produced the jihads out of which these states grew was not a new phenomenon in African history. Indeed the events in West Africa fitted into a wider movement in the Islamic world—the movement which produced, for example, the wahabiyya of Arabia. The degree of commitment to Islam in the different areas varied. Thus there are those who are inclined to argue that the leaders of the Sokoto jihad were more committed to Islam than al-Hajj Umar, for example. However that may be, the fact remains that once these movements got under way various other factors became operative and so transformed them into very complex affairs. This is proved by the two examples treated in this book—Samori Toure and Maba Diakhou Ba. Indeed the description of the latter as 'Scholar-Warrior of the Senegambia' sums up rather admirably the characters of most of the leaders of this type of states in West Africa.

From the above it is hoped that at least two points should have emerged. One, that events in nineteenth-century Africa developed out of situations which ante-dated that century; that there was a certain continuity in African history typified by the rise and fall of states and empires over time. Secondly, varied as the circumstances which produced these states were, there can be no questioning the fact that all of them were the products of responses to prevailing internal African situations. Where contact with Europeans played some part in determining the course events took, this constituted one of a number of factors and not always the most important one. Thus to seek to explain African history in the nineteenth century mainly in terms of European stimulus is to fail to see the basic factors which influenced the thoughts and actions of the Africans of that age. It fails to see the essential factor of continuity in African history.

Reformers and modernisers

The desire for reform in Islam produced a number of Islamic states in West Africa, as was pointed out above. However, it was not, it is true, in every situation that reform called for the creation of a new political entity. Quite often reform had to be carried out within the already established political entity. In all cases, however, reform necessarily meant a modification of existing institutions, the introduction of new ideas and new ways of doing things, a determination to achieve certain definite ends through planned action. Just as different circumstances produced different states, so did the situations out of which reformers arose vary.

In the earlier section we spoke of the rise of different states in the lake districts of East Africa. The very fact that there were a number of states meant on-going competition for primacy. Bunyoro achieved this primacy and held it until the opening years of the nineteenth century. Then she lost it to Buganda. The determination to regain this primacy was the main preoccupation of Kabalega who became ruler of Bunyoro in 1870. To achieve the end in view, however, he had to strengthen the monarchy and the fighting forces. His reforms were thus centred upon these institutions. In Ethiopia further to the north, the reforms begun by Theodore, continued by Yohannes IV and brought to greater fruition by Menelik, were the product of Ethiopia's experience in the one hundred and fifty years before the reign of Theodore. Ethiopia, a once powerful and well-led empire, had fallen into disunity and civil chaos for over a century. Province fought against province and central authority disappeared. This situation of anarchy produced a leader in the person of Theodore who sought to recapture the lost glory of Ethiopia. Theodore saw no other means of achieving unification than the repression of the powerful provincial rulers and the control of church and state. This meant for him the use of force. Force, however, failed to provide a lasting solution, and it was left to later rulers to find an additional if not alternative base for unification. The career of Menelik represents the most successful attempt in this direction.

Geography has always had a profound effect on history. The very geographical location of the states of North Africa has had a tremendous effect on their history down the ages. Thus Egypt at the eastern extremity of the Mediterranean has always been heavily involved with Arabia and various European activities in the Middle Ages of Europe. Separated from Europe only by the Mediterranean sea, this area not surprisingly felt the full impact of the Roman world in its heyday. In addition to pressures from Europe there were pressures from Asia, through Egypt especially after the Arab invasions of the tenth century. North Africa, which as a consequence of these invasions adopted Arab culture and speech, had nevertheless to be constantly aware of Europe just across the Mediterranean. In the nineteenth century, North Africa was subjected to unprecedented European pressure first as a consequence of the Napoleonic wars, then as a consequence of the industrial and technological developments in Europe and finally as a result of the new European imperialism in Africa. The problem which these pressures posed for North Africa was that of survival. Various rulers sought to contain these pressures in different ways. One ruler, however, realised that perhaps the best answer was to seek to meet Europe on equal terms both economically and militarily. He therefore determined to carry out far-reaching reforms in Egypt to make this possible. His name was Muhammad Ali, one of those treated in this book.

Resisters and collaborators

Muhammad Ali's reforms succeeded in preserving the sovereignty of Egypt (in fact if not in law) at any rate for the time being. His successors, however, had to face a Europe increasingly determined, for reasons of European diplomacy and economics, to carve up Africa among its member states. The last two decades of the nineteenth century witnessed the translation of this determination into positive action. The third part of this book deals with selected examples of African reaction to the European push in the age of the scramble and partition. Although the majority of the examples chosen are of persons who fought against European imperialism, there were also a few examples of those who collaborated with the Europeans. Even in states where the rulers took up arms in defence of their sovereignty, it was not unusual to find persons or groups who actively supported the Europeans.

In Lagos, the British bombarded Kosoko to submission with the overt support and blessing of Akintoye, a one-time Oba of Lagos, who had been driven off the throne by Kosoko and who was anxious to regain his throne. In Ghana, the Fante were for most of the nineteenth century allies of the British against their Asante neighbours. In the Tukulor empire there was a constant failure of the African group to come into a coalition against the French push as each group pursued what it saw as its own interests. In East Africa, the competition for primacy in the lake district already referred to, obviously determined the reactions of the various states to the British presence. Thus when Buganda realised that she could use the British to maintain and strengthen her primacy, she threw in her lot with the British against her African neighbours. But within Buganda itself there was a division of interests. The ruler who saw power slipping from his hands put up a fight. The new class of Christian elite which saw itself gaining power from the British presence teamed up with the British against their own ruler. The leader of this new Christian elite, Apolo Kagwa, is one of those treated in this book.

The point to be stressed therefore is that no meaningful study of African reaction to the European imperial thrust is possible without a full knowledge of the internal politics of the African states, knowledge of relations between various African states and knowledge of relations between different groups within individual states. The reactions of rulers and other leaders were always determined by their understanding of their own interests. Europeans were invariably fitted into intra-African feuds and alliances. The politics and diplomacy of European conquest and African resistance must thus be fitted into the politics and diplomacy of pre-scramble Africa.

This book therefore presents to its readers quite a spectrum of leadership in Africa in the nineteenth century. The collection demonstrates the variety of types of leadership which Africa boasted even in a century which, until recently, used to be regarded as a century of European activity and African slumber. It will be noticed that the categorisation is not absolute. Samori Toure belongs to the first as to the last category and shares some of the qualities of those in the second. Moshesh actually appears in two sections of the book, and many of those who are here presented as resisters were reformers before they became resisters. All of this means that our categorisation is essentially one of convenience of presentation. These leaders were all involved in the politics of their time—and politics can hardly be split up and sealed off into watertight compartments. It is our hope therefore that our readers will try to see these leaders in as full a perspective as possible, the categorisation notwithstanding.

Obaro Ikime
University of Ibadan
Ibadan, Nigeria

Shaka and the Rise of the Zulu

J. D. Omer-Cooper

The eastern coastland of South Africa in the area now known as Zululand and Natal is one of the most attractive places for human settlement in the whole of Southern Africa. From a hot and steamy strip along the coast itself the land rises through a series of terraces to the mountains of the Drakensberg range which separate the coastlands from the interior plateau. Winds from the Indian Ocean bring heavy rains in the summer months and numerous rivers and streams run down from the mountains to the sea. The warm waters of the Indian Ocean modify the climate and the area is spared the full bitterness of the southern winters except on the highest lands where snow is not uncommon in July and August.

In this area where the rich grass provides magnificent grazing and the fertile valley soils yield the heaviest crops in all South Africa, numerous tribes of the Nguni-speaking branch of the southern Bantu had their homes. Their ancestors had come down from lands farther to the north, absorbing or expelling the Bushman hunters and Hottentot cattle keepers that they found in the land, but by the late eighteenth century they had been established there for several hundreds of years and some of their fellows had pressed on farther south down the coastal strip to the Great Fish River and the rich lands of the Zuurveld where they encountered white settlers moving inland from the Cape.

Mixed farming

They were a people of mixed farmers. Cattle were their chief possession, the pride and joy of every chief and family head. A man's standing in society depended on the number of cattle he owned and cattle were the only offering acceptable as marriage dowry. In the centre of every settlement there was a cattle enclosure and this was the place where men gathered to talk about politics or settle disputes. So great was the importance of cattle in the life of the people that most of their proverbs contain some reference to them. Perhaps because it was thought so important, cattle herding was usually entirely reserved to men and boys, and it was thought unlucky for women to have much to do with the cattle or enter their enclosure. But though milk was an important item of diet and the hides provided blankets and cloaks, much of the food came from the agricultural work of the women. Millet, pumpkins and other crops were grown and the surplus corn was carefully stored to provide food in the winter months. From the millet corn a mild and healthy beer was made which enlivened social festivities and loosened the tongues of the old men as they sat and gossiped about the events of the day or the doings of neighbours.

Shaka Zulu

From child to man

The people lived in small hamlets scattered about the countryside, little circles of beehive-shaped huts, each with its central cattle byre. Most of these settlements were made up of members of a single family but the villages of chiefs were considerably larger and contained many persons who were not his close relatives. For the children of those days, life was full of excitement. Though they were expected to observe strict rules of politeness in the presence of their elders they spent much of their time with their playmates inventing all kinds of games and amusements. As soon as they were considered old enough the boys began to take part in cattle herding, driving the cattle out to graze on the open veldt and whiling away the time hunting smaller animals, making clay models of cattle and other beasts, running races or wrestling and fighting with one another.

The most important event in any boy's life came when he was old enough to think of taking on the status of manhood. He must then go through the ritual of circumcision and spend a month or more living in a temporary hut of branches away from the village, covering himself with white clay and wearing various distinctive emblems. During this period he would receive instruction on the customs of the tribe and the behaviour expected of a mature man. Then when the period of seclusion was over he would go at dawn to a stream or pond, plunge in and wash off the white clay. At the same time his temporary hut and all the clothing used while he was an initiate would be burnt and he would begin a new life. Boisterous horseplay and the lighthearted flirtations with the sweethearts of his boyhood must now be forgotten. He must marry and establish a family and behave at all times with the grave and dignified demeanour expected of a man.

Clan organisation

The people were organised in fairly small tribes, often largely made up of members of a single clan and containing no more than a few thousand members. Each tribe was politically independent and there were more than a hundred of them in Zululand and Natal alone. At the head of every tribe there was a chief who was the supreme head of the community in every way. He had the last word on all matters of law or policy and he was also the chief religious figure. He even regulated the planting and gathering of the crops and no one could eat any of the new year's harvest till he had held his first-fruits ceremony. But he did not rule as a despot. The tribe was divided into districts, each ruled for the chief by a sub-chief who was usually an important member of the royal family. In addition the chief had a number of officers called *indunas*, one of whom acted as his deputy when he did not want to undertake anything personally and could be likened to a Prime Minister. These indunas were generally chosen from families with no claim to royalty so that they would have no temptation to usurp the throne.

In the day to day conduct of affairs the chief consulted with an informal council of people living at his homestead, usually some senior members of his family, his chief induna and a few close friends or persons with a particular reputation for wisdom. On more important occasions all the district chiefs would be gathered together and the views of all sections of the community considered before a decision was taken. In theory the chief could override the advice of all his councillors but in practice this was an unusual and dangerous procedure as the important councillors were powerful men, often with a claim to the throne. If the chief went against public opinion they might start a civil war or simply break away with their immediate followers and establish themselves as independent chiefs.

Such division of tribes into two or more independent sections was very frequent, for in the malaria-free climate of South Africa where abundant grazing and farming land meant relative freedom from famine, population increased by leaps and bounds. As tribes became too large for easy government they split up. This often happened on the death of a chief, for it was unusual for the succession to be undisputed.

Changing conditions

In time the continual growth of population brought about a very different type of development, for grazing land began to become scarce and quarrels between tribes more frequent and serious. Previously wars had been minor affairs, cattle raids and skirmishes engaged in more from a spirit of adventure than a desire for conquest, but towards the end of the eighteenth century they began to take on a new character. Three great leaders emerged who thought of bringing large numbers of tribes under their control and creating tribal empires. One of these was Sobhuza, leader of a people who later became known as the Swazi. Another was Zwide, chief of the Ndwandwe tribe, one of the largest and most powerful in Zululand. The third was Dingiswayo, the famous chief of the Mthethwa.

As these rulers rose to prominence and wars became frequent and severe, the traditional initiation ceremonies could not be carried out without danger to the tribe. The newly circumcised youths could not take part in fighting and were in a very vulnerable position in case of an enemy attack. At the same time there was need for improved military organisation. Several tribes began to abandon the old customs and (using an idea which may have been borrowed in part from the neighbouring Sotho-speaking tribes of the interior plateau) to use the system of grouping by age which went with the initiation ceremonies as the basis of a new kind of military system. Instead of undergoing the normal ceremonies youths on the threshold of manhood would be gathered together and formed into a regiment with its own distinctive name. Thereafter they would be expected to fight together as a unit whenever need arose.

The unwanted child

It was while these developments were going on that a young man was growing up who was to change the history of most of South Africa and much of central Africa. His father, the chief of what was then a very unimportant tribe called the Zulu, had a sweetheart called Nandi from a neighbouring tribe. The chief was still an uncircumcised boy at the time and the elders were shocked to get the news that the girl was pregnant. They sent a message to her people that it must be a mistake and that an insect called U-Shaka was the cause of her swollen condition. When the child was born it was a boy, who came to be known by the name U-Shaka. It was a good name, for Shaka's whole personality and career were influenced by the fact that he was an unwanted, unrecognised child. His father, it is true, did marry Nandi but the marriage was unhappy. The lady had an uncontrollable temper and once slapped one of her husband's senior councillors. So she was driven away to take refuge with her own people. There Shaka spent a very unhappy childhood. He annoyed his playmates by his arrogant attitude and his insistence that he was the son of a chief, and as his father was not there to protect him they mocked and bullied him without mercy. So he grew up with a deep and bitter determination to prove his superiority and exercise power over men; a determination which made him careless of his own life and indifferent to the sufferings of others.

In the service of Dingiswayo

As a first step to fortune he joined Dingiswayo's forces and by his reckless bravery won himself a place of favour in the great chief's councils. But he found the warfare and policies of Dingiswayo too mild and badly organised for his liking. The regiments only assembled in full force from time to time when there was a campaign to be fought. They were armed with long-handled throwing spears, the traditional weapon for hunting as well as war. This meant that when a warrior had thrown his spear he was bound to retire from the front line. Battle could not be fought in orderly formation. They were very disorganised affairs which generally did not result in defeating the enemy very severely. Dingiswayo's policy towards the tribes he conquered was also rather gentle. He hoped to establish peaceful conditions by bringing many peoples to acknowledge his paramountcy, but he allowed those who accepted his authority a very great deal of autonomy and he did not seek to destroy his enemies completely. When his army returned from a successful campaign with booty of cattle he would keep only the oxen and send the cows back to the conquered people. Shaka saw that if instead of throwing their spears the warriors kept hold of them, advancing right up to the enemy and fighting hand to hand, a much more organised type of warfare would be possible. The regiment could move in an ordered line protecting itself behind linked shields until it came face to face with the foe. If they had disarmed themselves by throwing their spears they would be completely massacred. He also despised the easy-going attitude of Dingiswayo to conquered tribes. They should be brought under strict control or crushed completely, not left to gather strength to fight another day.

New tactics

His opportunity came when his father died and the Zulu needed a new chief. Shaka was not the rightful heir but he used his position at Dingiswayo's court to get the support of a *Mthethwa* regiment and with this he easily made himself the ruler of his father's people. He was then in a position to put his ideas into practice. One of his first acts was to give his men a practical demonstration of his new methods. He divided them into two groups each armed with reeds and made them fight a mock battle, one group throwing their weapons in the traditional way, the other holding them fast to use as stabbing weapons. The experiment was a complete success and thereafter the new methods were accepted wholeheartedly. This new way of fighting, however, needed careful and prolonged drilling and Shaka was led to introduce another important reform. Instead of the regiments assembling only on the eve of battle they were kept permanently on active service. Shaka thus had a permanent standing army. So long as Shaka remained subordinate to Dingiswayo his ambitious plans were kept within fairly narrow limits, but events were soon to remove this obstacle. The growth of the three tribal empires meant that sooner or later they would come into conflict. The first major struggle was between Sobhuza and Zwide. They fought over some farming land on the banks of the Pongola River, and Sobhuza was defeated. He fled with his people to central Swaziland and there continued his policy of conquering neighbouring tribes to lay the foundations of the present Swazi nation.

Collapse of Dingiswayo's empire

The retreat of Sobhuza left Zwide and Dingiswayo facing one another in central Zululand and in about 1817 war broke out between them. Dingiswayo marched to attack his enemy and sent a message to Shaka to bring his forces in support of his overlord. Some say that Shaka deliberately betrayed Dingiswayo into the hands of the foe; others that he merely arrived too late to affect the course of events. Whatever may be the truth of this matter, Dingiswayo left the main body of his forces to climb a hill from where he could look down on the battlefield. He found that he had walked into a trap and was seized by the Ndwandwe and put to death. The loss of their chief spread panic in the Mthethwa ranks and they dispersed without waiting for the enemy to attack. The empire which Dingiswayo had painfully built up disintegrated overnight.

The Zulu upstart

Zwide had apparently emerged the victor but Shaka still retained his forces intact. Zwide at first paid little attention to this minor vassal of Dingiswayo and Shaka took the opportunity to engage in a series of short campaigns, conquering several tribes and uniting their fighting force with his own. Once this came to Zwide's attention he determined on vigorous action and sent several of his sons with a powerful force to attack the Zulu upstart. In spite of greatly superior numbers the Ndwandwe were unable to defeat the better drilled Zulu regiments and the army was forced to retire, leaving several of the royal princes on the field. Zwide was enraged and later in the same year (1818), he launched a second attack with virtually the whole of his forces.

Faced with this massive invasion Shaka adopted elusive tactics, retreating ever farther into his territory, destroying all the food supplies as he went. At the same time he harried the advancing enemy with surprise night attacks. When the Ndwandwe had nearly reached the southern limits of the Zulu country on the Tugela River without making contact with their foe, hunger forced them to turn back towards their own country. Shaka shadowed them as they retreated painfully northwards until they were on the point of crossing the Mhlatuze River. Then choosing the moment when they were most exposed he threw his fresh and well fed regiments at the weary and half-starved Ndwandwe. A bitter struggle took place around the river but eventually the enemy broke and fled. Shaka had become the dominant power in Zululand.

Flight from Shaka's wrath

After this momentous battle there was no tribe in Zululand or Natal which could hope to stand against the Zulu regiments. The Ndwandwe did indeed find a place of refuge on the upper Nkomati River and recouped their forces until in 1826 they felt strong enough to attempt a comeback and invaded Zululand, but Shaka met them and administered a crushing defeat which broke them up completely. Every year after 1818 the Zulu armies went out on a major campaign. Steadily they extended the sphere of their operations till they had devastated the whole of Natal and passed beyond it to ravage the Pondo of the northern Transkei. The tribes they met were either conquered and absorbed or fled out of reach of the regiments carrying war and devastation to other peoples far from the original centre of disturbance.

After the battle on the Mhlatuse two sections of the Ndwandwe army broke away and fled into southern Mozambique. One, under a leader called Soshangane, built up an empire there; the other, led by Zwangendaba and usually known as the Ngoni, traversed much of modern Rhodesia, destroying the age-old Monomatapa empire on its way and then crossed the Zambesi to throw all east-central Africa into turmoil and establish a whole series of kingdoms in modern Tanzania, Malawi and Zambia.

Other tribes fled across the Drakensberg on to the central plateau. There they threw the Sotho-speaking peoples into confusion, devastating wide areas and causing many tribes to gather together under the leadership of Moshesh to form the modern Basuto nation, while others followed the indomitable Sebetwane on a fantastic journey to establish a kingdom on the flood plains of the upper Zambesi.

Military and political genius

In Zululand Shaka was able to give his military and political genius full rein. The youths of similar age, whether from his own or conquered tribes, were

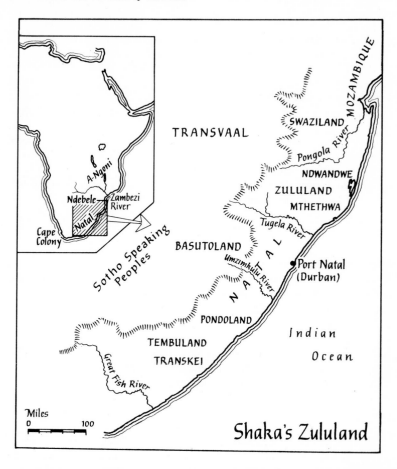

Shaka's Zululand

brought together and formed into regiments each with its own name, shields of a special colour, and other distinctive regalia. They were settled in military towns where they drilled and danced under the authority of officers personally appointed by the king, usually from families with no particular political influence. During their period of service the men were forbidden to marry or to wear the insignia of manhood. They were fed from the produce of the royal herds and regaled on the king's beer. They also received their weapons and other regalia from the ruler's stores.

Each military town was also a royal homestead and contained a section of the royal women. Shaka never officially married but he made himself the guardian of most of the young girls in his kingdom. They were gathered together in hundreds at the military towns and helped with the agricultural work needed to feed the army. They also took part in ceremonial dances, and for this purpose they were organised into age-regiments like those of the men, each with its own name. When Shaka felt that a regiment could be released from service he would dissolve a female regiment also and give its members as brides to the men.

Through this system Shaka was able to develop a new attitude of mind in his followers. As the youths of many different tribes drilled, danced and fought alongside one another, receiving everything from Shaka and reciting his praises at every meal, they came to think of themselves as first and foremost followers of the king, secondly members of particular regiments and only after that as members of a particular tribe or clan.

The system was not entirely perfect; sometimes, especially in the early days of his career, Shaka entrusted military power to persons who were chiefs in their own right. One of these was Mzilikazi, young leader of the Kumalo. About 1821 he took advantage of his position to defy his ruler. He was defeated by the loyal Zulu forces but escaped with his followers on to the interior plateau. He devastated much of the Transvaal in the course of building up a kingdom along Zulu lines. In 1837 after he had been attacked by the Boers of the Great Trek as well as the Zulu regiments of Shaka's successor Dingaan, he fled to modern Rhodesia, where his people the Ndebele (Matabele) still form a powerful element in the population.

Shaka's European vassals

In 1824 Shaka was faced with new problems when a party of English traders managed to land at Port Natal (present Durban) and arrived at his court. The Zulu king saw in the arrival of the traders an opportunity to acquire many useful commodities. He was particularly interested in the military possibilities of their weapons and though he felt that Zulu methods were more effective in mass battles he appreciated that firearms would be invaluable in certain military situations. He also heard from the interpreter Jacob and the traders themselves that the British Government was extremely powerful and he was anxious to remain on good terms with it. He thus gave the traders a privileged position in his kingdom and gave them permission to make use of a wide area around Port Natal which had been devastated by his regiments. The traders were allowed to assemble the remnants of the Natal population as their personal following and to occupy the position of semi-autonomous chiefs within his kingdom. In return he expected the traders to bring him valuable presents, to give him their advice, particularly on anything affecting relations between himself and the British Government at the Cape, and to take part with their followers in his campaigns when called upon.

The traders thus took part in the last battle with the Ndwandwe in 1826 and they also proved helpful on smaller campaigns where the nature of the country made it difficult for his regiments to come to grips with the enemy.

Despotism

The way that Shaka's kingdom was organised left tremendous powers in the hands of the king. The district chiefs who traditionally acted as checks on rulers were no longer in a position to do so as they no longer controlled their fighting men, most of whom were concentrated in the central army. Power had shifted from the traditional chiefs to the military indunas and only the generals were in a position to offer resistance to the royal will. But these were men of little standing. They were not of royal blood and they owed their position to the king. Shaka had no need to summon the old type of council and though he took pains to take the military leaders into his confidence he could always be sure of getting his way. He also discouraged the indunas of different regiments from meeting in his absence in case they should hatch conspiracies behind his back.

With the love of power which was such a part of his character it was not surprising that his rule became tyrannical. He obviously found great pleasure in the mere exercise of power, judging cases and ordering executions while taking his morning bath or forcing an induna to submit to his wrist being burnt with a magnifying glass which one of the traders gave him. The deaths of his grandmother and then his mother, the only person to whom he felt close, upset him deeply and he imposed intolerable sufferings on his people in the name of mourning for the Queen Mother. He planned to bring the year-long period of mourning to an end with a grand campaign against the tribes of the Transkei who separated his kingdom from the Cape colony. As these tribes could not be made to weep for Nandi's death they should be made to surrender their cattle instead of their tears. His purpose was not only to seize a great booty but to establish closer contact with the colony by smashing the intervening peoples. He was anxious, however, not to be involved in war with the colonial forces themselves, and for this reason he sent his most trusted indunas on an embassy to the Cape, in company with a Mr King, one of the traders.

Early in 1828 his army set out through Natal and began the campaign by attacking the Pondo. But the embassy had still not returned from the Cape and the trader Henry Fynn who accompanied Shaka on the expedition, warned him that the British regarded the Transkei tribes as under their protection. Shaka therefore decided to postpone his plans till he should have more definite information about the British reaction. He was determined not to be cheated of a major campaign, however, and ordered his army to turn about and proceed at once to the extreme opposite end of his domains and attack Soshangane, one of the refugee Ndwandwe leaders who was building up a kingdom in southern Mozambique. The great bulk of the fighting force went off on this expedition, leaving Shaka who stayed behind with such a small bodyguard that he sent after the army and recalled the young boys who had gone as weapon bearers and formed them into a new regiment.

'Oh! children of my father . . .'

By this time the sufferings he had imposed on his people had gone a long way to destroy their loyalty. They longed for an end to the unceasing wars and a return to normal life. Though Shaka had destroyed the power of the chiefs who in traditional society were usually the leaders of revolts, and had refused to marry and produce a legal heir who might come forward to contest his position, a possible focus of rebellion still remained, for several of the king's brothers were still alive though he had not allowed them to exercise any power. Sensing the dissatisfaction of the people, two of these, Dingane and Mhlangana, began to intrigue with the chief induna Mbhopa. The absence of the main bulk of the army provided an excellent opportunity and the conspirators laid plans to assassinate the king. One day Shaka was conducting an interview with some ambassadors from a Sotho-speaking tribe who had brought a tribute of cranes' feathers. Dingane and Mhlangana concealed themselves, spears in hand, behind the fence of the cattle enclosure against which the king was standing. Suddenly Mbhopa appeared and began beating the ambassadors and driving them away, cursing them for bringing the tribute late. Shaka was surprised, and while his attention was distracted asking Mbhopa what he was doing, Mhlangana raised himself above the level of the fence and stabbed the king in the back. Dingane stabbed him also, and Shaka staggered out of the enclosure shouting, 'Oh, children of my father, what have I done to you?' But the assassins had no mercy and he fell covered with wounds to rise no more.

A permanent mark

The mighty Shaka was dead but he had left a permanent mark on African history. In ten brief years of power he had brought together many different tribes to form a single kingdom. It did not disintegrate when he died, like Dingiswayo's empire, but continued to play an important role in South African history until it was finally brought under colonial rule in 1887. Even to this day the unity of the Zulu people which he created still survives.

Outside Zululand the devastations of his regiments and of other people thrown in motion by his campaigns led to the virtual depopulation for a time of wide areas in modern Orange Free State, Transvaal and Natal. This happened just when the Boer farmers in the Cape Colony, short of land and dissatisfied with the British Government, were looking for somewhere to settle away from British rule. They took the obvious opportunity and poured into the areas which had been temporarily emptied.

In the course of the wars started by the rise of Shaka some groups like the Ngoni and the Ndebele carried Zulu methods far into the interior. Others, like the Basuto of Moshesh, built strong states in sheer self-defence and a whole series of kingdoms came into existence which united the members of different tribes in a common loyalty. Some of the states created at this time have joined the community of independent African nations. Others still remain important sections within wider groupings. The names of Shaka himself, and of other heroes in the upheaval he started, remain alive in the memory of many peoples. A source of pride and inspiration to some, of fear and horror to others.

Moshesh and the Creation of the Basuto Nation—the first phase

J. D. Omer-Cooper

The interior plateau of South Africa between the Limpopo and the Orange was the home of a branch of the Bantu peoples who spoke languages belonging to the Sotho group. Those farthest to the west near the Kalahari desert spoke a different dialect from the others and are known as the Tswana (Bechuana). The remaining Sotho groups can also be divided into Northern and Southern Sotho but the differences between the languages of those groups, including the Tswana, are much less than those between them and the Nguni peoples of the eastern coastlands.

Like all the Bantu peoples of South Africa they had migrated into the areas they occupied at the beginning of the nineteenth century from lands farther to the north. Their ancestors had begun penetrating the area south of the Limpopo 200 or more years earlier, and the process of expansion was still continuing. There were still lands around the Orange River inhabited only by hunting bands of the Bushmen and the cattle-keeping

Moshesh as a young man

Koranna Hottentots, together with the half-white, half-Hottentot Griquas who had migrated out of the Cape Colony. Elsewhere within the area generally occupied by the Sotho peoples there were pockets of territory which had not been occupied and which still sheltered groups of Bushmen.

One of these was the central mountainous region of modern Basutoland. This difficult country, hard to penetrate but easy to defend, was hardly occupied by any Bantu peoples except in a few places where some Nguni-speaking groups from across the Drakensberg mountains had made their homes.

The northern and western fringes of the mountains, however, were occupied by many tribes of Sotho-speaking peoples. Like the Nguni of the coastal areas they were mixed farmers, and, though the languages of the two groups were too different for them to understand one another easily, their culture was very similar in many ways. The Sotho practised circumcision ceremonies as a means of initiation to manhood. They were organised in tribes with chiefs who ruled through subordinates who generally belonged to the royal family. Their tribes, like those of the Nguni, frequently split into fragments over succession disputes as growth of population made them too large for convenience.

There were some important differences, however. The Sotho tended to live in substantial villages instead of family hamlets dispersed over the country-side, and probably for this reason the ordinary man was able to take a more active part in politics than in the Nguni tribes. In addition to consulting with councils of chiefs and specially selected councillors the Sotho chief was ex-pected to hold public assemblies (*pitso*) in which vital policy could be fully discussed by all. Probably for the same reason also the circumcision cere-monies were a more public matter than was traditional among the Nguni peoples. The chief or sub-chief would decide when an initiation ceremony was to be held, usually when he had a son of age to be initiated; then all the youths of the village would take part in the ceremonies together with the prince. After initiation those who had gone through the ceremony at the same time formed a regiment with their age-mate prince as its leader. They were expected to fight together in times of war though they did not live permanently in barracks.

The land available for settlement in the Sotho area was much greater than on the narrow coastland strip as the Sotho had not moved so far south as the Nguni. So the problem of land shortage had not become acute and there was no development of multi-tribal empires such as happened in Zululand. The Sotho tribes were living in their traditional way, generally in peace except for minor quarrels between neighbours in disputes over succession, slowly ex-tending themselves farther to the south when they suddenly became involved in the disturbance which began on the eastern coastlands.

The wisdom of Motlomi

Towards the end of the eighteenth century there emerged an interesting figure among the Southern Sotho, a man called Motlomi. He was very interested in the cultures of different tribes and loved travelling. So although he was a chief in his own right he spent much of his life away from his people, visiting distant tribes. Wherever he went it was his custom to marry a daughter of the tribe he visited, and later leave her behind with cattle to support her and with permission to live with any man she chose. In this way he acquired in-fluence in many tribes other than his own. Perhaps because of his wide travels, or because of the visions which he is said to have seen, Motlomi became doubtful of some of the traditional beliefs. He questioned whether the witch doctors really detected magic practices or merely caused innocent people to be put to death, and he always emphasised the importance of peace and justice. Motlomi came to be regarded as a man of great wisdom and many chiefs brought their differences to him to be settled by arbitration. It was rather surprising, therefore, when he singled out a relatively unknown and insignificant lad for special attention. Moshesh was of royal blood but his father, though a senior member of the ruling family, was not the reigning chief of his tribe. This was called the Mokoteli, a small group which had broken away in times past from the Kwena in one of the innumerable succession disputes. Motlomi noticed signs of unusual intelligence and character in the boy and predicted that he would one day be a chief. He advised him always to prefer peaceful settlement to war, to beware of the machinations of witch doctors, and above all, to administer justice impartially between the strong and the weak.

The youthful Moshesh

As a young man Moshesh gave evidence of unusual initiative. He saw that the flat-topped mountains, of which there were many in the neighbourhood of Basutoland, offered excellent defensive opportunities. Anyone who established himself on one of them could set the rest of the world at defiance. So he left his father's settlement with the members of his age grade and established himself on the mountain of Butha Buthe in north-eastern Basutoland. There he was joined by adventurous young men from other tribes until he had a very respectable following. He set about making the best of his natural fortress site by building walls across the passes up the hillside to leave only a narrow gap through which no more than one beast could pass at a time. Look-out huts were also built near all the entrances, and caves in the mountainside were used as stores for surplus foodstuffs which might be needed in case of siege. These precautions were well advised, for about 1821 the peaceful life of the Southern Sotho tribes was suddenly and unexpectedly disrupted by the invasion of Nguni groups driven out of the coastal strip by the increasing fierceness of wars in that area, which accompanied the rise of Shaka and the Zulu people.

The warrior queen—Mma Ntatisi

The first of the Nguni groups to cross the Drakensberg were the Hlubi, led by Mpangazita. They swarmed over the mountains and fell unexpectedly on the powerful Sotho tribe of Tlokwa. The Tlokwa at that time were ruled by a woman called Mma Ntatisi, for their chief had recently died and the heir Sikonyela was not yet of age to succeed. Driven from their homes by the sudden onslaught of the Hlubi, the Tlokwa under their warrior queen began a long trail of wandering and fighting, attacking numerous other tribes, seizing their cattle and forcing them to a wandering life also. Because of their queen the Tlokwa came to be called Mantatees and such a terrible reputation did they acquire that this name was often applied indiscriminately to the numerous wandering hordes of the period.

Quite early in their career the Tlokwa attacked Moshesh on Butha Buthe mountain. Though they were in a great majority they were at a disadvantage in having to fight uphill and Moshesh's young followers charged down the hill so impetuously that the Tlokwa were forced right back into their own camp. As the fighting went on many of the Tlokwa cooking pots were over-turned and broken, and in spite of their numbers they were almost put com-pletely to flight when a woman called Maseile caught hold of one of the warriors as he was about to run away and began to abuse him and his fellows for being afraid of a much smaller force. This was a turning point in the battle and the Tlokwa warriors, ashamed at the woman's words, rallied and drove Moshesh's party back up the mountain again. They captured most of Moshesh's precious cattle but the mountain stronghold was too strong to be worth attacking and they moved off towards the west in search of easier prey.

Chief Matiwane

The departure of the Tlokwa gave Moshesh a brief breathing space. But his position remained far from secure. In the plains of what is now the Orange Free State the Tlokwa and the Hlubi continued to attack tribe after tribe, spreading havoc and destruction over a wide area. At any moment one or other of these powerful groups might turn back to attack Butha Buthe. At the same time a second Nguni tribe, the Ngwane of Matiwane, burst across the mountain chain and entered the boiling pot of tribal warfare amongst the Southern Sotho tribes.

The Ngwane were the most powerful of the tribes involved in the fighting in the Southern Sotho territory. Their warriors were organised in regiments rather like the Zulu, and being uprooted from their homes they fought des-perately for survival. They were deadly enemies of the Hlubi, with whom they had fought before either had crossed the Drakensberg, and shortly after they appeared on the plateau they moved off westward on the trail of their old foes. Moshesh, realising their strength, offered his allegiance to Matiwane and bought peace at the price of a tribute.

About 1824 the breathing space which Moshesh's people had enjoyed came to an end. The Tlokwa, after a long career of bloodshed and desperate battles with the Hlubi in which they were almost destroyed, came back to attack Butha Buthe in earnest. Moshesh sent a message to Sikonyela who was then old enough to lead the warriors, asking him to respect traditional rules of warfare; to fight only over the cattle and leave the agricultural crops, the basic food of the people, untouched. But Sikonyela was determined on a fight to the finish. Moshesh then tried magical means to ward off the enemy. A woman of his people believed that she had the power to call up a monster called Khoi Khoi which would frighten them away. She offered to stand in their path and turn them back. The Tlokwa, however, paid no attention to her incantations. They continued their advance and the woman fell into their hands. Then they laughed at Moshesh's magic, and chanting rude songs about the non-appearance of the supposed monster, they began a prolonged siege of Butha Buthe.

The Tlokwa siege of Butha Buthe

The defensive position which Moshesh occupied was strong enough to withstand any direct attack but the surface of the mountain top was not adequate to maintain very many cattle. His people began to suffer dreadfully from hunger and were reduced to eating their sandals and their leather cloaks. The Tlokwa also were growing weary of the siege but it looked as if success was within their grasp. Then Moshesh thought of a means to secure himself. He entered into an arrangement with a Nguni-speaking tribe to fall upon the Tlokwa while they were fully occupied in the struggle with Moshesh's people. (Who these people were is not very clear. Some evidence suggests that they might be the Ama Ngwane of Matiwane but we cannot be sure.) This tribe attacked the Tlokwa unexpectedly and drove them to flight. They rallied again soon afterwards but decided to abandon the attack on Butha Buthe. They went away but not very far, for they had learnt in the struggle how valuable mountain situations were and they established strong positions for themselves on two hills, Kooaneng and Yoalohoholo, at no great distance from Butha Buthe. There they were to continue to be a threat to Moshesh until he finally overthrew them in 1858.

The Basuto trek

The experience of the long siege had taught Moshesh that Butha Buthe was not adequate to face a really serious attack and he decided to lead his people in search of a stronger position. He heard that in central Basutoland there was another mountain which was ideal for his purposes. It had steep sides which would be easy to defend and its top was large enough to accommodate a great number of people together with their cattle. It was surrounded by fertile country where the people could support themselves in times of peace. The journey would be difficult and dangerous for by this time the depredations of the numerous wandering hordes had produced terrible conditions among the Southern Sotho. Most tribes had lost their cattle. Many had been completely broken up in warfare, and even the planting of normal crops had been brought to a halt by the disturbed conditions which made it unsafe for the farmer to go out to his fields. There was mass starvation and the country was infested by gangs of desperate men who would attack anyone for the sake of survival. Many had been reduced to such conditions that they had taken to cannibalism and lay in wait to fall on any passer-by. As Moshesh's people struggled towards their new home some fell behind and were seized by the cannibals. Moshesh's grandfather was captured and eaten. At last one night they reached their goal and gratefully installed themselves in the strong position which they called Thaba Bosiu (the hill of night). Moshesh's gamble had proved

A Basuto Warrior; a drawing based on a clay statue made in 1840. He wears a fur loin cloth, leather singlet and brass chest protector and carries a shield, stalking spear, throwing axe and a feather-stick which marked his position in the fighting force during battle.

successful and his people had found a position strong enough to resist every attack. Thereafter he was able to use his secure position as a base to extend his authority from a fairly small following to a great kingdom made up of many different tribes.

Diplomacy of Moshesh

His immediate task was to bring peace and order to the vicinity of his capital, to rally the remnants of broken tribes to himself and to win the support of the most important group of Nguni-speaking Ba Phuti, the first Bantu inhabitants of the mountainous part of Basutoland. The first part of this task was especially difficult because Moshesh's people were disgusted at the cannibal practices of the scattered refugee groups and thought only of a war of revenge to wipe them out completely. Moshesh realised that the cannibals had been forced to their practices by starvation and would be pleased to return to normal life if given the chance. But first he had to persuade his people to accept his plans and so he thought of a brilliant argument. The Sotho, like other Bantu people, believed in the power of the ancestors, especially the ancestors of chiefs, and their graves were sacred places which no one was allowed to disturb. So Moshesh told his people that the cannibals who had eaten some of their fathers, including his own grandfather, were like living graves. They were sacred to the spirits of the ancestors and could not be killed. Then he began to put his policy into practice. He offered peace to the cannibals and lent them some of his own cattle so that they could use the milk on condition that they should stop their evil habits and accept his authority. Most of them were glad to do so and settled down to normal life, becoming some of his most devoted followers. In the second part of his task he was equally successful, for after a brief struggle with the powerful Ba Phuti chief Morosi, Moshesh treated him so generously that he became one of his most loyal vassals.

Towards a common loyalty

Thus Moshesh's following began to expand into the Basuto nation and as it grew so it attracted more and more tribes to come and seek security within it. To organise and control this evergrowing mass of different peoples Moshesh was in no position to impose the type of military system used by the Zulu. That was the result of conquest, while Moshesh's kingdom grew mainly by peaceful attraction. He therefore used more traditional means. Where tribes had lost their chiefs or were fairly small he placed them under the rule of members of his own family. Where they were large and powerful like the Phuti he left them under their own chiefs so long as his paramountcy was recognised. At the same time he encouraged a feeling of common loyalty by bringing the leading men of all sections into his councils and discussing important matters in public assemblies which any of his subjects could attend.

Divide and survive

While Moshesh was extending his influence in this way his military position remained precarious. The Ngwane and the Hlubi had continued their old quarrel in a series of bitter fights on the plains of the present Orange Free State. Finally they fought an all-out battle and the Ama Ngwane of Matiwane were victorious. The Hlubi were broken up, one group fleeing to the Transvaal, the rest joining with their conquerors. Matiwane was now supreme between the Orange and the Vaal rivers and Moshesh as his vassal was forced to pay a heavy tribute. To free himself from this difficult position he decided to play one major power against another. He had already taken the precaution of offering his allegiance to Shaka and sent him a valuable tribute every year of crane's feathers and other materials used as regalia by the Zulu regiments.

One year he stopped the tribute and when it was demanded he pleaded that the marauding activities of the Ngwane made it impossible for his people to collect the materials required. Shaka sent an army to the High Veld which attacked Matiwane, but it was only a small force and it retired without winning a definite victory. Matiwane, however, ran into difficulties with another neighbour, Mzilikazi, the Zulu general who had broken away from Shaka and established himself with his followers in the Transvaal. When some of the Hlubi entered the area in their flight from Matiwane's victorious warriors they were captured and brought to Mzilikazi. They joined his followers for a time but later they broke away and tried to escape home. Mzilikazi's regiments pursued them, but as they passed through the territory occupied by the Ngwane some of the other Hlubi who had been forced to join Matiwane's men went to the help of their comrades. So Matiwane became involved in a quarrel with Mzilikazi and began to think of leaving the area to look for happier hunting grounds. Before he left, however, his people urged that Moshesh should be punished for his treachery, and though Matiwane does not seem to have approved, his followers launched an attack on Thaba Bosiu.

The Ngwane surged up the mountain side but Moshesh's men, perched on the heights, sent volleys of stones and spears hurtling down the narrow gulleys up which the invaders must pass. They wavered and as they began to beat a retreat the exultant defenders poured down the slopes and put them to headlong flight. Matiwane's prestige as the dominant power in the Southern Sotho area was gone, and shortly afterwards he withdrew to enter the territory occupied by the coastal tribes near the colonial frontier where he met his final defeat at the hands of British forces.

Generosity to the defeated

Moshesh had thus emerged as the dominant power on the inland plateau between the Orange and the Vaal, but north of the Vaal River Mzilikazi's regiments were scouring the country for cattle and it was only a matter of time before they extended their raiding activities to the Southern Sotho. In 1831 a Ndebele army sent out to retaliate for a raid made by the Tswana chief, Moletsane, on their king's cattle, approached Moshesh's territory and commenced an attack on Thaba Bosiu. Even the superb Zulu-type discipline of the Ndebele regiments, however, was no match for the defensive advantages of Moshesh's mountain stronghold.

Two desperate charges were made but the missiles of the defenders brought them both to a halt and the Ndebele drew off. Moshesh realised that this was not an outright victory. Only a fraction of the Ndebele forces had been involved and they could return to the attack time and again until resistance was worn down. He hastened to secure a diplomatic advantage by an act of conspicuous generosity in his hour of victory. He sent a gift of cattle after the defeated Ndebele with a message to say that Moshesh assumed they must have been hungry to attack him unprovoked. He was sending them cattle that they might eat and leave him in peace. Mzilikazi was greatly impressed when he heard the news and his regiments never attacked the Basuto again.

Learning from the enemy

Though Moshesh by war and diplomacy had survived the attacks of his most formidable Bantu enemies, peace was not to come to the Basuto country.

The Griquas (half-caste Hottentot whites) and the more pure-blooded Korannas with their horses and guns took advantage of every opportunity to swoop down on unprotected Bantu cattle. As the devastations of years had swept away most of the cattle in what is now the Orange Free State and Mzilikazi's regiments made raiding in the Transvaal too dangerous, they turned their attention to Moshesh's country. They attacked Thaba Bosiu without success, but for the most part they restricted themselves to guerrilla-type warfare; sweeping down unexpectedly on small villages, alarming the inhabitants with their guns and riding off with the cattle before pursuit could be organised. Moshesh's people were reduced to dire straits but they began to organise effective counter-action; waiting till the Griquas camped for the night, then making a sudden charge and capturing horses and guns. Moshesh saw at once the value of these new military means. He encouraged his people to acquire horses and learn to manage them as well as accumulating as many guns as possible. Within a very brief period the Basuto became a nation of mounted gunmen with their own breed of horse: the Basuto pony.

Servants not masters

During 1832 a Christian Griqua named Adam Krotz visited Moshesh at Thaba Bosiu and told him of the work of white missionaries amongst the tribes. The chief was greatly interested, for not only were many Sotho, who had fled to the colony in the period of disturbance, streaming into his kingdom with tales of their experiences under the white government, but Boers from the Cape were grazing their cattle from time to time in the angle between the Caledon and Orange rivers, an area which Moshesh felt should be occupied by his own expanding people. He thus despatched two embassies with gifts of cattle to the C.M.S. Mission station of Phillipis on the Orange River with a request for missionaries to be sent to him. All the cattle were stolen by Griquas on the way, but the second embassy arrived in time to persuade three French missionaries of the Paris Evangelical Society to visit the Basuto king. They were received with open arms and soon opened a series of stations in Moshesh's kingdom. The Basuto ruler had acquired new allies who were to be vital in helping him understand and deal with pressure from white governments and who could wield influence in Europe in his support.

The coming of the missionaries was not unaccompanied by difficulties, however, for as their success depended on the support of the king they naturally tried to persuade him to come and live with them on their station at Morija. Moshesh seems to have been persuaded at first, but he was determined not to place himself under the authority of anyone else and he soon saw that it would be militarily suicidal to abandon Thaba Bosiu. So the missionaries were disappointed, but Moshesh remained master in his own home.

Missionary complications

A more complex problem arose from the fact that the relative peace and stability of Moshesh's kingdom continued to attract new peoples to come and join him. The French missionaries were responsible for introducing some new groups, including the old war leader Moletsane who had so much annoyed Mzilikazi in past years. He established himself near Moshesh's old capital of Butha Buthe and became one of the Basuto king's most important vassals. In 1833 a more serious development occurred when the Wesleyan missionary Archbell, who worked with the Tswana tribe of Ba Rolong in the south-western Transvaal, led his flock on a migration to the Basuto country and settled alongside one of Moshesh's stations at Thaba Nchu. Moshesh welcomed these new arrivals as an addition to his people and gave them permission to occupy land which he regarded as his own. But the Wesleyan missionaries did not want to see their flock under the authority of a chief who worked with another society and the Rolong chief himself was naturally anxious to maintain his autonomy. The position was worsened when the Wesleyans extended their work to the Tlokwa of Sikonyela, for a link was thus established between the new arrivals and Moshesh's oldest enemies.

Accomplishments of the first phase

The year 1836 marks the natural end of one phase in the life of Moshesh, for this was the year of the Great Talk and thereafter for the rest of his life the great chief would be mainly concerned with maintaining his still imperfectly consolidated nation against pressure from land-hungry whites. The transition is not absolute and abrupt, for problems of the first phase entered into the second and the process of expanding and assimilating the Basuto people was still incomplete. Nevertheless there is a definite change of emphasis.

In the first phase of his career Moshesh had successfully laid the foundations of a multi-tribal kingdom in face of almost overwhelming odds. Whether as a result of the influence of wise old Motlomi or purely of his own personality, he had developed from the leader of a small band of youths into a real statesman.

He had demonstrated his outstanding skill in diplomacy as well as war; his capacity to adopt new ideas without losing his balance; his ability to win the friendship and make use of the councils of missionaries without falling under their influence. Perhaps, above all, he had demonstrated that deep sense of humanity which is his most striking characteristic. All these were qualities that would be sorely needed in the turbulent second phase of his career.

Kimweri the Great: Kilindi King of Vuga

G. O. Ekemode

Kimweri the Great, who ruled the Kilindi kingdom of Vuga from about 1803 to 1868, was certainly the greatest nineteenth-century African monarch and statesman in the area which is now the modern state of Tanzania. His greatness was recognised not only by his own subjects who gave him the appellation of *Za Nyumbai*—of the house—on account of his patience and forbearance, and addressed him as the *Simbamwene* —son of the Lion—because of the firmness of his rule, but was also acknowledged by his equally famous contemporary, Seyyid Said of Zanzibar. The German missionary, Dr. J. L. Krapf, and the British explorer, R. F. Burton, who visited Vuga between 1848 and 1857, were much impressed by the effectiveness of his government and the stability of his kingdom.

Unlike Mirambo, the powerful Nyamwezi ruler, Rindi, the great Chagga chieftain, or Mkwakwa, the warlike Hehe chief, Kimweri the Great was not simply the ruler of his Shambala people, but was the powerful king of a multi-national kingdom. In the early part of his reign, especially in the third decade of the nineteenth century, his kingdom included the Pare people in the north-west, all the districts of Usambara and Bondei, a greater part of the Zigua country and the coastal strip from the island of Wasin in the north to the region south of Pangani inhabited by the Digo, the Segeju, the Swahili and the Arabs. In a rather conservative estimate in 1848, Dr. Krapf estimated the population of the kingdom to be about half a million and its extent approximately 60 miles from north to south and 140 miles from east to west. The British explorer, R. F. Burton, who was Kimweri's guest in Vuga in 1857, put the population of the royal capital, Vuga, at about 3,000. But another British contemporary, Cooley, records the estimate of his Swahili servant who put the population of Vuga as three times as large as that of the town of Zanzibar. However, the significance of the reign of Kimweri the Great for East African history does not lie solely in the creation of an extensive multi-national state in the north-east of modern Tanzania—the precursor of the present African state—but also in the bringing to a successful culmination of the process of state formation which had begun in Usambara at about the end of the first quarter of the eighteenth century.

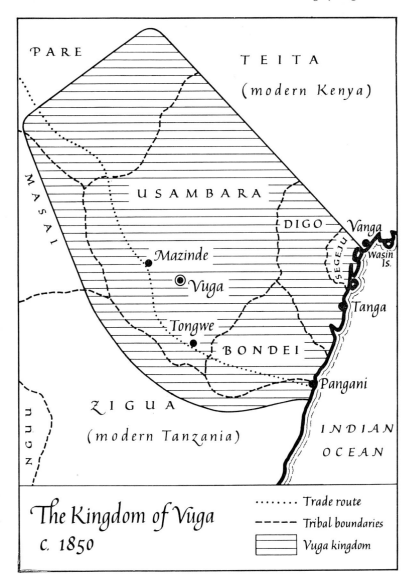

The Kingdom of Vuga
c. 1850

········ Trade route
----- Tribal boundaries
Vuga kingdom

Consolidation and expansion

When in about 1803, Kimweri the Great succeeded his father, Shebuge Kinyasi, as the fifth king of Vuga, he inherited the twin problems of consolidating the rule of his Kilindi clan and extending the frontiers of his kingdom into the territories of its aggressive neighbours. These were extremely difficult problems, since the defeat of his father by the Zigua immediately before his accession had exposed his people to the danger of

Dr. J. L. Krapf

Zigua raids for slaves and cattle and his kingdom to that of possible disintegration. This situation would have brought an abrupt end to the process
of state formation begun by Mbega of Nguu, who in about 1725 founded
the kingdom by transforming the existing pre-Kilindi Shambala tradition
of vague political precedence of one clan over others into something much
more concrete by completely institutionalising the leadership of his Kilindi
clan over all Usambara.

Since the basis of the acceptance of Kilindi leadership was the peace and
prosperity which it gave the country, Kimweri realised that he could only
consolidate Kilindi rule in Usambara by pursuing a dynamic policy of
expansion at the expense of the neighbouring peoples. He also knew he
would not be safe until he had subdued the Zigua who had caused his
father's death and until the coastal Arabs and Swahili, through whom
they obtained arms and who sponsored most of their slave raids, had been
brought under the effective control of Vuga. Kimweri also had other considerations. The annexation of the Zigua plains would itself add to his
kingdom an extensive area where elephants could be hunted in large numbers for their ivory which was an important article of trade, and which
would greatly increase the royal income. In particular, the conquest of the

Zigua country and the neighbouring coastal region would bring Kimweri into contact with the coastal peoples—Arabs and Swahili—from whom weapons could be obtained not only for the hunting expeditions for the collection of ivory, but for the conquest and annexation of more districts to the kingdom. This contact would also eliminate the services of the Zigua, Arab and Swahili middlemen, who, like the Fante of the nineteenth century Gold Coast, were making a handsome profit through their control of the trade between the coast and the interior.

But before embarking upon his expansionist policy, Kimweri had to keep his house in order by quickly crushing an internal revolt by certain Shambala who had taken advantage of the death of the previous ruler and the confusion that followed it to declare themselves independent of the central authority in Vuga. He then turned his attention to the northern frontier where there were intermittent raids by the Teita and the Kamba. After frightening off these rather distant enemies, Kimweri moved south to deal with the Digo, the Zigua and other coastal peoples. It is said that the Bondei, who like the Zigua and the Nguu belong to the Zigua nation or cluster of peoples, which speak languages that are mutually intelligible, accepted Kilindi rule during this period not as a result of a formal act of conquest but because they wanted to benefit from the wise leadership of the Kilindi. However, the Digo, the Zigua and other coastal peoples resisted Kilindi control and had eventually to be forcibly annexed. By 1848 when Krapf first visited Usambara, Kimweri the Great was already exercising effective power on the coast between Pangani and Vanga through his representatives.

Privileges for Muslims

In the solution of the administrative problems posed by the inclusion of non-Bantu peoples like the coastal Arabs and Swahili in his kingdom, Kimweri proved himself a wise ruler. He quickly realised the danger of imposing the norms and institutions of a Bantu people on the Arab and Swahili traders and therefore worked out a different administrative policy for them. On the coast, the established Kilindi policy of ruling the towns and villages of the districts had to be set aside in favour of a policy of appointing non-Kilindi headmen as the representatives of the King of Vuga. Krapf, who met some of these royal representatives, says they were supposed to uphold the influence and authority of Kimweri among his coastal subjects. Since the Swahili and Arab subjects of the king were not taxed, and were generally accorded freedom of trade and movement not allowed the ordinary Shambala, the functions of these headmen must also have included the promotion of trade with the outside world by creating a peaceful atmosphere through the enforcement of law and order.

These coastal headmen were allowed certain privileges of office not permitted the Kilindi princes who were the governors of the various districts of Usambara and Bondei. For instance, they were allowed to wear sandals and carry umbrellas of state. They could also walk about preceded by musicians. In addition, they were probably allowed to own property; for it is likely that many of them had been successful traders before their appointment. In any case, it is inconceivable that men unaccustomed to the intricacies of coastal life and trade would have been appointed to administer what were essentially trading communities. These extraordinarily liberal privileges were, no doubt, calculated to induce and maintain the loyalty of these men to their sovereign who lived in distant Vuga, and to ensure the security of the economic basis of royal power. This policy resembled that of the West African kingdom of Dahomey which also employed 'foreigners' to administer the coastal district and its population of foreign traders.

It is easy to come to the conclusion, as Krapf did, that Kimweri's reason for allowing his coastal Arab and Swahili subjects all this freedom was to prevent them from becoming dangerous to him, since they could easily obtain European fire-arms in Zanzibar. It must, however, be stressed that apart from ensuring the security of his kingdom against possible revolt of hostile Arab and Swahili subjects, Kimweri the Great, a politically wise ruler, might not have wished to offend his Muslim subjects by forcing them to accept the practices of pagan society. What was important to Kimweri was his control of the coast, and if this could be achieved by giving some concessions to those living there, the better for him. As long as the customary tributes and presents flowed to Vuga in recognition of his sovereignty, Kimweri the Great considered himself the effective sovereign of all parts of his kingdom, be it the coast or the interior.

Island sultan and inland king

The extension of Kimweri's power and influence to the coast also had political and diplomatic implications, for it led to a clash with Seyyid Said, the powerful and energetic Sultan of Zanzibar. This clash was caused by their conflicting claims to the coastal strip extending from the island of Wasin in the north to Pangani in the south. Kimweri the Great claimed the territory by right of conquest; so did Seyyid Said who, after crushing the Mazrui of Mombasa in 1837, had taken over that part of the coast which the Mazrui themselves had previously taken by conquest. As long as Seyyid Said did not care about the administration of the coast but only concerned himself with trading activities, there was no immediate clash between the island sultan and the inland king. It was only when he began to assert his control over the coast after 1852 by appointing his representatives in the coastal towns that an open clash became inevitable.

By this time, Seyyid Said really wanted to show that he was in effective control of the coast, in order to dispel rumours circulating in European circles in Zanzibar, especially among the French, that the Sultan of Zanzibar's authority did not extend to the coast. These rumours had gained ground as a result of a conversation between Krapf and the French Consul in Zanzibar in 1852, during which Krapf said that Kimweri had actually levied tributes on the coast. As there were fears that France might colonise

Seyyid Said

part of the East African coast during this period, great pressure must also have been put on Seyyid Said by the powerful Arab interests in Zanzibar, as well as by the British Consul, Aitkins Hamerton, to make his claim to the coast effective in order to keep out the French. In trying to do this, however, Seyyid Said came face to face with the already established power of Kimweri the Great.

The details of the dispute between island sultan and inland king are unknown. It probably led to clashes in a few places along the coast, especially in important commercial centres like Tanga and Pangani, between the supporters of Seyyid Said and the loyal subjects of Kimweri the Great. But the disagreement between the two rulers seems to have been of very short duration; for, writing home in April 1853, Erhadt, the German missionary, reports that after having a long conversation with Seyyid Said about Usambara, the sultan offered him a letter to Kimweri. He says that Seyyid Said had received letters from his agents on the coast saying that the difficulties with Kimweri the Great had been solved and that peace would soon return to Usambara. However, it was in an agreement reached later in 1853 that the conflicting claims of both rulers were finally resolved.

Arab-Bantu condominium

According to the terms of this agreement, which formed the basis of a treaty of friendship between Kimweri and Seyyid Said, an Arab-Bantu condominium was established in the disputed territories on the coast. Seyyid Said was empowered to administer the important coastal towns of Tanga and Pangani. These towns had a large Arab and Swahili population and had been important commercial centres in the Arab trade network. Kimweri, on the other hand, was allowed to control the rest of the coast, and appoint the Jumbe or headmen. It was, however, stipulated that these coastal Jumbes should have their appointment confirmed by the Sultan of Zanzibar, who would take the opportunity to give them presents and request protection of his interests. This treaty was significant because it not only recognised the right of Kimweri to the coast but was in itself a recognition of the sovereignty of Kimweri the Great by Seyyid Said. It also led to improved relations and promoted trade between the two states. The advantages of mutual cooperation between the two rulers soon became apparent when Seyyid Said came to help Kimweri stop the Zigua raids which were interrupting the caravan trade between Pangani and Usambara, especially at a time when Kimweri's old age and constant illness were making it impossible for him to ensure the security of the caravan routes in his kingdom. Seyyid Said was then permitted to erect a fort near Mount Tongwe in which he placed a garrison of twenty-five Baluchi soldiers.

Growing Arab and Muslim influence

The extension of Kimweri's power to the coast also had important cultural results, for it brought the kingdom of Vuga into close and friendly contact with Arab and Muslim influences. By the time of Krapf's second visit to Vuga in 1852, two influential Muslims from Zanzibar, Osman and Manioka (possibly islamised Swahili) were advisers at the court of Kimweri. As a result of the improved relations between Zanzibar and Vuga, Arabs and Swahili were employed by Kimweri as private secretaries and soldiers, as the career of Abdallah bin Hemedi, the author of the *Habari za Wakilindi*, a compendium of Shambala oral traditions, clearly exemplifies. It was as a result of Arab influence that the King of Vuga became known as Sultan, a title which was most probably first given to him by the Arabs and Swahili, but which later came to be accepted as the official royal title of the Kings of Vuga. Arab influence on the court and kingdom of Vuga was also manifested in the dress of the people. Royal dress began to include the clothes imported by the Arab and Swahili traders, and royal princes and the king's courtiers began to wear the *Kanzu* in the Arab fashion.

Another by-product of Arab influence was the spread of Islam into the kingdom. During his second visit to Vuga in 1852, Krapf observed that two of the king's sons—Khatib and Abdallah—were good Muslims. Growing Muslim influence and the opposition of his advisers did not prevent Kimweri from granting Krapf's request for the establishment of a Christian mission station at Tongwe. Little wonder Burton has described him as a 'pragmatic pagan'. Kimweri's attitude could, however, be best understood in relation to his desire to adapt himself and his kingdom to the changing conditions of the modern world, an ambition whose realisation offered no place for any involvement in racial or religious conflicts. On the other hand Christianity may have been welcomed, as it would be in the kingdom of Buganda, as a counterbalance to the growing Muslim influence.

Seeds of disintegration

However, Arab contact with Vuga had not been completely positive, for it also brought in its train negative and disintegrating influences. For example, the opportunities of trade which the contact with Arab and Swahili traders afforded, led inevitably to the gradual undermining of royal authority, and tended to encourage centrifugal forces within the kingdom. This was because it became increasingly difficult to maintain the royal monopoly of the export and import trade on which the economic and political stability of the kingdom largely depended, since there were now excellent opportunities for individuals within the kingdom to engage in private and illicit trade with the Arab and Swahili traders who stood to gain from such a development. The result was that some of the royal princes, who were the governors of the districts of the kingdom, were able to acquire large private fortunes and thus became less dependent upon the King of Vuga. They were greatly encouraged by the decline of the central authority in Vuga which began in the fifth decade of the nineteenth century when Kimweri's old age made it impossible for him to carry out the customary inspection tours of all parts of the kingdom to control and supervise the administration of the royal princes. Freed from strict royal control, the provincial governors began to enrich themselves by diverting a large section of the trade of the kingdom into their own hands. A particular example of this was the case of Semboja, one of the many sons of Kimweri, who was the governor or chief of the village of Mazinde, an important caravan trade centre. Semboja not only took advantage of his position to engage in profitable but illegal trade with the caravans but also enriched himself considerably from the tolls he collected from them. As a result of his wealth and important connections with powerful Arabs on the coast from whom fire-arms could be obtained, Semboja not only defied his father's authority shortly before his death, but also refused to recognise the authority of his (Semboja's) nephew, Shekulwavu, who inherited the Vuga kingdom in 1868.

The most disintegrating aspect of Arab influence on the kingdom of Vuga was the involvement of Arab and Swahili traders and professional soldiers in the politics of the kingdom. But for Arab intervention, the disagreement which broke out within the ruling Kilindi clan after the death of Kimweri and which led to the Usambara civil wars of 1868 to 1890 could have been resolved. Even if the civil wars had broken out at all, it would have been much easier to bring the warring factions to a peace settlement, especially with the intervention of the missionaries. It was the intervention of powerful Arabs who wanted to fish in the troubled waters of Usambara that intensified the civil wars and led to the disintegration of the social, economic and political organisations of the kingdom.

The king and the Kitala Kikuu

It is necessary at this point to consider how the kingdom of Vuga was organised under Kimweri the Great. To uncritical nineteenth-century European observers, the political system of Kimweri's kingdom was a pure and unmitigated absolutism. Krapf said that the king was a despot whose absolute powers were taken for granted by his people, but he justified the royal absolutism because it enthroned peace and order by keeping the people, who might otherwise have remained unruly, under effective control. Burton was less sympathetic in his remarks about Kimweri's rule. As far as he was concerned, the king was a 'petty despot who rules at home like a right kingly African king by selling his subjects, men, women, and children, old and young, gentle and simple, singly or, when need lays down the law, by families and by villages'.

It is important to note that Burton's observation about the existence of the slave trade during the reign of Kimweri the Great is not completely true. Although there were domestic slaves in the kingdom, it does not appear that Kimweri greatly relished the sale of his subjects as Burton claims. The king seems to have known how to put these slaves, most of whom were captured in wars during the early part of his reign, into productive use by making them work on his plantations. The true picture is that the slave trade was very restricted during the reign of Kimweri, for only certain categories of criminals were sold. These were mostly deserters from the ranks, murderers and members of the families of runaway prisoners. The existence of a state prison, which Krapf reported, certainly implies that not all criminals were sold. The slave trade only reached alarming proportions in Usambara from 1868 onwards during the period of the civil wars which followed the death of Kimweri.

It is equally untrue that Kimweri simply exercised an autocratic power over a subject population whose position approximated to that of slaves. Admittedly, the king ruled firmly and effectively, even to the point of controlling the kingdom's external trade and regulating the relations of the Shambala with foreigners; nevertheless this firm control does not necessarily imply autocracy, since there were effective controls within the kingdom's political system on the actual exercise of royal power. For instance, the participation of a council of advisers, called the *Kitala Kikuu* or the Great Council, whose members were drawn exclusively from the commoner clans, tended to act as a check on the exercise of arbitrary power by the king at every stage of decision-making at the royal court. Since these royal advisers or councillors were the heads of their clans, whose interests and views they represented, any decisions jointly arrived at by the king-in-council could be regarded as representing the wishes of the people. In fact, the democratic basis of royal authority can be explained not only in terms of the independence of the royal advisers from absolute royal control, since they were not appointed and could not be removed by the king, but also in terms of the popular acceptance of the Kilindi dynasty by the elders and people of Usambara, since Kilindi rule in Usambara was not imposed by conquest.

The Walau

Kimweri the Great ruled the royal capital of Vuga and its neighbour-hood directly and other towns and villages of the districts indirectly through governors or chiefs who were royal princes and princesses. In order to maintain the loyalty of the royal governors to the King of Vuga, royal officials called the *Walau* were appointed to serve as the link be-tween the district and the central administration by communicating the king's instructions to the governors and ensuring their execution. With the effective use of the Walau system, Kimweri was able to maintain his hold on an apparently decentralised administration. But in this arrangement, which offered excellent prospects of unity and stability, were inherent weaknesses capable of wrecking the very foundations of the kingdom. For example, as the powers of the governors were not delegated by the king but were derived from their membership of the same ruling Kilindi clan, there was the possibility of these governors developing their districts into independent chiefdoms—which was what happened after the death of Kimweri. This development revealed the fragility of the whole constitu-tional structure, which could only be maintained by the forceful personality of Kimweri himself.

Realising that an efficient and stable administration depended on an effective system of revenue collection, Kimweri devised various methods of collecting revenue. Burton, who observed the kingdom's system of revenue collections says 'cattle-breeders contribute the first fruits of their flocks and herds; elephant hunters offer every second tusk, and traders are mulcted (fined) in a portion of their merchandise. Cultivators annually pay ten measures of grain.' The king also had other sources of income. Principal among these were the tributes collected from the districts through the royal governors, the booty of war, the fines imposed by the royal courts and revenue raised from royal estates, from caravan fees and from the king's monopoly of the export trade.

The military

The bulk of the royal revenue was spent on the maintenance of the court—the payment of the courtiers and messengers and the upkeep of the royal harem. The king also had to provide for his body-guard, which formed the nucleus of his army. Burton says this corps of royal guards consisted of 400 musketeers whom Kimweri the Great called his *Waen-grezi*, or Englishman, probably because of their use of English fire-arms. This body performed strict police functions in peacetime, but in war they formed the vanguard of the peoples' militia. Although all able-bodied men were expected to serve their king in times of war, Kimweri sometimes re-cruited mercenaries for his campaigns, and these mercenaries had to be paid by him. The absence of a standing army in the kingdom not only

reduced the cost of administration, but also meant the complete subordination of the military to the civil authority. This made for order and stability
in the kingdom; very different from the arguments which occurred after
the death of Kimweri when professional Arab and Swahili soldiers began
to intervene in the politics of the kingdom, thereby widening the gulf between the rival Kilindi factions and making the settlement of their disputes
impossible.

Thus, before his death, after a long and memorable reign of about 65
years, Kimweri the Great gave the kingdom of Vuga a well-ordered social,
economic and political organisation which not only surpassed that of most
states on the East African mainland but also excelled that of the more
famous empire of Seyyid Said of Zanzibar. But as in Seyyid Said's empire,
it was the personality of the king that welded the various parts of the
kingdom together, especially during the latter part of Kimweri's reign when
external influences began to undermine the authority of the king and the
stability of the kingdom.

It is thus tragic that Kimweri the Great left his kingdom to a young and
impetuous ruler, his grandson Shekulwavu, who was determined to be a real
king, and to a host of ambitious governors or chiefs of the districts, who
were equally determined to cling to the privileges, bordering on virtual
independence, which they had enjoyed towards the end of Kimweri's reign.
It was this inevitable clash of interests that produced the crisis within the
royal clan, which led to the Usambara civil wars and the eventual disintegration of the kingdom. But although the kingdom which Kimweri the
Great so well consolidated and expanded is no more, and in spite of the
efforts of the German colonial administration to destroy traditional
authority in German East Africa, Usambara still bears the mark of Kilindi
rule. For even today when the nationalist government of Tanzania has
removed the chiefs from the field of local administration, Vuga and its
neighbourhood of Soni is still administered through a civil servant who is
a descendant of Kimweri the Great!

Maba Diakhou Ba: Scholar-Warrior of the Senegambia

Charlotte A. Quinn

Although the Gambia is now one of the smallest of Africa's states, the area of the Gambia valley has been of far broader historical significance than its size on a map might indicate. For over five hundred years a strip of Mandingo settlements has extended along the river's banks from the Futa Jalon plateau (one of the principal sites of Mande settlement in West

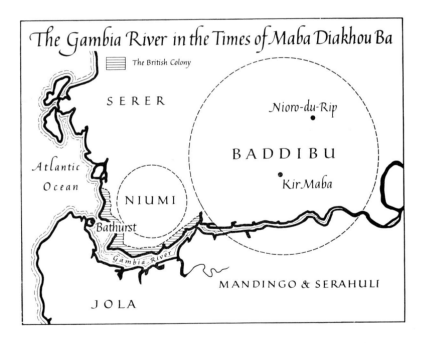

The Gambia River in the Times of Maba Diakhou Ba

The British Colony

SERER

Nioro-du-Rip

BADDIBU

KirMaba

Atlantic

Ocean

NIUMI

Bathurst

Gambia River

MANDINGO & SERAHULI

JOLA

Africa), to the Atlantic Ocean, and the Gambia river, one of the most accessible and navigable waterways in West Africa, has attracted important ethnic groups such as the Fula, Wolof, Serahuli and Jola. During the second half of the nineteenth century events taking place in that area affected the lives of people living as far north as the Senegal river and as far south as the Casamance. It is interesting to contrast the relative obscurity of the Gambia valley today with the attention it received in Paris and London during certain periods of Europe's expansion overseas.

The revolution which broke out in 1861 in the Kingdom of Baddibu, on the north bank of the Gambia, was to have far-reaching repercussions for the populations of the whole of the Senegambia (the region drained by the Senegal and Gambia river systems) and it was also to have a marked effect on European politics.

During the eighteenth and nineteenth centuries a wave of Islamic reform was sweeping through West Africa and much of the Islamic world, and one of the main causes of the Baddibu revolt was the long-standing oppressions suffered by the state's Muslim minority at the hands of the traditional ruling class. The leader of the revolution was Maba Diakhou Ba, a devout Marabout scholar of Torodbe ancestry who was able, during the brief span of his political career, to conquer much of the Senegambia and to establish there the beginnings of Islamic rule. His revolt marked an important stage in the spread of the strict observance of Islam in West Africa and was the achievement of a thoughtful scholar who spent most of his life studying and teaching the Koran.

Maba was called from his peaceful studies by the needs of his fellow Muslims and he died fighting for the establishment of a purified Islamic state. His greatest achievements were the spread of Islam and the unification, however briefly, of Mandingo, Fula and Wolof peoples behind a single

cause. He fought principally against pagans and against Muslims who were careless in their observances, but he also, in establishing his rule, came into sharp conflict with the leaders of the expanding French colony on the Senegal river whose ambition was to establish routes to the upper Niger and the Western Sudan.

Influence of al-Hajj Umar

Maba was the eldest son of a Muslim priest who had come to Baddibu from the Senegal valley at the beginning of the nineteenth century. His education was started under his father and continued under scholars in Cayor and Jolof, the Wolof states to the north of the Gambia. When his training was completed, he stayed on teaching in Jolof, where he married the king's niece, Matti N'Jie, and attracted a substantial following within

A Wolof boy. This woodcut was taken from a nineteenth-century book—*Les Français au Niger* by Pietri

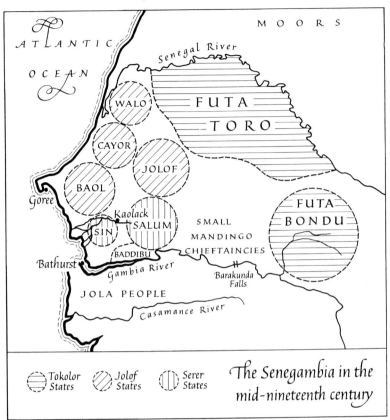

The Senegambia in the mid-nineteenth century

Tokolor States — Jolof States — Serer States

the state. He remained in Jolof after his father's death until his younger brothers persuaded him to return to Baddibu to become head of the family there. At this time the Tijaniyya leader, al-Hajj Umar, was gathering support for his attack on the states of the upper Senegal valley, and in 1850 Maba arranged a meeting with him. According to tradition the two men prayed together for three days and Umar told Maba of the significance of the Tijaniyya brotherhood and the *jihad* (holy war) he proposed to bring to the Senegambia. It is said that he and Maba divided the area between them, and that Maba was to be responsible for carrying the jihad to the Gambia valley. But Maba returned to his teaching and studies and remained in Baddibu for the next ten years. He founded a small town called Kir Maba (Wolof: Maba's town), which now lies north of the Gambia–Senegal border. There he was joined by a number of his *talibes* (student disciples) from the Wolof states to the north.

Oppression of the Marabouts

At this time, Baddibu was one of the chain of small Mandingo kingdoms which lined the River Gambia from its mouth to the Barakunda Falls, some three hundred miles up river. For several centuries Baddibu had been ruled by families directly descended from the first Mandingo settlers who had come to the river from the east, over four hundred years before. These families still controlled most of the economic, social and political benefits which the Gambia valley had to offer, because their long residence entitled them to authority over the use of land. By the middle of the nineteenth century, however, their power was much diminished, for the old traditions on which their rules were based were outdated. Life along the Gambia had changed and people who had settled near the river after the royal families were deeply involved in the groundnut trade. When Maba began his jihad, the wealthiest man in Baddibu was the *alkali* (headman) of a Marabout town, but Muslims were excluded from political positions outside their own settlements.

Thus, the people of Baddibu—as well as those of the other Gambia states—came to be divided into two opposing factions. These were labelled 'Soninke' and 'Marabout', and the division cut right across families and traditional political boundaries. The symbol of the difference between the two groups was the drinking of, or the abstention from, alcohol.

The Soninke party, the 'drinkers', was composed of the king and his supporters who were pagans or indifferent Muslims. The Marabouts, however, were generally devout, and were careful observers of the laws of the Koran. By 1860 they had attracted to their cause many of those dissatisfied with the King of Baddibu's rule, who complained that he and his men imposed illegal taxes upon them, stole their women, slaves and properties, and rode about the country disturbing the Muslims. Many of the Marabouts, being traders and the richest segment of the population, were likely to bear the greatest burden of taxation and to suffer the most from the demands of the Soninkes. Furthermore, by the 1860s, the king had lost most of his power to his followers and the country was suffering from the widespread lawlessness associated with the decay of a centralised authority.

A Fula member of the Marabouts. Woodcut from *Les Française au Niger*

The British contribution to the chaos

Baddibu was one of the most fertile areas along the river's banks, producing a large share of the groundnut crop which then, as now, was the principal river export. In 1861 the farmers of Baddibu sold their groundnuts to the British and French traders who were established in the river states. A small British colony which was located on an island at the mouth of the Gambia and which was dependent on the groundnut trade for its revenue, was drawn into the explosive situation in Baddibu in an attempt to protect this trade. Hostilities between Soninkes and Marabouts had resulted in damage to property which the British claimed as their own, and a military expedition was sent from the colony to restore order and punish Soninke raiders. In the course of their operations the British troops burned Marabout towns as well. Maba persuaded the invaders to spare his own community but the British demanded excessively

One of the Drinkers party—a Soninke man. Woodcut from *Les Français au Niger*

heavy fines from the Soninke rulers of Baddibu and left the state in greater chaos than they had found it.

The jihad begins

In the confusion that followed the British intervention, the town of Kir Maba became a centre of the dissatisfaction with what remained of Soninke rule. Suspecting treachery on the part of the Marabout leader, the king sent a party to kill him. Maba drove the Soninkes off, killing the king's son, and summoned the Marabouts of the kingdom to rally together under his leadership. A small Marabout force besieged the king's town and killed the king. In a few weeks the Soninkes were driven from Baddibu into neighbouring states in the north and south.

The transformation of Maba from scholar and teacher to warrior and political leader is an interesting one. He is said never to have carried weapons or to have personally fought in any of the wars that followed. Instead, he led the prayers before and during battle, surrounded by a following of blind priests, and wrote amulets for the warriors to carry with them. In 1862, immediately after the Marabouts' brilliant victories in Baddibu, he wrote to the British Governor at Bathurst saying that, having rid the country of the Soninkes, the institution of kingship had been abolished and with it all forms of authority maintained 'by plundering the property of others'. Instead of assuming power in the state himself, he said, he was returning to his farm to continue his teaching, for he was a man of peace and study, not a politician.

It was impossible for Maba to remain in retirement, however. Marabout communities elsewhere in the Gambia called for his help and the Soninkes, exiled from Baddibu, attempted repeatedly to return. Within the year, Maba's followers were fighting in Niumi, a small Mandingo state west of Baddibu, and Maba himself was forced to lead an army into Salum, to the north, in pursuit of a Soninke band. As a result he came into conflict with the king of Salum whom he drove from the state, replacing him with the king's father, a converted Muslim. The deposed king fled to a small French post which had been established near his capital and Maba's army was defeated by French artillery at Kaolack in 1862.

The jihad spreads to Serer and Wolof

At the time, this was but a temporary setback for the Muslims. During the next three years Maba extended his rule over most of the north bank of the Gambia. He even started to penetrate the south bank states as well, but was driven out by the Soninkes who rallied there against him. Such was the initial success of the jihad that the Soninke clans ceased to be a significant political factor along the Gambia for many years. Only in individual towns—such as those on the south bank which resisted Maba's

The formal dress of the damel of Cayor

invasion—were local Soninke authorities able to withstand the sweep of the Marabout revolution.

Even the French were forced to recognise Maba's rule in Baddibu and Salum. Together with other Marabout leaders, Lat Dior, *damel* (king) of Cayor, and Albury N'Jie, the *bourba*-Jolof (king of Jolof), Maba and his army overran the territory from Jolof to the river Gambia. In 1865 overtures were made to the Tokolor states of the Senegal valley, and to the Moors in what is now Mauretania, in an effort to construct under Maba's leadership a grand alliance of Muslims against both pagans and the, by then, intruding Europeans.

A description of Maba at this time shows us an exceptionally tall man, with a striking pock-marked face, whose qualities of leadership and persuasiveness attracted a following among many of the region's ethnic groups and inspired both fear and admiration in the Europeans who encountered him. The British Governor wrote that he had never seen so imposing an array of soldiers—in 1865 they numbered more than ten thousand—nor so well-disciplined a force as that which followed Maba. To the English he was known as a man who kept his word but whose success could prove dangerous to a continued European presence on the Gambia. They were alarmed to see that in spite of their long established policies of divide and rule, there was the likelihood of a unified African state controlling the banks of the river and its trade. Lacking sufficient funds to mount a full-scale attack on the Muslims, however, the British colonists tried by economic pressure and threats of armed intervention to overthrow the Marabout leadership.

The French fear a powerful state

It was, however, the French who most actively opposed the spread of Marabout rule in the Senegambia. In a series of letters which passed between Maba and Faidherbe, the Governor of the French colony on the Senegal, Maba accused the French of allying themselves with infidels against the faithful. He urged them to accept his divine mission and his political objectives—which were in fact incompatible with the

General Faidherbe—Governor of Senegal. Woodcut from *Les Français au Niger*

Europeans' desire for peace and stability and a free route for trade. Despite a peace treaty signed by both French and Muslim leaders in 1864, Faidherbe saw Maba as nothing more than a piratical warrior chief whose talk of holy war was simply a cover for plundering the area. Maba's alliance with the kings of the Wolof states seemed to the French an attempt to drive them from the Senegambia and they moved aggressively to destroy the Marabouts before they could establish their power. Two expeditions went into Salum and northern districts of Baddibu, burning crops and villages and destroying the countries' wealth. Although the French were not able to destroy the Marabouts' power during Maba's lifetime, they crippled the movement by these attacks and prevented the Muslims from moving freely into the Senegal valley. Whenever the Marabouts were drawn into open conflict, French artillery eventually defeated them, although the cost to the European forces was high. Each time they were defeated, the Muslims returned to southern Baddibu, reassembled their ranks, and pushed again into the north. By the end of 1865, however, these pressures from the outside were beginning to bring out latent conflicts within the Marabout movement itself.

Wolof domination

The territory controlled by the Muslims was divided into provinces, ruled by *qadis* (magistrates) chosen from among the generals of Maba's army. Theoretically a central authority was located at a town in northern Baddibu, Nioro-de-Rip, but in fact Maba was forced to move about continually fighting, and little control was maintained over the separate districts of the loosely-knit empire. Many of the provincial qadis had been members of the group of Wolof talibes who had first come to Baddibu with Maba during the 1850s. Thus to members of Mandingo communities in the Gambia states, Maba's movement was dominated by 'strangers from the north'. As a result, throughout his career, Maba was threatened by challenges to his authority from within the Gambia provinces. As Maba's attention turned more and more to the Senegal, and the cost of the war continued to bear on the Mandingo communities of the Gambia, their dissatisfaction increased. In 1865, as Maba's grand alliance with the Moors and the Tokolor seemed on the point of realisation, a revolt by Mandingo Muslims broke out in Baddibu against Maba's representative there. Maba was forced to return to the banks of the Gambia and never again was he able to grasp the opportunity of uniting the whole of the Senegambia behind him.

After restoring order in Baddibu, a period of inconclusive fighting followed in Salum. In 1867 Maba Diakhou Ba invaded Sin, a Serer state north of the Salum river. In the battle of Somb, the Marabouts were defeated and Maba was killed. His head was sent to the French at Goree to prove that after many victories and close escapes, the Muslim leader had indeed died. His body was buried at Gossos on the frontier of Salum and pilgrimages are made there to this day.

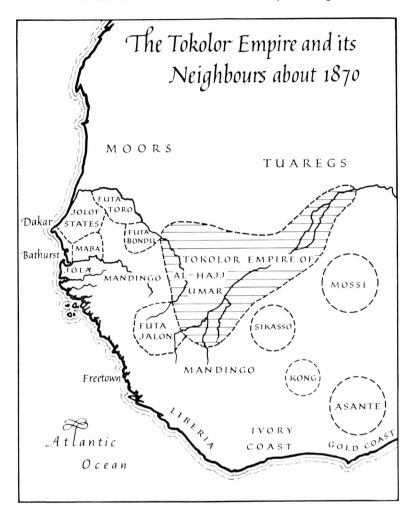

Maba was succeeded as *almamy* of Baddibu and Salum by his brother, Mamour n'Dary, but no one appeared to take his place as leader of Muslims throughout the Senegambia. Although Mamour n'Dary could, as late as 1873, call upon fifteen hundred armed men to follow him, no one after Maba was able to bring Mandingo, Wolof, Fula and Serahuli into a single unity within Islam. A few years after Maba's death the remaining leaders of the movement were fighting among themselves for political power.

The spread of Islam

Although no permanent structures of theocratic rule emerged from Maba's holy war, his primary purpose, the spread of Islam, was accomplished. Throughout his lifetime Maba took care to maintain the purity of the jihad, allying himself only with good Muslims or with those who were converted at his instruction. Both the kings of Cayor and Jolof were converted by Maba during the 1860s and both continued to convert others after his death. Prisoners taken during the wars were given a choice of pronouncing the declaration of faith and renouncing alcoholic drink, or of dying. And despite the diversity of their backgrounds his followers impressed observers with the uniformity of their belief. The British Governor in 1865 was astonished to see the entire army prostrate itself as one man for the evening prayers. He reported that dying Marabout warriors were congratulated by their companions on their good fortune and prospects of being accepted into heaven.

Thus, Islam was carried throughout the Senegambia, and the seeds of conversion were planted which flourished in the twentieth century. Today over eighty per cent of the people of the Gambia are professed Muslims, while a hundred years ago the majority were considered pagan or at the most indifferent observers of Islam.

Notes

Al-Hajj Umar-Khalifa of the Tijaniyya Tariqa in the Western Sudan. Between 1848 and his death in 1864 he built an empire between the Senegal and Timbuctu. Umar was a Tokolor of the Torodbe class from Futa Toro. See Hunwick, J., 'The Nineteenth Century Jihads' in Ajayi and Espie, *A Thousand Years of West African History*, Ibadan and Nelsons, 1965, pp. 262–278; Trimingham, J., *A History of Islam in West Africa*, Oxford, 1962, pp. 181–6; Abun-Nasr, J., *The Tijaniyya*, Oxford, 1965, pp. 101–141; Webster & Boahen, *The Revolutionary Years: West Africa Since 1800*, Longman, 1967.

Almamy—From Imam; The political and religious leader of a Muslim community, the title of the rulers in the Futa kingdoms and later adopted by Samori Toure.

Fula—In Hausa, Fulani (plural) and Ba-Fillaci (sing.); in their own language Fulo (sing.) and Fulbe (plural); in French Peuls or Peulhs; in Arabic Fellaci; their language is Fulfulde.

Jola—People located south of the Gambia river. It has been suggested that the Jola were responsible for the building of the stone circles of the Senegambia. See Mahoney, F. and Idowu, H., 'Peoples of the Senegambia' in *A Thousand Years ....* pp. 142–3. Also Beale, P. O., 'The Stone Circles of the Gambia and the Senegal', in *Tarikh*, ii, 2, 1968.

Lat-Dior—Damel of Cayor 1862–3 and 1871–1882; died 1886. In the struggle for supremacy among the Wolof, while the bourba-Jolof sought the support of the French, thus opening the country to their penetration and ultimate dominance, Lat-Dior turned to al-Hajj Umar who was then conquering a large empire on the upper Niger. Thus the struggle among the Wolof became a part of the larger struggle between the French and the Tokolor led by Umar, for control of the Niger–Senegambia region. Lat-Dior was driven off the throne in 1863 with the help of the French. In his years in exile he allied with Maba in an effort to get back his throne. When the French were defeated in Europe by Bismarck in 1870, they lost their grip in the Senegambia. Lat-Dior won back his throne but in the resurgence of French imperialism in the 1880s he lost it again. See Monteil, V., Lat-Dior, 'Damel du Kayor 1842–1886 et l'Islamisation des Wolof', *Archives de Soc. et des Relig.*, No. 16, 1963.

Marabouts—Muslim holy men or priests. On the Gambia river the word came to mean all devout Muslims who sought the overthrow of pagan rulers.

Qadis—Muslim magistrates or judges.

Soninke of the Mande-speaking peoples—The dominant people of the ancient empire of Ghana. Spread out widely over the Western Sudan as long-distance traders. Samori Toure was of Soninke origin. On the Gambia river it came to refer to all those who adhered to the pagan or nominal Muslim party against the Marabouts who supported Maba.

Serer—Prior to 1300 the Serer lived in the area now occupied by the Wolof. With the Wolof migrations into the area some Serer moved south and founded the kingdoms of Sin and Salum. Islam did not gain influence among the Serer as it did among the Wolof. Leopold Sedar Senghor, famous poet-philosopher of negritude and president of the Republic of Senegal, is Serer. For the history of the Serer see Mahoney and Idowu, 'Peoples of the Senegambia' in *A Thousand Years, ...*, pp. 136–140.

Torodbe—The dominant caste among the Tokolors of Futa Toro. Among the Tokolor the most important families, owners of large estates, religious and political leaders were Torodbe. Individuals were expected to marry within the caste.

Wolof—In the fourteenth and fifteenth centuries the Wolof people were united under the bourba-Jolof (King of all the Wolof) and organised into four provinces, Jolof, Walo, Cayor and Baol. In the sixteenth century the ruler of Cayor took the title 'damel' (king) and sought complete independence. Baol followed suit. By the nineteenth century all the former provinces were independent but a certain respect was reserved for the bourba-Jolof because he represented the common ancestral origins of the Wolof people. The majority of the people were pagan although Muslim scholars worked and taught among them. In the nineteenth century both Lat-Dior, damel of Cayor, and Albury n'Jie, the bourba-Jolof, were converted by Maba. There followed a mass turning to Islam so that the Wolof people today are thoroughly Muslim.

Samori Toure

R. Griffeth

History is a hard judge of war leaders. The winning general becomes a great hero, far-sighted, intelligent, full of virtue and honour. The losing general becomes a goat—short-sighted, stupid, devoid of honour and driven by base motives. However, a special place is reserved for those war leaders who fought a brave fight even though they lost the final battle. Such a leader was Samori Toure, creator of a vigorous military state in the

Samori Toure

Upper Niger region. The French soldiers who finally conquered this empire praised its creator for his undoubted military skill. They even conceded that he was a worthy and an honourable opponent, although they went on to write harsh opinions about some of the methods of war which he used.

As a war leader Samori was forced to commit many desperate and cruel acts which affect his reputation to this day. As we have said, history judges war leaders with a very special brand of severity. To some Samori was a great hero, an almost superhuman leader who directed the most determined resistance ever placed in the path of French conquest. To others, and especially to those Africans who were innocently caught between Samori's armies and the French columns, he has become a veritable devil, a destroyer of villages, a ruthless slave master, a degenerate seeker of booty.

Between these two extremes of passionate feeling, both of which reveal a greatly exaggerated picture, is the story of a real man. This man was possessed of a special genius and, almost certainly, a great sense of mission in life. His special genius was something rare among strong and determined leaders, the ability to see clearly and respond effectively to changing circumstances. His great mission in life was to build and constantly to defend an empire which was largely the product of his own personal energy.

But it was Samori's fate to see his efforts defeated by forces which even this extraordinary figure could not control. Finally, change and respond as he might, no alternative courses of action were left open. The supplies necessary to sustain his armies had been cut off and in every direction the occupation of his lands by a militarily superior power was becoming a fact.

Samori's long career is usually divided into three phases. The first phase includes his years as a growing boy and young man (1830—52) which he spent learning to become a trader. During the latter years of this part of his life he travelled extensively in the far western part of the Sudan.

Somewhere around the year 1852 a new phase began. His mother, Masorona, had been taken as a captive by Sori Birama, the chief of Bissandugu. In order to gain her release Samori voluntarily became a soldier in the army of this king. His life was thus transformed. From the peaceful life of a trader he was introduced to that most tempering experience for a young man, the rigorous training of the warrior. And it was also at this time that his obvious leadership talents came to the surface. Samori quickly rose to an important position in Sori Birama's army.

This second phase of Samori's career (1852–82) was taken up with the great tasks of construction. First he gathered a large following of ambitious young men and allies. With these followers he set out both by force and by diplomacy to build up from among the many small and independent communities of the Upper Niger region a strong and unified state. These years witnessed the fulfilment of Samori's manhood. He created an empire of which he was the unquestioned leader.

While this monumental task of state-building could easily stand as an achievement worthy of our undivided study, it is the last phase of his career, from 1882 to 1898, which has attracted by far the greatest attention. For during this decade and a half Samori was locked in a desperate struggle with French military forces who were slowly transforming the Western Sudan into a French colony. In this long and drawn-out conflict Samori's one great purpose was to save from destruction the empire into which he had poured the enormous energies of his life.

We must look, then, at the events of all three major phases of his long career, and not just at the last sixteen years of it, if we are to understand and appreciate properly the life and work of Samori Toure.

His youth

While the exact date of Samori's birth is not known, the best estimates place the event near the year 1830. His birthplace was the village of Manyambaladugu (near the town of Sanankoro) where his father, Lafiya Toure, worked a farm and raised cattle and sheep. The majority of the peoples of this area were Malinke (an important group within the Mande-speaking language family). Some of the Malinke were good Muslims, but the practice of the religion was not especially strong at the time except among those called 'Dyula' who were the men of commerce.

Lafiya Toure, even though he was a farmer, traced his descent from this good Muslim trading class. The Toure clan had originally lived around Jenne in the very heart of the old Mali Empire. When Songhai replaced Mali as the greatest state of the middle Niger region in the fifteenth century, some of the Toure clan, including Lafiya's paternal ancestors, left Jenne and moved into areas further up the river. There they married local Malinke girls and over time settled down to work farms. Such was the case with Samori's parents and grandparents. Lafiya took as his first wife a woman named Masorona. She belonged to the local Malinke clan who called themselves the Kamara. Lafiya and Masorona's first child was Samori.

Thus we can see that through his father's family Samori was indirectly connected with the great Dyula trading community. His maternal relations, on the other hand, attached him to the settled community of local farmers. From his earliest years, therefore, he may have received some instruction in the Islamic faith; but at the same time he was quite naturally initiated into the proper Malinke age-grade association. In this, Samori's upbringing was no different from that of most of his neighbours. One might strongly profess Islamic belief if the need, or desire, arose. This need did arise in Samori's case when he became a trader by profession

The first years of his life were spent in his father's village. At the age of seven, or thereabouts, he was sent to live with his mother's sister, Nyale Konate, and her husband, Kagbefere, who lived some twenty miles away in another village. After spending some time with them, he then accompanied a son of Kagbefere, Nyalemori, to an even more distant village. There he remained under his cousin's supervision until he was ready to return to his father's village to be initiated. After he had received the ceremonies of circumcision and initiation he remained with his father to help care for the farm and its cattle and sheep.

Lafiya took this opportunity of his eldest son's residence with him to encourage the young Samori to remain in Manyambaladugu and assume his proper duties in the family. Samori, on the other hand, was by then setting his sights on a more exciting profession. By all accounts the slow daily routine of the farmer held little appeal, and he yearned for a life with more action and excitement. So by the time Samori was seventeen or eighteen his spirit of fierce independence was becoming apparent already. He therefore asked his father's help so that he might become a Dyula (a trader). Lafiya was reluctant to agree, but he finally gave his son's proposed enterprise his blessing. Samori was given some calves as the first property which he might sell. He was then dispatched, with proper gifts and instructions, to live in the village of a good friend of his father's, Katsyanterna Mara, the chief of the Eastern Kuranko region. This chief became Samori's patron and protector.

The first duty Samori undertook as a trader was to supply his patron with rifles and gunpowder. On trips which he took to acquire these goods he thus began to familiarise himself with market towns over a wide area. He may have travelled as far as the coast itself, perhaps to Freetown, in order to obtain firearms. But he traded in many other items as well: kola, which he took from the Loma area (in Liberia); cattle and sheep which he bought in the Wassalu region (southern Mali) and from points even further distant in the east; and horses which may have been obtained from as far away as the Bobo territories (Upper Volta). And, like most other long-distance traders of the time, he certainly dealt to some extent in the slave trade.

Since all these activities caused him to travel for long periods to distant places, Samori soon came to know, and be known by, many of the important persons in the Dyula trading network. Looking ahead to later years, the knowledge which these new acquaintances gave him may have been extremely important when he became so actively engaged in building up and defending his state. For all the things he may have learned as a trader would be equally important to the soldier and to the head of a state: where and through whom to obtain weapons and horses; political conditions in the various villages and towns of the Malinke lands; persons who might rally to his cause from memories of past friendship and association.

In the service of Sori Birama

One other feature of this period of his life was to become centrally important: Samori's adherence to Islam. The profession of Muslim faith and formal obedience to the requirement of public prayer were two absolutely essential matters for anyone who became a Dyula. While it is extremely difficult to determine whether Samori went through a period of deep religious feeling at this time, he must, nevertheless, have become fairly regular in his formal profession of the outward forms of Islam. At the same time he may also have achieved some familiarity with such common Islamic notions as that of the jihad (war against unbelievers); for he was certainly aware of jihads that had been waged in territories not far from his homeland. Thus while many writers have accused Samori of having been a very poor Muslim, the accusation is probably quite unfair.

As most of his later acts proved, he was at least as strong in the faith as most of the rulers in Malinke-land at the time.

The great change in the direction of his life came some time around the years 1851–2. During one of his numerous long trading trips a friend came to him with the information that Sanankoro had been raided by the troops of Sori Birama, the king of Bissandugu. He learned with horror that during the raid his mother, Masorona, had been taken captive and led off to Bissandugu. Upon hearing this news he then considered what action he could take that would gain his mother's release. With an audacity that was to characterise so many of his actions, he finally resolved to go straight to Sori Birama and to offer this chief his services in return for his mother's freedom. This offer was accepted, and Samori voluntarily committed himself to seven years' service in Sori Birama's army.

Quite soon it became apparent that the new recruit possessed exceptional qualities of military leadership. He became a popular and an effective commander. He waged no large-scale campaigns, for his forces were small. But he did become skilful in the art of leading raiding parties, and he also matured his notions of how to deal with enemies and unfaithful friends by employing the gentler strategy of diplomacy and negotiation. All the time while he was serving another master he was certainly planning for his own independent future.

Civil disturbances of the kind which Samori himself, as a raider, helped to perpetuate, were constantly troubling the peace of Malinke-land. No one chief or king was strong enough to impose peace on the whole land. It therefore became Samori's ambition to create a force strong enough to achieve this elusive end. In the beginning his efforts were necessarily modest. Others began to attach themselves to the small band of warriors whom he personally led, partly because they were drawn by the strength of Samori's personal leadership. After a few years Samori felt himself strong enough to declare his independence from his master, Sori Birama, and to begin acting entirely on his own initiative. He was greatly assisted by members of his own family, whom he appointed sub-commanders over his forces, and by close friends and followers who saw in Samori's plans the fulfilment of their own ambitions. For the rest, some chiefs willingly agreed to serve his cause; others were persuaded by a combination of bluff, diplomacy and occasionally force to rally to his side.

Samori's organisation

Sanankoro became the main town of this new army. From there it began to push out in all directions. Throughout the late 1860s and 1870s the ever-growing Samorian armies campaigned regularly, so that by 1879 the limits of the area under his rule extended from Sierra Leone in the west to Ivory Coast in the east, and from a point near Bamako in the north to the Liberian frontiers in the south. When in 1879 Samori finally placed the major trading centre of Kankan under his direct rule, he held sway over all the major groups of Malinke peoples.

As more and more territory and ever-growing numbers of people were brought within the jurisdiction of Samorian rule, new forms of organisation were developed in order to make the state run smoothly. Previous states, like old Mali, had not paid much attention to everyday affairs on the local level except in the central territory of the capital and in important trade centres. The technique used to control local rulers was to require them to pay an annual tax, or 'tribute', to the king's treasury. But in the Samorian state (which was smaller and thus more easily governed) even local matters came under the direct supervision of Samori and his

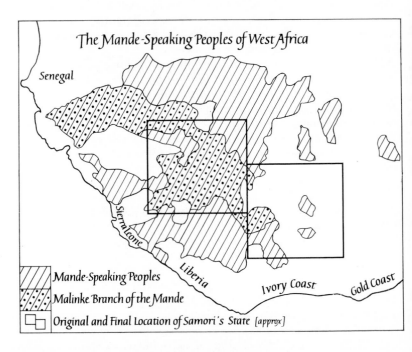

The Mande-Speaking Peoples of West Africa

Senegal

Sierra Leone

Liberia

Ivory Coast

Gold Coast

Mande-Speaking Peoples

Malinke Branch of the Mande

Original and Final Location of Samori's State [approx]

appointed officials. It was in this sense, then, that the Samorian state represented something quite new for the Malinke peoples.

The traditional territories of this Upper Niger region were re-organised into provinces. There were three provinces located in the valley of the Milo branch of the Niger river over which Samori and his ministers exercised direct control. Surrounding these three core provinces were seven others, each of which was governed by an appointed military official. This military governor shared his authority with a civil official, a *qadi* (judge), who was also the local head of the religious community. Both these officials were directly responsible to Samori himself who, as the *amir al-mu' minin* or *almami*, was the civil and religious chief of the entire state. This form of direct control carried right on down to the level of the village, several of which were grouped together to form a district within the province. All this elaborate organisation did not come into being at once. This efficient structure was built up over a period of at least twenty years. Similarly, it was not always the same size, for its extent depended upon Samori's success or failure in maintaining military control and friendly diplomatic relations with those in the more distant reaches of the state.

Samori's army

From this description we can see that the army was the most important element of Samori's authority. This fact remained unchanged throughout the life of the state. While Samori had the undoubted prestige which surrounded his religious title of almami, his power finally rested upon his command of an intensely loyal army. Here once again Samori's position can be seen to differ from that of some of his contemporaries such as Ahmadu, son of al-hajj 'Umar, whose religious authority was always greater than his political and military authority.

The most striking feature of the Samorian army was that its ranks were filled mostly with captives—young boys who had been trained to serve as professional soldiers. Unlike the Fulani troops in Sokoto and Macina, these soldiers were infantrymen who carried rifles. They were called *sofa*, and very few among them owned horses. Even though the sofa were recruited by the provincial commanders they owed their first loyalty to Samori himself, for the commanders were frequently changed and moved about from province to province. During times when major campaigns were undertaken, this standing army of professional sofa could be greatly expanded by calling upon a conscripted reserve (one man in ten in every village was required to answer a general call for more soldiers), a volunteer 'militia' consisting of those who owned horses and who could become the cavalry force in a large army corps, and other troops sent by chiefs who were outside the central state but under Samori's protection. The size of the army thus depended upon the military needs of the moment; and in periods of intense crisis as many as ten to twelve thousand fully equipped soldiers might be available for duty.

Even more striking than the large numbers of trained and reserve soldiers which made up the Samorian army, were the efficient ways in which it was used for various purposes. In fact, one should properly speak of the Samorian 'armies', for, until the very last months of the state's independent existence, units of the army were operating both at the centre and at the furthest corners of the territory. Some of these units were small, highly mobile forces employed in the north to put constant pressure on the French communications outposts. Larger units undertook such difficult military tasks as laying siege to fortified towns, such as Sikasso. Still other units protected the capital, or trade caravans, and went on small-scale raids. Each of these units, large and small, formed a reserve which could be dispatched to the point where it was most needed. The key point here concerns not the number of soldiers which Samori could call upon, but the efficient way in which he always used them. This is certainly a major subject in itself and lies at the very heart of what was special in Samori's genius as a war leader.

But as any student of military affairs would be quick to inform us, trained soldiers, regardless of their numbers, and however shrewd the strategic use of them, constitute only one part of the chance for success. Armies must always be backed up by assured and constant sources of supply. The supply of the Samorian armies presented special difficulties: Malinke-land lay far inland from the coast, and therefore far distant from supplies of firearms; it was also difficult to raise horses in this area, and they had thus to be

Hauts fourneaux et forgerons.

Samori's *forgerons* and blast furnaces

imported from outside the state, from the Volta region to the east or from the mid-Niger region to the north. Food presented less of a problem since the heartland of the state was basically agricultural in character. Even so, transport of foodstuffs to armies in the field required careful organisation. It was a singular achievement that, throughout the long years of state expansion and resistance to the French, these great difficulties of supply and transport were successfully met. Perhaps it was Samori's knowledge of trade routes, learned during his career as a Dyula, that came to his assistance when he was faced with organising the economic means of keeping his forces properly equipped. On the other hand, the talents of special workers in the state were wisely used: the *forgerons* (metal workers) were exempt from military service so that they might use their skills to cast replacement parts for imported rifles, and to manufacture cartridge cases and other types of military hardware. Necessary imports were thus supplemented by the growth of local industry harnessed to military needs.

First encounters with the French

This growing and prosperous new state met its first challenge from the French in 1882. The year before, a Samorian army had laid siege to the village of Keniera (near the modern city of Siguiri in Guinea). Since the French were, at that time, attempting to secure their lines of communication by establishing a series of fortified posts of which Siguiri was one, they saw the presence of Samori so near their line as a definite threat. The commander of the French forces, Lt. Col. Borgnis-Desbordes, sent an emissary to Samori asking that the siege of Keniera be withdrawn. The request was refused by Samori, and when the emissary returned to his chief and reported the outcome of his talk, Borgnis-Desbordes decided to employ a show of force. He sent out a column of some two hundred infantrymen, accompanied by a section of artillery, in hopes that Samori might thus be forced to withdraw from Keniera. The first shot was fired when this column made contact with an advance cavalry reconnaissance element from Samori's army. This mounted force was successfully repulsed by the French, but Borgnis-Desbordes' orders prevented him from following up this minor victory by pursuing Samori's main army.

A second encounter took place in 1883, after one of Samori's commanders had led a raid in which the telegraph line between the forts at Kita and Bamako was cut. At the same time a number of captives were taken from villages in areas which the French declared were under their protection. The engagement took place a short distance from Bamako where, at first, Samori's troops seemed to gain the upper hand. Borgnis-Desbordes was forced to order his troops back into the fortifications of the city. In a series of subsequent actions the French succeeded in demonstrating the superiority of their firearms as against those possessed by the sofa armies, and Samori reluctantly faced the prospect of having to alter his military tactics from those of direct confrontation with the main body of French troops to the more limited ones of planned raids by small numbers of highly mobile soldiers. This became the pattern of warfare for the future. Samori was able to preserve a partial advantage by the means of never over-committing his forces.

In 1885 a Col. Combes replaced Borgnis-Desbordes and soon found himself faced with this new situation. He saw that a critical weakness affecting the use of his troops was the fact that his telegraphic communications system could easily be broken by raids. He therefore sought to strengthen the garrisons at key points along the line. One such point was the village of Nafadie, between Siguiri and Niagassola, which was commanded by Captain Louvel. Nafadie had become nearly isolated, since numerous small parties of Samori's troops were raiding almost at will throughout the surrounding countryside. Combes dispatched a column to relieve Louvel, in the hope that the strengthened garrison could then set about pacifying the whole area. Numerous encounters followed and while the French nearly always managed to achieve victory in face to face combat, Combes was unable to win a decisive triumph over the Samorian army. In addition, many of Combes's troops had been recruited from among the Malinke, and these refused to fight against Samori. As a result of all these things Samori's reputation grew larger in the eyes of the local population.

A Franco-Malinke peace

The French were now coming to see that their task was not to be a simple one. Around the end of 1885 a large concentration of troops was built up at Niagassola. Their main goal was to contain Samori, since they saw that defeating him outright was not possible with the forces at hand, and to limit his sphere of operations to the area south of the Tinkisso branch of the Niger. At the same time Samori saw that he was faced with a similar problem, for the French with their superior weapons could not be decisively beaten. So the almami sent messengers to the French, indicating that he would like to open negotiations for a treaty of peace and a delimitation of territories.

Emissaries from both sides finally met at a place called Kenieba-Koura where a treaty bearing that name was signed. By its provisions Samori was granted sovereignty over the lands south of the Niger where it joined the Tinkisso. North of that boundary was to be the sphere under French protection. Samori clearly rejected the French suggestion of any form of protectorate over his state, a matter which troubled the French sufficiently to cause them to seek a re-negotiation of the treaty two years later. This

Samori receiving a French mission

task was undertaken by Captain Peroz who led a mission to Samori's capital at Bissandugu. A new document was drawn up which contained very similar clauses to the old one, but in language which was rather more specific on the question of the boundary. The greatest importance of this visit for us today is that Peroz subsequently wrote a full account of it, which has become one of our prime sources of information about Samori's state when it was at its height. Peroz had an opportunity to see and learn a great deal about how the state was organised and got to know some of the leading figures in it. He had a number of interviews with Samori himself and he has written with a certain measure of real admiration for the qualities of leadership, strength and warm hospitality which he found in the almami's character.

But while the treaty itself gave Samori a period of respite from French interference, it also checked the drive to expand his army. He was now forced to redirect his efforts, and so turned eastwards into areas which seemed by the treaty to fall within his guaranteed sphere. His first main object was to bring the important town of Sikasso under his control. In this ambition Samori probably made a grave strategic error, for Sikasso, under its own aggressive leader, Tieba, was also well into a period of expansion itself. Sikasso was a well-fortified place and thus Samori had to employ a lengthy siege-and-starve operation in the attempt to overpower it. For sixteen months the pressure was kept up, but to no avail. Tieba held out, partly owing to assistance given him by the French. This instance of French aid to a ruler whose country Samori declared to be within his sphere of influence so angered him that he declared the treaties broken.

Once again bands of the sofa began to raid north of the boundary line and the French seized the opportunity to retaliate. The breathing period had mainly benefited the French for they were able to pursue other adversaries free from any worry created by Samori. The almami on the other hand had suffered an important reverse, since the central object of his attention during the same period had resulted in no gain. Now that the battle was once again joined a last attempt at negotiations was made. The new French commander, Archinard, sent representatives to Samori in 1889. One last treaty, called the Convention of Niako, was dutifully and solemnly signed by both parties. But the issue was already clear: the French would tolerate no independent state anywhere within the Western Sudan, so that whatever treaties were signed were temporary by their very nature. It was equally clear to Samori that the means of an independent existence was being badly undermined by the French presence. By 1891, therefore, an unrelenting and implacable hostility came to characterise the attitudes of these two adversaries.

Scorched earth

On April 3, 1891, Archinard set out at the head of an impressive French army to invade and destroy the very heartland of the Samorian state.

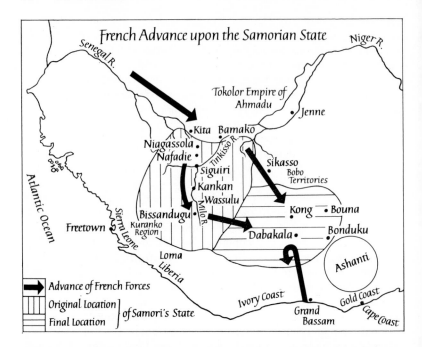

Elements of Samori's mobile forces kept up an attack on the advancing column, but it nevertheless reached the main city of Kankan on April 7. By April 9 the capital of Bissandugu was taken and the French had made good their first objective. Throughout the remainder of that year and during 1892 the French devoted themselves to securing this new territory effectively.

Meanwhile, Samori, his armies, and a major part of the population of his state, had withdrawn from the Milo valley to set up a new headquarters in the east. The tactic of withdrawal employed now was to level and burn all that was left behind so that the French would find it difficult to remain once they had taken possession of his lands. This 'scorched earth' policy characterised his major moves from now on, and it has done much to earn Samori that unpopular part of his reputation as a desperately cruel leader. It is quite beside the point here to attempt either to apologise or to condemn Samori's conduct in humanitarian terms. War produces inhuman actions from all parties involved in it, and this was true of the French as well as of Samori. But a significant point is that Samori, with an army that was poorly equipped when compared with that of the French, adopted one of the few tactics that held out any hope for the preservation of the state. Slave-capture and scorched earth policies were dreaded by the local peoples; yet both these practices were intimately connected with the problem of the survival of Samori's state. This explanation in no way justifies these cruel measures, but it does make clear why Samori used them.

By 1893 Samori had been forced to retreat from the major centres of his empire and had, as a consequence, rebuilt his capital at Dabakala (in the north-eastern Ivory Coast). Elements of the sofa now scattered to the east where they raided numerous communities. Frequently there were encounters with the French, but none of these amounted to a large scale battle. Back in the Upper Niger valleys the French continued to push on in spite of the terrible difficulties created by Samori's land-ravaging retreat. At the same time the French were planning a massive campaign which was designed to encircle Samori completely, cutting off any possible escape route. Columns were to advance from bases in the Sudan and others were to be dispatched from the Coast to join them, in an all-out effort to run their adversary to ground.

The closure of the ring

This grand operation got under way in 1894. From all areas of West Africa under French occupation detachments were sent to assist. Numerous columns from the French Niger forts converged on the newly created posts of the upper river valleys. Others came by way of Sikasso in the north-east. Yet a third column was sent up from Grand Bassam under the command of Col. Monteil, who had recently brought a large contingent of seasoned forces from Equatorial Africa to that place. Monteil set out in late 1894 to push through the forest towards Kong, but he met such fierce resistance from the Ivoiriens in the south that the column made painfully slow progress. By 1895 it had gone as far as Dabakala only to find that Samori had withdrawn. Monteil's troops were by this time crippled with disease, far beyond the limits of effective supply, and totally demoralised by the constant fighting they were forced into by the coastal peoples. He retreated to Grand Bassam without having made contact with either the main Samorian force or the other French columns.

The failure of this major offensive gave Samori sorely needed time to rebuild the strength of his army further and to attempt diplomatic alliances with other African leaders. But the time when such alliances might have proved workable now seemed past. He opened negotiations with the leaders of Kong, but nothing certain was settled between them. He also sent emissaries in the direction of Ashanti, hoping for an alliance between himself and King Prempeh, the reigning Asantehene. These ambassadors and their escorts were halted by a large English force near Bonduku, thus putting an end to the possibility of any co-operation from that direction. At an earlier time Samori had tried to secure the friendship and assistance of the English. He had for a long time received traders from the English areas into his state and had purchased weapons and gunpowder from them. But his action regarding a treaty with Prempeh had raised sufficient alarm with the governor of the Gold Coast to prevent any hopes of further friendly aid from the English. The story seemed to be similar in other places. Wherever Samori turned in search of allies he was confronted by the fact that the French and English expansion had cut him off from prospective friends.

As the isolation increased, military needs became more and more acute. In order to acquire goods for trade, Samori redirected his forces northwards. In April of 1895 he launched a vigorous attack against Kong. In spite of his former profession of friendship to the town's rulers, his sofa pillaged the territory, burnt the city, made captives of its able-bodied men and took the rest to be sold as slaves or to be executed. It is to this deed, particularly, that those critics of Samori who have regarded him as a cruel fanatic have pointed. In this instance, his critics appear to have the better of the argument. But one must not forget the extreme pressure which was being applied to Samori from all sides at this time. Survival had become by now a matter lived out day by day.

The last three years of Samori's history as an independent ruler form

The city of Kong before its destruction

a record of desperate resistance and overwhelming frustration. French attacks upon his sofa were met by counter-attacks, though there were also occasional attempts to re-open peace negotiations. When three emissaries were sent forth to petition the French, the French interpreted their arrival to mean that at long last Samori was willing to accept a protectorate. The ambassadors, on the other hand, insisted that their instructions were only to sue for peace and the establishment of a new set of boundaries. The almami was still to be guaranteed an area over which he alone would exercise sovereignty. But the French would have no less than their protectorate. Disheartened, the emissaries were forced to convey this bitter news to their leader.

Samori responded to the French demands by stating that he wished only for a treaty of peace and commerce in which both sides could live in amity. But as to accepting the protectorate, he replied that 'You (the French) are able to close off the route to the South much as you have already closed off the routes to the North and to the West, but the road East remains open to me and the land of God is large: amen.'

Thus ended the possibility of an easy solution for the French. The following year, 1897, a major incident took place which sealed Samori's fate by bringing down the wrath of both the French Government and popular opinion on his head. Captain Braulot, the officer who had previously met with Samori's emissaries, was leading a column near Bouna when he encountered a sofa regiment led by Samori's son, Sanatieni-Mori. The two groups did not engage each other in battle, but met on amicable terms since peace negotiations were presumably still going forward. However, while the two forces were camped together an incident arose in which some of the Senegalese riflemen accompanying Braulot aroused the anger of a few sofa. In the disturbance which followed, shooting broke out and Braulot, his lieutenant, a French sergeant and ninety-seven Senegalese were killed. When Samori received the news of what had happened he was furious, for the incident made it appear that he had permitted a terrible and treacherous act. He dispatched his deep apologies to the French for these acts committed by his men, but he was as unwilling as ever to give in to the French political demands.

In the meantime the French set about sealing off that last route to which Samori had referred—the East. In May of 1898 a company under the command of Colonel Audeoud captured the city of Sikasso from Tieba's successor, King Babemba. Samori's last hope was now to make one final move, in the direction of the forest, to Liberia. There he hoped that a strongly fortified mountain position might be defensible. But the French set out immediately to follow his trail. Step by step the almami moved westwards, burning each village as it was vacated, and leaving small contingents of sofa to fight rearguard actions. This tactic was rapidly depleting his forces, but it also cost the French men and human suffering.

The end for Samori came in September of 1898 when a surprise attack was made on his encampment by a small company led by Captain Gouraud. Employing the ambush tactic, Gouraud caught Samori's exhausted guards off balance, and the almami was taken prisoner before he could gather his forces to counter-attack. All the weapons were collected and destroyed. Samori and his immediate family were transported first to Kayes and then, after some months' detention, they were exiled to Gabon. Samori died there two years later, bitter over the years of disappointment met in opposing the French encroachment on his lands, but happy in the knowledge that his followers had remained unflinchingly loyal to him until the very end. His sofa was broken up and the men were sent back to their original villages. Thus came to an end a resistance movement which had, over the course of more than sixteen years, proved its effectiveness in face of overwhelming odds.

Preservation of the state

Samori had begun the task of state-building before the French had arrived in the Sudan. At first, therefore, they seemed to be only one more adversary to fight, no different from other African opponents. They might, in fact, have become friendly allies. Only later did the French intention to establish an empire over all the Sudan become apparent to Samori; and when it did, he resisted with all his might. In adopting effective means to carry on the military aspects of resistance, Samori showed himself to be flexible and wholly receptive to using the best means at his disposal to achieve freedom from outside control. His manufacture of parts for the most modern weapons, his highly realistic diplomacy, and finally his scorched earth strategy were all geared to this end. At its heart, then, Samori's fight was a political one in which the major point was always the preservation of his state.

One of the greatest strengths of Samori's state contained also a great weakness. The fact that he ruled over a group of related peoples, the Malinke, of which he was also a member, gave his first empire a large measure of internal unity. But when he was faced with a powerful opponent like the French, he found it very nearly impossible to act in concert with other rulers such as Tieba, Ahmadu of Massina, and Prempeh against what might have been considered by all as the common enemy. His attempts to establish alliances came too late to be of any help. Islam, which might have served as the cement needed to hold a more widely based empire together, proved instead a liability when the almami was placed on the defensive. For when religion was made to serve the ends of state above all, it suffered a bad reputation for non-religious acts of cruelty committed in its name. For non-Muslims of the area, then, Islam came to have the worst possible connotation—capture, slavery, or death.

Upon viewing these many considerations in the career of Samori Toure it should now be clear that sweeping judgments, either in praise or condemnation, hide and distort much that we should like to know. First, he did not begin as a resistance leader. Samori created out of conditions of political chaos in the Upper Niger region a strong, centralised state which was rooted in certain traditions of political reform which had swept the Western Sudan in the nineteenth century. But before the state could achieve any measure of equilibrium, and while it was still in the phase of rapid expansion, it was confronted by another, militarily superior expansionist power in the form of French soldiers. Slowly perceiving what this meant, Samori marshalled his strength and by both negotiation and shrewd use of his limited forces sought to preserve his freedom of action. That he finally lost was not because it was beyond his intelligence to win; it was rather the result of his lack of command over the resources necessary to sustain the fight.

Reviewing his career, then, Samori's early years were marked by a long and constructive phase of state-building. This was followed by fifteen years of an often dramatically successful struggle to avoid being swallowed up by a mighty alien intruder. While these attempts and their purpose do not necessarily excuse the acts of cruelty which were committed in the name of military need, the long resistance does demonstrate the admirable strength of Samori's personality, the genuinely inventive character of his leadership, and the vigour to sustain a defence of the state which he had so painstakingly built through long hard years of supreme challenge. Thus while the argument will undoubtedly continue between those who admire and those who dislike Samori, his importance as a leading figure in the history of West Africa during the nineteenth century will remain undisputed.

Notes

Note that Samori Toure is often spelled Samory Ture; the Mande speaking people are often referred to as Malinke, Mandinka, Mandingo or Mende. Most books about Samori are in the French language. One particularly good (because it is written in simple and easy French) is Niane, D. T. and Suret-Canale, J., *Histoire de l'Afrique Occidentale*, Présence Africaine, 1961, pp. 119–128. This is beautifully illustrated and is a textbook for Secondary schools in the Republic of Guinea.

Muhammad Ali, Moderniser of Egypt

R. T. Tignor

In examining the career of Muhammad Ali, ruler of Egypt from 1805 until his death in 1849, a historian must decide what aspects of this man's diverse career to emphasise. Should he concentrate on Muhammad Ali's military exploits? Should his primary concern be the complex and important diplomatic problems of these years, the impact of Egypt upon Eastern and international diplomacy? Or should the historian present Muhammad Ali's career in more traditional form by means of a chronological political narrative? I have decided to follow none of these perfectly valid approaches, but rather to examine Muhammad Ali as a moderniser of Egypt. Because of present-day interest in problems of modernisation, there seems to be some virtue in analysing his impact upon Egyptian society in these terms. What aspects of Egyptian society were most profoundly transformed, what aspects less so, and what were the reasons behind the modernisation programme?

What is modernity?

A word is in order about the term modernisation. Modernisation is an effort by which a country strives to become modern. In this sense, then, all countries that are not modern must sooner or later attempt to modernise if they are to survive as independent units. But to become modern does not mean to become Western, even though the countries of Western Europe were the first to develop modern institutions. There are, in fact, many approaches to modernity, and many different ways in which countries can be modern. The modern Western world is the result of pressures for modernisation interacting upon traditional Western institutions. By the same token we can expect that the pressure of modernity will interact with traditional institutions in the non-Western world.

For purposes of analysis I should like to divide the characteristics of modernity into four categories: economic, political, social, and intellectual.

The most obvious characteristic of modernity is that found in the economic sphere—industrialisation. Whereas in traditional societies the vast majority of the population lives on the land and engages in subsistence agriculture, in modern societies a larger percentage of the population lives in cities and produces manufactured goods. The agricultural sphere is also rationalised and mechanised, permitting a proportionately smaller population to produce foodstuffs not merely for themselves, but for the urban population as well. Rural self-sufficiency, so characteristic of traditional, agricultural societies, gives way to interdependency, trade, and the use of monetary exchange between rural and urban areas.

The modern political sphere is somewhat more difficult to analyse. It used to be a cardinal belief of most Western European and American scholars that democratic institutions were a requisite of political modernity and maturity. Now these scholars are not so sure, for they have numerous examples of successful modernisation being effected by means of authori-

Muhammad Ali 1769–1849

tarian, non-democratic regimes. Other characteristics of political modernity are more universal. The first is the emergence of the nation-state. Whereas empires and loosely-organised kingdoms were common in traditional societies, these have given way in modern times to the nation-state. Moreover, an important part of the organisation of the nation-state is the loyalty of the individual to his government. The ability to mobilise vast numbers of people for political and economic action, and to involve vast numbers in state programmes, is another characteristic of political modernity.

In the social sphere the essential characteristic is a high level of social mobility. This entails movement from place to place as well as from job to job. A person's occupation is determined primarily by the capacity he shows for doing certain jobs, rather than by his birth, family connections, religion, and so forth.

In the intellectual sphere modern societies are characterised by the growth of scientific knowledge and the use of the scientific method. Whereas in traditional societies knowledge of the natural world was accorded a lower priority than knowledge of the supernatural, this relationship has been reversed in modern societies. The scientific method leads to verifiable knowledge, that is, knowledge which can be checked over and over again by means of experiment.

Here then are a few characteristics of modernity, though these have been presented in outline only. They could be amplified a lot, and, of course, they are not universally agreed upon. With this framework in mind, and remembering that Egypt was a traditional society in 1800, we can now examine Egyptian modernisation under Muhammad Ali.

Securing political control

Muhammad Ali was not an Egyptian, but rather an Ottoman Turkish war leader, who was sent to Egypt by the Ottoman Empire during Napoleon's invasion of the country. French troops under Napoleon had invaded Egypt in 1798. Egypt was still a part of the Ottoman Empire, although it was more or less self-governing under a ruling oligarchy of Mamluks, a military class, originally ex-slaves and of foreign origin, who had ruled Egypt since the eighteenth century. The Mamluk army was thoroughly defeated by the French troops, and the Ottomans, fearing the extension of French campaigns into the rest of the Empire, despatched their own troops into Egypt. Eventually the French army was forced to withdraw from Egypt, and a three-cornered power struggle ensued. This involved the Mamluks, the legitimate representatives of the Ottoman Empire, and Muhammad Ali, who, instead of retiring from Egypt as the Ottomans commanded, wanted to carve out an empire for himself. By 1805 Muhammad Ali had established enough power to win reluctant recognition from the Turkish Empire as the Viceroy of Egypt. The Mamluks had been temporarily defeated, and those who had not succumbed to Muhammad Ali had retreated to Upper Egypt, a traditional area of refuge for rebel groups in Egypt. Muhammad Ali lay in wait for these opponents, however, and in 1811, on the pretext of negotiating with them, he invited the Mamluks to Cairo. Those who came were slaughtered by the Viceroy's troops as they sat at a banquet, and from that year—1811 —Muhammad Ali's power was unchallenged within Egypt. Once having solidified his power, the Viceroy turned his attention to modernising his society.

That Egypt would in any case have begun to modernise in the early nineteenth century seems probable. The encounter with the French troops had been decisive, and, no matter which of the three contenders for power had obtained control of the government, there would surely have been some effort to alter Egyptian society. What the encounter with the French had shown was the overwhelming military superiority of the Western world. But the shape of Egyptian modernisation was decisively effected because it was Muhammad Ali who came to power. He was not a Mamluk, so he felt no obligation to preserve any of the basic Mamluk institutions. Nor was he the agent of the Ottoman Empire, so his own reform programmes did not have to be tied to those of the Ottoman Empire. Had they been there could be no doubt that they would have been less successful, because Ottoman reform met many obstacles which made it less effective than Egyptian modernisation.

Military modernisation

The cornerstone of Egyptian modernisation was military reform. This could not have been otherwise. In the first place, Muhammad Ali was himself a military man. Secondly, it was the military superiority of the West which had so far impressed the Middle Eastern leaders. Thirdly, Muhammad Ali rightly feared the designs of the Ottomans. He was an intruder in Egypt who had deprived the Turks of control over this rich territory. He realised that the Ottomans would be anxious to reassert control over Egypt if they had the opportunity to do so, and that, if he allowed military modernisation to lag, the Ottomans would easily be able to overrun Egypt. Perhaps most important, Muhammad Ali was an ambitious man. He wanted to secure a powerful place for himself and his family in the Middle East. Egypt was to be his base of operations, for extending his sphere of influence throughout the area while, of course, retaining his control over Egypt. A strong military machine was to be the instrument for attaining these goals.

Once Muhammad Ali had consolidated his power in 1811, he was free to turn his attention to military modernisation. He recognised Egypt's lack of trained military personnel, and he looked primarily to France for expert assistance. Although Muhammad Ali was willing to employ foreign technicians from all over Europe, French technicians and institutions gradually came to occupy the predominant role in Egyptian modernisation. Men who had served with Napoleon's army and found it difficult to adjust to a less militaristic society in France were attracted to Egypt.

Educational modernisation

The Viceroy was not a shortsighted man. He realised that a more general modernisation would be required to support the reforms in the army. Consequently, Egyptian modernisation was carried into many other areas. Muhammad Ali realised the need for far-reaching changes in Egypt's system of education. The technological and military superiority of the West derived from its system of education, and Muhammad Ali was well aware that Egypt would remain behind Europe, or dependent upon it, until Western education was introduced into Egypt. Thus the Viceroy launched a two-pronged programme for modernising Egyptian education. First, European scientists were brought to Egypt to serve as teachers in the new schools. Second, the best Egyptian students were sent from these schools to pursue their studies at advanced levels in Europe. The ultimate goal was to bring European science to Egypt, and, through the training of Egyptian students, to free Egypt from its dependence on Europe.

Military considerations were an important aspect of Egypt's modern educational system. The first new schools created by Muhammad Ali were military ones, designed to turn out an officer corps for his army. Egyptian students sent to study in Europe were expected to study technical subjects: engineering, medicine, and so forth. Most were subsequently employed by the Egyptian army. Nevertheless, there was no clear-cut distinction between the military and the civilian in Egypt, and many of the educational reforms affected non-military spheres. Ultimately, schools of Engineering and Medicine were created. One of the most important schools was the School of Translations, founded because of the need for men skilled in making translations from European languages into Arabic or Turkish. It was in this school that many works were translated from European languages into Arabic, thus bringing a great deal of European science to Egypt.

The financing of these expensive programmes of modernisation, in addition to the Egyptian military campaigns, put a much greater burden on the resources of Egypt than ever before. Thus major efforts were made to modernise the economic system.

Agricultural modernisation

Egypt is the gift of the Nile. Without Nile irrigation waters the land could not support cultivation. The traditional system for irrigating the land was known as basin irrigation. Basins with earthen walls around them were prepared along the side of the Nile, and the flood waters were led into them and allowed to remain there for a fairly long period, while they deposited the silt they were carrying with them. After this period of time had elapsed, the waters were returned to the main Nile channel and were carried to the sea. This system was employed from Pharaonic times until the beginning of the nineteenth century. But it had some basic weaknesses. Since only flood waters were used for irrigation, the soil could support only one crop a year. Most of the land was cultivated in subsistence crops, and only a small percentage of the crops could support an urban population. High and low floods were disastrous. The high floods would spill over the banks of the Nile and rush uncontrolled through the basins, bringing destruction to the land and villages. Low floods did not bring enough water to enable all the regularly cultivated land to be irrigated. Famines were a frequent occurrence in Egypt. Finally, many of the most economic crops could not be grown, because their growing season coincided with the low Nile season when irrigation water was not available. Cotton and sugar—two crops which could have been exported—were grown only in the summer, which coincides with low Nile months.

These were the problems facing the modernisers of Egypt if they were to increase the economic resources of the country. What Muhammad Ali did in addressing himself to the problem was to introduce a full-scale agricultural and hydraulic revolution that has continued unabated to the present. The transformation came about because of the Viceroy's desire to grow summer cash crops, particularly cotton and sugar. To do this he needed to make irrigation waters available for summer cultivation. And he solved this problem by digging deep canals capable of carrying low Nile waters to the land. A number of European hydraulic engineers were brought to Egypt to implement these reforms. These engineers also began work on the first major Egyptian dam across the Nile, which was located at Cairo. This dam was designed to raise the summer Nile waters, thus enabling more summer irrigation water to be carried to the land. Although the dam at Cairo was not completed until a later period, it was the first of numerous dams designed to control Nile water and permit the cultivation of two, or even three, crops a year. This development in Egyptian hydraulics is now culminating in the enormous new dam being constructed at Aswan.

With the introduction of this system of controlled irrigation, Egyptian peasants and landlords could now cultivate a crop which was to become Egypt's great export—cotton. Egypt began its first cotton exports to Europe in the 1820s, and by the end of the nineteenth century cotton was to account for more than eighty per cent of all Egyptian exports. Moreover, because of the favourable soil and climate Egyptian cotton was a specially high-quality product which always held a strong position in the world market.

To increase state revenues as much as possible Muhammad Ali introduced a system of state monopolies by which certain products grown in Egypt had to be sold to the state at prices fixed by the state. Cotton, sugar, and other export items were on this list. These products were bought by the state from Egyptian cultivators at low prices and then sold to European merchants at much higher prices. The state thus obtained new sources of revenue. But, of course, the Egyptian peasantry were still forced to live at bare subsistence level, now compelled to farm their lands more than once a year, but enjoying little benefit from the increased economic productivity of the lands.

Industrialisation

Another aspect of Egyptian modernisation was industrialisation. Muhammad Ali's desire to be independent of Europe for manufactured products led him to embark upon an industrial programme. Once again, European technicians were brought to Egypt. A steel and iron foundry was established. Ship-building plants were constructed in Alexandria. Textile mills were established throughout Egypt, and, during the time that this experiment flourished, Egypt manufactured a large proportion of the textiles purchased in the country. On the whole, however, industrialisation was expensive and not successful. The machinery had to be imported. There were not enough technicians to keep machines in a proper state of repair; when there were breakdowns, machines were allowed to lie idle. Nor were Egyptian industries competitive with European industries; they existed only because of high protective tariffs. Moreover, Egypt did not have cheap fuel sources, and most of the machinery was run by animal power. When, in fact, the protective tariffs were abolished, the experiment in industrial development collapsed.

Military exploits

Egyptian modernisation depended upon military success, and so we must now turn to the military campaigns of Muhammad Ali. There is no virtue in giving a detailed narrative of these military efforts. Rather, a simple enumeration of them, a description of the general goals, and an indication of the outcome should suffice. Muhammad Ali's overriding goal was to secure for himself and his successors a safe and unchallenged position in the Middle East. All of his campaigns had this aim. There were forays into the Sudan, which were designed to extract its wealth and make available new supplies of army recruits. Mainly, however, the campaigns of Muhammad Ali involved the Ottoman Empire. In the early part of his career he fought on the side of the Ottomans, primarily because the Turks desperately needed military help. He helped put down a revolt in the Arabian peninsula and then unsuccessfully tried to crush the Greek nationalist rebellion. Through these campaigns the Egyptian Viceroy hoped to win concessions from the Ottoman Empire which would secure his position in Egypt. Eventually, though, Egypt and the Ottoman Empire were destined to clash, because the Ottomans were not content to let Egypt slip from their grasp, and because Muhammad Ali's ambition was ceaseless. War broke out twice in the 1830s, and on both occasions the Egyptian forces defeated their Ottoman adversaries. Had it not been for European intervention, Muhammad Ali might have been able to invade Istanbul and proclaim himself Sultan of the entire Ottoman Empire.

European intervention, led by Britain and Russia, was, however, to prove the undoing of the Viceroy's plans. Neither Britain nor Russia wished to see the collapse of the Ottoman Empire, or its take-over by Muhammad Ali. The British regarded the continued existence of the

Empire as a safeguard to the various routes to India and the Far East. They were determined that the two major routes, which went through Egypt and Syria, should not both be controlled by an ambitious man like Muhammad Ali. The Russians desired a weakened Ottoman Empire, dependent upon Russian strength for its existence. Accordingly, they feared the designs of Muhammad Ali. There was another important element ranged against the Viceroy: the European commercial community. European merchants wanted to trade freely in Egypt, and they were fundamentally opposed to Muhammad Ali's state monopolies which cut into their profits. Through the combined efforts of these groups Muhammad Ali was forced to halt his advances into the Empire and in 1841 he was compelled to sign the Treaty of London. The main features of this Treaty were that the size of the Egyptian army was to be reduced drastically and that Egypt was to abolish its protective tariffs and accord a favourable position to European merchants. The Treaty did, however, recognise the right of Muhammad Ali and his successors to rule over Egypt as a self-governing province within the Ottoman Empire.

The Treaty of 1841, limiting the size of Egypt's army, undercut the goals of Egyptian modernisation. Once the military ambitions had been frustrated, there was little pressure to carry on the other programmes of modernisation. Moreover, the abolition of the existing trade barriers and the gradual suppression of state monopolies undermined industrialisation and reduced state revenues. Reform programmes were allowed to slacken. Schools were shut down. Education missions to Europe were slowed. European technicians were sent back to their countries. From 1841 until 1848, when Muhammad Ali died, there was a marked decline in Egyptian modernisation, a decline which continued during the reigns of Muhammad Ali's two successors, Abbas (1848–54) and Said (1854–63). Modernising activities were not to reappear until Ismail came to the throne in 1863.

Egypt and other modernising societies

Egyptian modernisation can be compared with modernising programmes carried out in other societies. In order to modernise a society must, of course, begin to develop in the direction already indicated. Quite often the two most serious obstacles to modernisation are the lack of technical skill and the shortage of capital (the large sum of money necessary to buy machinery to start industry or to finance the mechanisation of agriculture). Muhammad Ali's efforts to solve these two problems can be compared with solutions found in other countries.

The first and obvious point is that Egypt borrowed its technical skills from Europe on a very large scale. Europeans were brought to Egypt for almost all modernising projects. They were put in charge of the army, navy, educational system, public health services, agriculture, hydraulics, factories, commerce, and general economic planning. Moreover, Egyptians were sent to Europe in large numbers to obtain advanced scientific training. The borrowing of technical skills from economically and technologically more advanced societies has been adopted by almost all late modernising societies, and even some early modernisers. Indeed the only country which did not use this technique to some extent was the first moderniser, England, simply because it had no technologically advanced society to borrow from. Even the early modernising Western European states—Germany and France—borrowed technical skills from England, although not

The Mosque of Muhammad Ali in Cairo

so systematically as did the Egyptians because they were not so far behind and had modern schools.

The second obstacle to modernisation is capital formation, and here one country's experience differs radically from another. In England, capital was formed largely by private entrepreneurs. Other countries were not so liberally endowed with capital and were forced to look for new approaches. In France and Germany important new banking institutions were created in the nineteenth century which immensely stimulated the formation of capital for industrial purposes. Communist Russia employed another technique. The Russians had less capital available in their society. Yet through the collectivisation of peasant farms and through a system of central economic planning the state was able to squeeze capital from the peasants and use it for industrialisation.

It is surprising how much Muhammad Ali's programmes foreshadowed the policies of Stalinist Russia. The Egyptian Viceroy did not collectivise the peasantry as did Stalin. Indeed, there was a significant growth in private property during this period. But he did impose a set of state monopolies on most agricultural, commercial, and industrial products sold in Egypt. Thus he was able to buy cheaply and sell dearly. The profits realised swelled state revenues and provided the funds for modernisation. Money was squeezed from the population by keeping them at low levels of living. Egyptian peasant suffering was acute, as it was in Russia under Stalin. Peasants deserted their farms rather than work under this system, but most were brought back by the state.

The Treaty of 1841 ended the state monopolies and this source of state revenue. When Egypt began to modernise again—under Ismail—another, more popular, technique for overcoming the lack of capital was employed. Money was borrowed from Europe. As happened so often in the nineteenth century, capital borrowing led to European political intervention in Egypt, and ultimately to the establishment of European political control.

Assessment

Another way to look at Muhammad Ali's modernising efforts is in the light of the four categories of modernisation previously mentioned. To what extent was Egypt moving toward modernity and to what extent was it not? In the economic sphere there were quite substantial efforts to industrialise and develop a cash economy for agriculture. The first programme failed; the second succeeded and Egypt's rural economy was gradually transformed from a subsistence one, enjoying a large measure of self-control, to an export economy tied to the world economy. In the political sphere Egypt has always had a political compactness not found in many other traditional societies. This compactness or centralisation has come from the irrigation system of the country which must be administered by a centralised government. Moreover, Egyptians have always lived in the basin of the Nile, partly removed from other populated areas in the Middle East and Africa by deserts. Egyptians had a sense of their own identity. Nevertheless, this compactness did not mean that Egyptians in the past had developed a national consciousness or loyalty to a nation-state. In fact, traditionally Egypt had been governed by alien military oligarchies which exploited and oppressed the Egyptian populace for its own purposes. This situation was little altered under Muhammad Ali, for he was himself an alien conqueror who brought his own protégés to Egypt and exploited it as ruthlessly as his predecessors. He did not really try to promote an allegiance to the Egyptian nation-state on the part of the Egyptian populace. But there were many unintended consequences of his modernisation drive favourable to the development of national feelings. Although Muhammad Ali tried to reserve top positions in the army and the administration to Turks like himself, many Turks were disinclined to enter non-military positions and so Muhammad Ali had to turn to the Egyptian population. Turks were especially reluctant to enter the new non-military schools or the civilian professions—medicine, engineering, and teaching. These were accordingly monopolised by Egyptians. Egyptian peasants for the first time were recruited into the army. Egyptians were also sent to Europe where they experienced concepts of European nationalism and carried them back to Egypt. Finally, economic modernisation led to greater contact between rural and urban Egypt and gradually began to break down rural self-sufficiency.

In the social sphere there was an obvious increase in the movement of people about the country, and a growth of urbanisation. The major cities of Cairo and Alexandria began to expand at a rapid rate. Other new cities were founded in the Delta.

The changes in the intellectual sphere were also self-evident. Western science was brought to Egypt, and its mastery gradually became the standard by which a person was judged. This development put new emphasis on merit as the measure of a man rather than birth. At the same time traditional Muslim learning co-existed with the new learning. There were two sets of schools in Egypt, one leading into the modernised institutions and the other into the Islamic institutions. There were inter-relations between these two spheres of activity, but in time the scientific, modernised institutions came to assume the predominant position in Egypt.

Emperor Menelik II of Ethiopia

R. Pankhurst

Menelik, who reigned as King of Shoa from 1865 to 1889 and as Emperor of Ethiopia from 1889 to 1913, was perhaps the greatest of Ethiopia's rulers. His reign was of considerable importance in that it witnessed the reunification and modernisation of his country, as well as a great increase in its position in world affairs.

Ethiopia, though a powerful state in ancient and medieval times, had in the middle of the eighteenth century fallen on evil days. The powers of the monarchs had been usurped by the feudal lords and centralised government had been replaced by the autonomy of the various provinces whose rulers warred among themselves.

Menelik II; a drawing based on a picture in the
Museum of Anthropology and Ethnography, Leningrad

The reorganisation and resurrection of the ancient state had first been attempted in the middle of the nineteenth century by the Emperor Theodore (1855–1868) and had later been partially accomplished by his successor, the Emperor Yohannes IV (1872–1889). It was, however, left to Menelik to bring this work to fruition, as well as to withstand the pressure of the European powers in the scramble for Africa, and to lay the foundations of a modern state.

Menelik, the grandson of one of the most famous of the kings of Shoa, Sahle Sellassie (1813–1847), had been brought up at the court of the Emperor Theodore from whom he learnt much. The young man was kept there as a prisoner, but was treated with considerable respect and consideration. In 1865, he succeeded in escaping from Theodore's fortress at Magdala and made his way to his native province of Shoa whose government he then took over.

Menelik—the man

Menelik's personality, his innate intelligence and ability, his grasp of world affairs and his interest in modernisation, impressed all observers. 'During the many interviews I had with him,' recalls the British diplomat, Rennell Rodd,

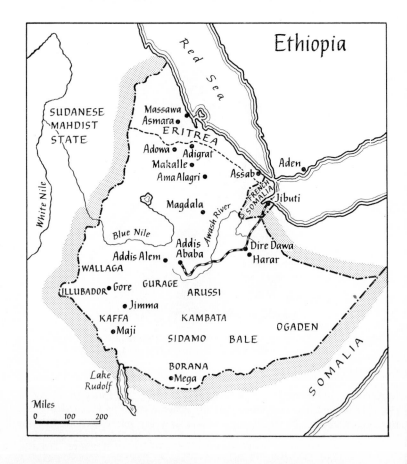

'I formed a high opinion both of his intelligence and his character. . . . His energy was astonishing. By rising before dawn and beginning his day with prayers in chapel at 6 a.m. he made time to attend personally to every detail of the administration in a country constituted of many heterogeneous elements. Accessible to all his subjects from the highest to the lowest, he had succeeded in winning universal regard and affection.' Other observers tell a similar tale. Thus the French traveller Vanderheym noted that Menelik got up early and was constantly occupied with one project or another and might be seen inspecting, for example, the mechanical saws, the water system, the repair of artillery or guns, the making of mule collars or shields or the planting out of vegetables from newly imported seeds. The sovereign's physician, Dr. Merab, confirms this picture, adding that Menelik embodied law and order in his person and guaranteed justice to all, being called the 'father of his people' by all his country's numerous tribes, Amharas, Gallas, Gurages and Shankellas, etc.

Menelik—the monarch

The homely yet impressive character of the monarch must also be emphasised. He was always willing to participate in manual work of any kind and wished to give dignity to occupations traditionally regarded as inferior. Vanderheym, for example, records that it was by no means unusual for this remarkable sovereign to get off his mule and set an example by himself taking part in any work which was in hand. The British envoy, Hohler, relates that Menelik often assisted in such varied work as church-building and grass-cutting. It was not therefore surprising that the Emperor should have issued a decree castigating his people for their traditional dislike of manual work, and declaring the farmer more important than the king. 'All mankind,' it added, 'is descended from Adam and Eve; there was no other ancestor. Discrimination is the result of ignorance. God said to Adam: "In the sweat of thy brow shalt thou eat bread!" If we do not carry out this injunction and everyone is idle there will be neither government nor country. In European countries when people undertake new kinds of work and make cannons, guns, trains and other things revealed by God, the people concerned are called engineers; they are praised and given more assistants, not insulted on account of their craft. But you with your insults are going to leave the country without people who can make the plough; the land will thus become barren and destitute.'

Menelik's character may be further illustrated by his behaviour during a great famine which occurred in 1889–1893 when he set an example to his people by himself working in the fields. The official chronicler of the reign relates that the monarch used both pick-axe and hatchet and symbolically despatched implements of these kinds to the provincial rulers with the message: 'Imitate me!' A British observer of this time, Captain Wellby, confirms this account. He records that Menelik 'formed a big camp, and setting the example to his people with his own hand . . . tilled the soil, and in due time handed over to the sufferers the fruits of their labours, an example that encouraged others to do likewise. I was told these years he ate no beef for he argued: "Why should I enjoy plenty while my people were in want?" I doubt if any European ruler would have denied himself to the same extent for a similar cause.'

Leadership of this quality seems to have made a deep impression. The Ethiopian historian, Afewerk Gabre Yesus, says that when the people saw their ruler bleeding after cutting down brushwood they were moved to tears. 'Everyone, not only dignitaries, but also ecclesiastics and priests, each seized a spade or axe and went to work in the woods.' Himself greatly impressed, the Ethiopian historian goes on to liken Menelik, who had dug the ground and cleared the brushwood for his people, to Christ who had bent down to wash the feet of the apostles, and adds: 'Menelik II, seizing the axe, with the same hand as he held the crown, cleared the land, and his foot, because of the spines, became a pool of blood. A true king is like that.'

Menelik—the moderniser

Menelik was above all a modernising ruler and, as such, greatly interested in machinery of all kinds. The foreign travellers of the time provide many anecdotes, often humorous, to that effect. Thus the missionary Martial de Salviac reports that one of his colleagues once brought Menelik a sewing-machine which had been taken to pieces for packing. After several attempts at putting it together the priest confessed his inability to do so. Menelik, however, spent the whole night with the machine, carefully examined each of the pieces, tried them together and by the next day had the whole thing working perfectly. Other travellers describe Menelik carefully examining such varied articles as an oil traction engine, a circular saw and a mechanical stone cutter about which he became 'so excited', Hohler says, that it was 'impossible to do business' on other matters. On the arrival of the first motor car the Emperor insisted on being driven in it. One eye-witness account describes him as 'laughing and puffing for breath, with his goggleless eyes streaming, as happy as a schoolboy, while the now-galloping escort was left somewhere on the horizon'. It was not long, however, we are told, before the Emperor learnt to drive 'fairly expertly'. Dr. Merab fully confirms the Emperor's interest in scientific matters. He says that Menelik would have been 'as happy as an angel' to attend one of the great industrial exhibitions in Europe, and of this proof notes that his master took a keen interest in astrology, was a founder member of the French Astronomical Society and was perhaps the only crowned head to watch the eclipse of the sun by the planet Mercury in 1908.

Menelik's interest in innovations was well summed up by an Italian envoy, De Castro, who observed that 'if a builder of castles in the air came with a plan to erect an escalator from the earth to the moon the Emperor would have made him build it if only to see whether it could be done'.

The Emperor's approach to new machinery was, however, by no means childish, but imbued with a realisation of the needs of his country. His interest in innovation owned much to his belief that Ethiopia could only preserve its independence in the face of European colonial expansion by adopting many of the techniques which had been adopted in Europe during the period of Ethiopia's long isolation.

The story goes that early in his reign President Grevy of France sent an envoy with an old cannon and a musical box as presents. According to one account the envoy pointed repeatedly at the weapon and said that with it 'one could make *boum-boum*'—as though Menelik had never seen a cannon in action. The Emperor at all events felt insulted, and, turning to the envoy, said: 'You will thank the President very much for having known that I was a grandfather. These presents are in truth excellent toys for my grandchildren.' He is then said to have conducted the envoy to his arms depot where there were to be seen cannon and rifles of the latest type. 'These,' he said, 'these are *my* toys!'

World affairs

Menelik's intellectual curiosity extended to the whole world as can be seen from his conversations with visitors from abroad. He had 'heard of the Himalayas', observes the British traveller Vivian, 'and had a very good idea of the part of India where they were to be found'. He asked another Englishman, Powell-Cotton, if he had ever visited Russia. 'No,' Powell-Cotton replied. 'Ah,' he said, 'you should go, for it must be a great country.' This seemed to open up a fresh train of thought, for the next question was: 'Does England allow the native princes of India to have as many soldiers as they like of their own?'

The American envoy, Skinner, reports that Menelik 'knew of our war with Spain', and had 'heard evidently a good deal' about President Theodore Roosevelt 'whose personality interested him much'. A French traveller, Michel, says that the Emperor asked him for detailed information on the French campaigns in Madagascar, inquiring how the Hovas had resisted the invaders, how the latter had captured the capital Tananarive, what was the importance of that town, and how the houses were built there. After listening attentively to Michel's replies, he commented: 'The Malagash are more industrious than us, but they know less how to fight.'

The Emperor's questions, according to the English traveller, E. A. Pease, 'were always direct and searching'. 'We talked of many things,' he adds, 'of English political parties, and the Transvaal War, of war and its evils, of international jealousies, of Abyssinian suspicion of the European Powers. . . . I explained to him, in answer to a question, that I was a Liberal in politics, because that party was, in my opinion, associated with the work of raising our own people, and working for the amelioration of suffering humanity everywhere, and averse to aggression. . . . He asked why I opposed the present ministers. I said I opposed the present Government because it was, in my opinion, reactionary and extravagant with the national resources. He said to me, after we had talked over these things: "I am a Liberal. I am a man of

peace. I want no wars, it is bad for all. I want friendship and understanding."
Menelik, however, did not always agree with the foreigners with whom he
conversed. The French envoy, Klobukowski, reports a conversation in which
the Emperor questioned him on the working of the French parliamentary
system. After the envoy had alluded to various political difficulties, Menelik
asked, 'Then the Government is not the master in your country?' 'It is,'
Klobukowski replied, 'but on condition of being approved by Parliament.'
'And if Parliament does not approve?' 'It must wait,' was the reply, 'take up
the questions afresh, modify them, discuss the matter again.' On hearing these
words the sovereign is said to have wrinkled his eyebrows and to have commented: 'Here that would not work.'

Foreign servants

What were the main events and achievements of Menelik's reign? His
genius may be seen in many directions. His desire to modernise the country
led him to make greater use of foreign technicians than any of his predecessors.
As early as June 14, 1874, he wrote to the Khedive of Egypt—a country with
which Ethiopia had long had strained relations—requesting assistance in
finding persons with a knowledge of the arts and crafts. The request appears
to have been fruitless, but a few years later in 1877 Menelik sent a message
to a Swiss trader at Aden with whom he had business contacts, asking him to
send him some Europeans skilled in various crafts. They were to serve as
instructors to Ethiopian workers and be employed as government engineers.
The trader informed some of his compatriots of the sovereign's desire with
the result that three young Swiss technicians arrived in 1878, one of whom,
Alfred Ilg, remained in Menelik's service for many years and played a useful
part in the country's development in both the technical and diplomatic fields.

The story of Ilg's rise in his master's favour illustrates the recurrent interest
in fire-arms which can be seen in so many of Ethiopia's innovating monarchs. It is said that soon after Ilg's arrival Menelik asked him to make him
a pair of shoes. Ilg replied that he was unacquainted with such work, but the
sovereign insisted that he should obey, which he did. The ruler was enchanted
by the shoes and requested that the young engineer should then make a
rifle. Ilg again protested his ignorance, adding that it would cost much more
to manufacture the weapon than to import one from abroad and that the
finished product would inevitably be far inferior. Menelik brushed these
arguments aside, remarking that the cost was a matter of no account and that
it was important to see whether a rifle could be made in the country with the
resources available. Ilg thereupon yielded to the monarch's entreaties and
constructed the required rifle.

Weapons for survival

Menelik was also greatly interested in the import of fire-arms and was much
more successful in obtaining them than any previous Ethiopian ruler. Pos-

sessing fairly convenient access to the coast through the ports of the French Somali colony and the Italian port of Assab, which were being improved in this period, he had the additional advantage that the French and Italian governments were both for reasons of their own strongly in favour of his obtaining arms. The French hoped that by supplying him with arms they would win his friendship which would be useful to them in their rivalry with the British, while the Italians were no less anxious to win his co-operation or at least neutrality in their conflict with his nominal overlord the Emperor Yohannes, the ruler of the north.

Menelik for his part devoted much of his attention to the import of arms and was willing to pay very high prices for them. The French poet, Rimbaud, who engaged in the trade, reported that old rifles could be purchased in Europe for 7 or 8 francs each and resold in Ethiopia for 40 francs. An extensive trade in fire-arms soon developed. Menelik is estimated to have obtained no less than 25,000 rifles between 1882, when the arms trade for practical purposes started, and 1887 when he occupied Harar, thereby rendering easier his contact with the coast. In January of the following year the Italian Prime Minister, Francesco Crispi, sent Menelik a gift of 1,000 Remington rifles with the message: 'May these increase your power and carry destruction among your enemies and those of my country.' Further sales and gifts followed with the result that Menelik soon had by far the best equipped army of any independent African state.

The Italians and 'perpetual peace'

On the death of the Emperor Yohannes in March 1889, Menelik succeeded him as Emperor and was crowned on November 3. The first years of his reign were clouded by difficulties with the Italians who had seized the Red Sea port of Massawa in February 1885, and began to advance on to the Eritrean plateau not long after the death of his predecessor. This was the period of the scramble for Africa, which had become particularly fierce in 1885. To avoid disputes among themselves the European powers had devised the General Act of Berlin which was signed on February 26 that year. Article XXXIV stated that 'any power which henceforth takes possession of a tract of land on the coast of the African Continent outside of its present possessions, or which, being hitherto without such possessions, shall acquire them, as well as the Power which assumes a Protectorate there, shall accompany the respective act with a notification thereof, addressed to the other Signatory Powers of the present Act, in order to enable them, if need be, to make good any claims of their own.'

Notwithstanding growing Italian interest in East Africa, Menelik had been on friendly terms with Italy until his accession as Emperor. On May 2, 1889—less than two months after the death of Yohannes—he signed a Treaty of Perpetual Peace and Friendship with Italy. This treaty, which was destined to be of crucial significance in the history of Ethiopian relations with the European powers, contained articles of benefit to both signatory powers.

Menelik recognised Italian sovereignty over the Eritrean plateau including Asmara, while the Italian Government recognised Menelik as Emperor of Ethiopia and agreed in Article VI that he was entitled to import arms and munitions through Italian territory. The most important article, however, was Article XVII which was soon the basis of a dispute between the two signatories. The quarrel arose from the fact that the treaty had two texts, one in the Ethiopian language, Amharic, and the other in Italian, the sense of which though identical in other respects differed materially in the aforesaid article. The Amharic text stated that the Emperor Menelik should have the power to avail himself of the services of the Italian authorities for all communications he might wish to have with other powers. The Italian text, however, made it obligatory for the Emperor to conduct all his transactions with the other powers through the Italian Government. Though the Italian formula was soon used by the Italian Government to claim that it had established a Protectorate over Ethiopia, the time was not yet ripe for an open conflict.

The Emperor's cousin, Ras Makonnen, went to Italy to negotiate further details for the implementation of the Italo–Ethiopian agreement, while General Baldissera, the officer in charge of Italian expansion in Africa, prepared to advance on to the Eritrean plateau in accordance with the Ucciali treaty. On August 2, 1889, Baldissera issued a proclamation for the occupation of Asmara, and on October 1 Ras Makonnen signed an Additional Convention to the Ucciali treaty. By the terms of this new agreement Italy again recognised Menelik as Emperor of Ethiopia, while Ethiopia recognised the sovereignty of Italy over her Red Sea colony on the basis of the frontiers actually in existence at that time. Article IV stated that the Emperor could issue coins of his own which would be made in Italy and would also circulate in the Italian colonies, money produced for Italian colonial use being on the other hand guaranteed a circulation in Ethiopia. Article VI laid down that the Italian Government would give the necessary guarantees to enable an Italian bank to grant the Emperor a loan of 4,000,000 lire. Half this loan was to be paid in silver and the other half was to be deposited in Italy. It was agreed that the revenue of the Harar customs should be used as a guarantee both for the interest on the loan and its eventual repayment.

Italy miscalculates

The Italian Government, which was by this time in control of the Eritrean plateau, now felt that it was in a position to proclaim to the world that Italy had obtained a Protectorate over Ethiopia. This was done on October 11, over five months after the signing of the Ucciali Treaty. The Italian diplomats were to inform the governments to which they were accredited that 'in conformity with Article XXXIV of the General Act of Berlin' Italy was serving notice that 'under Article XVII of the perpetual treaty between Italy and Ethiopia . . . it is provided that His Majesty the King of Italy consents to avail himself of the Government of His Majesty the King of Ethiopia for the conduct of all matters which he may have with other Powers or Governments.'

Britain, which accepted the Italian claim, accordingly entered into three Protocols with Italy, dated March 24 and April 15, 1891, and May 5, 1894, whereby the boundaries between British colonial territory and the alleged Protectorate were defined.

The Emperor, however, refused to accept this interpretation of the Ucciali treaty. On September 27, 1890—eleven months after the announcement of the Italian claim—he wrote to King Umberto I of Italy declaring that on re-examining the two texts of Article XVII he had discovered that they did not agree. He added: 'When I made the treaty of friendship with Italy, in order that our secrets be guarded and that our understanding should not be spoiled, I said that because of our friendship, our affairs in Europe might be carried on with the aid of the Sovereign of Italy, but I have not made any treaty which obliges me to do so. I am not the man to employ the aid of another to carry on my affairs, your Majesty understands very well.'

Determined not to become further dependent on the Italian loan the Emperor stopped drawing on it and began paying back the part he had already used.

Whose dignity?

Italo-Ethiopian relations had thus reached a deadlock which could only be solved by resort to war. The Italian envoy, Count Antonelli, said to Menelik: 'Italy cannot notify the other Powers that she was mistaken in Article XVII, because she must maintain her dignity.' The Emperor's consort, Empress Taitu, who was present at the interview, exclaimed: 'We also have made known to the Powers that the said Article, as it is written in our language, has another meaning. As you, we also ought to respect our dignity. You wish Ethiopia to be represented before the other Powers as your protectorate, but this shall never be.'

After a delay of over two years, which he turned to good advantage by im-porting very large quantities of fire-arms especially from France and Russia, Menelik at length denounced the Treaty of Ucciali on February 12, 1893; a week or so later, on February 27, he informed the European powers of his decision, declaring: 'Ethiopia has need of no one; she stretches out her hands unto God.'

Victory at Adowa

Fighting began in January 1895. The invaders were at first victorious and succeeded in occupying a large stretch of territory including Adigrat, Makalle and Amba Alagi. Later in the year, however, Menelik moved north with a large and moderately well armed force and, himself commanding operations, won significant victories over the Italians at Amba Alagi in December and at Makalle at the turn of the year. The Italians were obliged to fall back on Adowa.

The first weeks of 1896 witnessed a period of inaction on either side, neither the Italian nor the Ethiopian army desiring to take the initiative. Finally on February 25, Crispi, exasperated by the delay, telegraphed to General Baratieri: 'This is a military phthisis, not a war . . . a waste of heroism, without any corresponding success. . . . It is clear to me that there is no fundamental plan in this campaign, and I should like one to be formulated. We are ready for any sacrifice in order to save the honour of the army and the prestige of the Monarchy.'

Baratieri's reaction to this telegram was to order his army to attack; accordingly the battle of Adowa opened in the early morning of March 1.

The Emperor from the outset was in a relatively good position. He had the wholehearted support of the local population, whose patriotism was intensified by the fact that the Italians had been expropriating a sizable amount of land in an attempt to settle Italian colonists. The inhabitants of the area in which the battle was fought were therefore most willing to show Menelik's troops the best paths and to bring news of enemy movements. The Italians, on the other hand, had to face the enmity of the local people and had no accurate maps to help them. Their army therefore moved in the greatest possible confusion.

The Ethiopian army moreover was much larger than that of the Italians. Not counting soldiers with spears it had well over 100,000 men with modern rifles. The Italians for their part had somewhat more cannon—56 as against

The Battle of Adowa; a drawing based on a picture
in Haile Selassie University, Addis Ababa

Menelik's 40—but only about 17,000 men, of whom 10,596 were Italian and the rest Eritrean levies.

The result of the battle was the complete defeat and rout of the invaders. Official Italian figures record that 261 European officers, 2,918 non-commissioned officers and men, and about 2,000 *askaris*, or native troops, were killed, and that a further 954 Italian soldiers were permanently missing and had therefore to be presumed killed. Total Italian casualties thus amounted to over 7,560, or nearly 43 per cent. of the original fighting force of 10,596 Italian and about 7,100 native troops. The Italians also abandoned all their cannon, as well as about 11,000 out of the 14,519 rifles with which they started the battle.

Fruits of victory

As a result of this battle Menelik gained enormous local and international prestige. On October 26 the Italians agreed to the Peace Treaty of Addis Ababa, whereby they accepted the annulment of the Treaty of Ucciali and recognised the absolute and complete independence of Ethiopia. Menelik, on the other hand, did not consider himself in a position to insist on an Italian withdrawal from Eritrea though he had often expressed a desire of obtaining access to the sea. In the months which followed, the French and British Governments sent diplomatic missions to sign treaties of friendship with Menelik; other missions came from the Sudanese Mahdists, the Sultan of the Ottoman Empire and the Tsar of Russia. Addis Ababa thus emerged as a regular diplomatic centre where several important foreign powers had legations.

Though wooed by the Great Powers of the day, Menelik was able to maintain a policy of absolute independence. In 1898 he sent one of his generals, Ras Tassama, as far as the White Nile, where the latter was supposed to make contact with a French force under Captain Marchand who was marching thither from the west African coast. Marchand failed to appear when he was expected, and Tassama was soon obliged to withdraw because his men, who were accustomed to live in the mountains, were suffering from the fever which was prevalent in the marshes of the Nile. Marchand subsequently arrived at Fashoda, but withdrew in the face of British pressure. Menelik thereafter realised that he could not rely very heavily on France. His independence of the Great Powers was referred to by the British envoy Harrington, who, writing of his fellow European diplomats, observed: 'I have not yet seen that any of us have what I could really call influence, i.e. influence that would make Menelik do what he did not want to do. Influence to the detriment of others is plentiful here, but to one's own advantage is decidedly infinitesimal.'

Empire-building

The last quarter of the nineteenth century was a period of Ethiopian empire-building in which Menelik succeeded not only in resurrecting the greatness of

Ethiopia, but also in extending his frontiers farther than any previous monarch of whom we have record. In 1875 he acquired parts of Gurage. In 1881 his general, Ras Gobana, marched into Kaffa which agreed to pay tribute, Jimma, Limmu, Gera and Guma at the same time becoming tributary states. In 1882 Menelik sent his first expedition to Arussi. In 1886 Ras Gobana occupied Wallaga, while Ras Darge completed the occupation of Arussi. In 1887, Menelik defeated Emir Abdullahi of Harar, and, at the other end of the realm, Illubabor was annexed. In 1889 the acquisition of Gurage was completed, while Ras Walda Giyorgis annexed Konta and Kulo. In 1890 the occupation of Kambata was begun and was completed in 1893. In 1891 the Ogaden, Bale and Sidamo were occupied. In 1894 Ras Walda Giyorgis brought Gofa under his control, and Walamo was conquered. In 1896 a first expedition was sent to Borana, which was more effectively occupied in the following year when Fitawrari Hapta Giyorgis built a fort near Mega on the Kenya frontier and took over Konsa on his return march. In the same year Kaffa, which had refused to pay tribute, was conquered. In 1898 Menelik gained control over Beni Shangul on the Sudan frontier, while Ras Walda Giyorgis received the submission of Goldea and Maji, and reached Lake Rudolf. In the same year Ras Tassama, marching from Gore, subdued the Massonge and Gimirra tribes.

The Scramblers

The later years of Menelik's reign saw a deterioration of his relations with the three neighbouring colonial powers, Britain, France and Italy. Hitherto they had been rivals in Africa and when in difficulty with one Menelik could usually count on help or co-operation from another. In 1906, however, expectation of his imminent death caused the three powers to draw closer together, and on December 13 they signed a Tripartite Convention for mutual cooperation to maintain the status quo in Ethiopia. In the event of the status quo being disturbed, they agreed that they would work together to safeguard their own interests which were specified as comprising: (1) a British interest in the Nile Valley and hence in the area of the Blue Nile; (2) an Italian interest in Eritrea and Somaliland and hence in the adjacent areas of Ethiopia; and (3) a French interest in the French Somali Protectorate and hence in its hinterland.

When the agreement was in due course presented to the Emperor, he replied: 'The Convention of the three Powers has reached me. I thank them for having acquainted me with their desire to consolidate and maintain the independence of our Realm. But this actual Convention, and the agreements of any of them are subordinate to our authority. It is known that they cannot in any way find our decision.'

Foundations of a modern state

Menelik's reign was characterised by numerous innovations, particularly after the battle of Adowa. The result was that though the way of life of the average Ethiopian was little changed from what it had been hundreds of years earlier the foundations of a modern state were slowly but surely being laid.

One of the most notable developments of this time was the foundation of a new capital, Addis Ababa, which took place around 1886. The town rapidly acquired all the characteristics of a boom city and by 1910 was estimated to have a population of about 70,000 resident and 30,000 to 50,000 temporary inhabitants.

The construction of bridges in modern times also dates from this period and was important in beginning to improve the country's difficult communications. Menelik, who expressed great interest in communications, gave orders to the Swiss engineer Ilg to build the first bridge over the Awash River in 1886. The work was described by Ilg, in a humorous though nevertheless revealing letter. 'Shoa,' he says, 'has advanced a step forward. . . . The beams had to be carried 15 kilometres on human shoulders. For the bridgeheads I had to square up the stones on the spot. I even had to burn coal in order to forge the nails, rivets, screws and bolts required. Add to this a tropical sun with all its dangers, heavy rains with resultant dysentery, intermittent fever and cyclones which almost pulled out my beard and carried the tent in all directions. At night the hyenas almost stole our leather pillows from under our heads; jackals and other rabble plundered the kitchen and obliged me to obtain respect with strychnine.'

In 1892 Menelik, by this time Emperor, reorganised the system of taxation and extended the principle of tithe for the upkeep of the army so as to terminate the traditional system whereby the soldiers were allowed to requisition or loot whatever they liked from the peasantry. Menelik's official chronicler says that the new regulations followed the proverb that one should give according to one's capacity, and were very popular with all concerned.

Two years later in 1894 the Emperor issued Ethiopia's first national currency 'in order', as an official proclamation declared, 'that our country may increase in honour and our commerce prosper'. Though the new Menelik dollar, which was produced in France, never really displaced the long-established Austrian Maria Theresa dollars, the units of smaller denomination were of considerable advantage to retail trade.

Improving communications

The postal system meanwhile was being brought into existence. The country's first postage stamps, ordered like the coins from France, were put on sale at the end of 1893, the formal decree establishing post offices, etc., being issued in the following year. French advisers were used by the Emperor in developing the service, and Ethiopia in due course joined the International Postal Union in 1908.

A concession for the construction of a railway from Addis Ababa to the French Somali port of Jibuti was granted by Menelik to Ilg as early as March, 1894, but the technical, financial and political difficulties involved were so great that the line, which was constructed with French capital and skill, did not reach Dire Dawa until the end of 1902 and Akaki, 23 kilometres from Addis Ababa, until 1915; the first train services from the coast to the capital were inaugurated in 1917.

Two telegraph and telephone systems had meanwhile been established at the turn of the century. One, constructed by the engineers responsible for the railway, followed its track from Addis Ababa to the coast, while the other, erected by Italian technicians, linked the Italian colony of Eritrea in the north as well as with a number of provincial centres in the south and west.

Early in the twentieth century the first modern roads were constructed between Addis Ababa and Addis Alem and between Harar and Dire Dawa, with the assistance of Italian and French engineers respectively, while at about the same time the capital's wood supply was greatly improved by the introduction of the eucalyptus tree from Australia.

Modern institutions

The later years of the Emperor's reign saw the establishment of a number of modern institutions. The Bank of Abyssinia was founded in 1905, as an affiliate of the National Bank of Egypt.

Ethiopia's first modern hotel, the Etegue, was another innovation, the chronicler of the reign carefully noting that unlike the old system of hospitality it was necessary at the hotel to pay for all dishes consumed.

The Menelik II School, the first institution of its kind, was set up with the help of Coptic teachers from Egypt in 1908. Menelik had already shown his interest in modern education by sending students for education abroad: the first three went to Switzerland, while six others went shortly afterwards to Russia.

The Menelik II Hospital, founded to replace an earlier medical establishment operated by the Russian Red Cross from 1897 to 1907, was erected with the assistance of various foreign doctors in 1910.

A state printing press came into existence in the following year.

Politically the personal character of Menelik's administration was retained till the latter part of his reign, when failing health and the increasing complexity of government appears to have caused him to decide on establishing Ethiopia's first cabinet. This decision was taken in October 1907, and, according to the chronicler of the reign, stemmed from his master's desire of 'implanting European customs in our country'.

An examination of the reign of Menelik thus reveals that it was an important and formative period in the country's history in which the foundations of modern Ethiopia were laid.

Kabalega and the making of a new Kitara

G. N. Uzoigwe

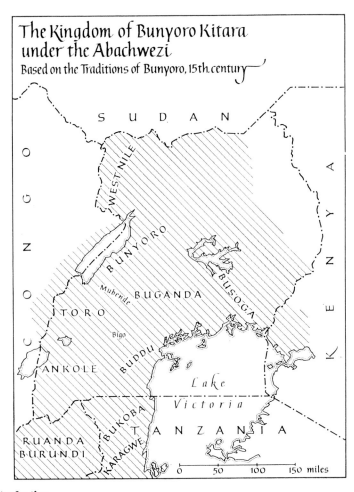

The Kingdom of Bunyoro Kitara
under the Abachwezi
Based on the Traditions of Bunyoro, 15th. century

Introduction

The Abachwezi empire of Kitara was at the height of its power and influence some time during the fifteenth century. True, the existence of such an empire has recently been questioned, but the balance of learned opinion is that the

Kitara empire did exist. Only its extent and the nature of its control are still in doubt. We can safely say that it was similar to most contemporary empires in other parts of Africa: far-flung, culturally varied, and loosely administered. In some cases the subject people was required only to make an occasional payment of tribute to Kitara and formally accept its sovereignty. Viewed in this light, the Abachwezi empire of Kitara covered the present Republic of Uganda (with the possible exception of Karamoja) and included parts of the Congo to the west, and parts of Karagwe and Rwanda to the south. Undoubtedly, it was the most important empire of its day in eastern Africa.

The Abachwezi dynasty was inherited by the *Ababito* (kings), to which line Kabalega belonged. The last of these Biito monarchs, Sir Tito Winyi, the son of Kabalega, (deposed in 1967 as a result of the Ugandan republican constitution) believed that the Biito were grandsons of the Bachwezi. The empire inherited by the Biito was still extensive but certainly smaller than that of their grandfathers. Ankole, for example, had broken away before the arrival of the Biito, and Buganda seceded before the death of the first Biito king of Kitara, Isingoma Mpuga Rukidi ('the multi-coloured one').

The rise to power of the Biito over Kitara can be placed somewhere in the sixteenth century. From then to about 1830 the *Abakama* (kings) of Kitara were constantly feuding with those of Ankole and Buganda. More importantly the Biito princes also displayed a remarkable appetite for quarrelling among themselves.

By the end of the eighteenth century the Biito empire of Kitara was clearly in decline, gradually eclipsed by the growing power of Buganda. Ankole had also extended its frontiers at Kitara's expense. The principalities of Busoga maintained a slippery sort of independence, paying tributes now to Kitara, then to Buganda, according to their shrewd estimation of where power lay. During the reign of Omukama Dukango I Cwa Mujwiga (c. 1731–1782), Kooki and Bweru (Buddy) unilaterally declared their independence of Kitara. In the reign of Omukama Kyebambe III Nyamutkura (c. 1786–1835) his sons, complaining that he was too old, proceeded to divide up what was left of the empire. Kaboyo, the favourite prince, carved out Tooro—where he was *saza* (provincial) chief—for himself. Tooro's first independence of Kitara lasted from about 1830 to 1836. This automatically meant the loss to Kitara of the profitable salt trade at Katwe. Two other princes, Isagara Katiritiri and Kacope seized control of Chope country in northern Kitara (where they were saza chiefs) and divided it among themselves. The attempt of the fourth prince, Karasama Bugondo Bwamusugu, to cut off his saza of Bugungu on the eastern side of Lake Albert was foiled, but the Omukama's authority over Bugungu remained for some time ineffective.

The reign of Nyamutukura marked the beginning of the end of the empire of Kitara. Any hopes of giving it a new lease of life appeared impossible until Omukama Cwa II Kabalega (1870–1899) made a determined bid to stop the rot. This is the major importance of Kabalega in the history of Uganda and why he merits this study.

Kabalega: the man and his ideas

What sort of man was Kabalega? The European travellers—with the exception of Emin Pasha—who had dealings with him misunderstood and misrepresented the man. Subsequent writeis, drawing largely from these sources, have either repeated the old stereotypes or made feeble attempts to portray the essential Kabalega; feeble in the sense that there has been little attempt to study the man and his ideas. The result is that we still know little of the personality of Kabalega. But our knowledge of him as a soldier and an anti-imperialist is abundant. Why then did he fight? Why was he a resister?

There are two sides to his character: on the one hand, he was a difficult and complex personality; on the other, he was a man who genuinely loved his people. Certainly, he was ruthless towards the rebellious. But he displayed a remarkable kindness and liberality towards his *abarusura* (army) as well as towards all others whose loyalties were not in doubt. He was deeply interested in guns and in all things military. In actual combat he was imaginative and brave.

This picture hardly matches up to either the whimpering, drunken coward of Baker's description or the bloodthirsty savage who indulged in barbaric orgies that Casati portrayed in his book. The truth was that both Baker and Casati were unreliable witnesses. But such impressions, unfortunately, are still current among teachers and school children even in Bunyoro. Teachers and students will enthusiastically take visitors to the royal village of Mparo where Kabalega lies buried and point out the tree where he was supposed to have hanged many innocent people. This accusation of indiscriminate hanging based largely on European accounts, is difficult to prove. Kabalega certainly imposed severe sentences, including the death penalty, on his subjects. Those executed were normally convicted criminals who were handed over to the saza chief, Iretta Byangome, who was also the commander of the Ekirwane division of the abarusura. Iretta was the chief prosecutor/executioner. The section of the army responsible for the actual execution was called the *ababogora* (military police), who did not hang the victims but clubbed them to death. This point has been stressed merely as an example to show that many of the contemporary stories about Kabalega should be carefully checked.

Kabalega was born in 1850. His mother, Kanyange Nyamutahingurwa, was probably a Muhuma lady from Mwenge (now in Tooro). She belonged to the Abayonza clan. Kabalega's early youth was spent in Bulega where he and his mother had taken refuge when some rebellious Biito princes had temporarily chased his father, Omukama Kyebambe IV Kamurasi (1852–1869), off the throne. This incident probably left a strong impression on the mind of the young boy. It is believed that when he was brought back to the palace he was given the name Akana Ka Balega, signifying the one who came from Bulega. Later on it was shortened to Kabalega.

He grew up in the palace with his elder brother, Prince Kabigumire. They played together and like all young boys discussed their ambitions and aspirations. Kabigumire's ambition was to slaughter all his father's servants when he became king and replace them with those of his choice. Kabalega's ambition was to turn these servants into soldiers when he became king. There was no point in killing them, he argued. As soldiers they could be profitably used in maintaining internal stability and in raiding neighbouring countries. Moreover, successful raids would make them rich and contented. The stage was thus set for the succession war which was to break out within a few years.

Kabalega the king

During this period Kabigumire and Kabalega were placed under the care of Kamihanda Omudaya, the younger brother of Kamurasi. He was instructed to study them and note which of the two exhibited kingly characteristics. At the same time he taught them courtly etiquette and the history of the kings of Kitara. It soon became apparent that Omudaya was impressed with Kabigumire. He found him more royal and refined in behaviour. Kabalega, on the other hand, was impulsive, headstrong, proud, opinionated, and short-tempered. Despite the views of Omudaya, however, Kamurasi indicated his preference for Kabalega as his successor. He must have been impressed by his younger son's single-mindedness, aggressive qualities and obvious interest in the common people. Kabalega used to chat with them and give them gifts. They adored him. But the majority of the royal family hated him. They appear to have been apprehensive of him and to have made up their minds that he would never be their king.

As a young man, Kabalega was slim like his father but slightly shorter. He was about five feet ten inches in height and very light in complexion. With age, however, he added so much weight that he is generally described as a big, sturdy, fat man. He had big, bright eyes, a large mouth, and prominent but very white teeth, the upper two of which were missing in later life. He spoke with a deep, refined voice but 'occasionally roared like a lion'. He had the curious mannerism of speaking with a stern countenance when in good humour and with a smile when in a rage. He was extremely neat and clean and his 'hands were beautifully kept'.

Usually a cheerful man, he became in later years 'as changeable as the weather'. Essentially a soldier, he demanded implicit obedience, strict discipline and efficiency. He tolerated no arguments. He was merciless towards those of his royal guards who failed in their duty. Intelligent and practical, he did not suffer fools gladly. He spoke several languages including Runyoro, Swahili, Arabic, and probably Luo.

We have seen how, by the end of the reign of Nyam-utukara, the Biito empire of Kitara had broken up. Nyabongo II Mugenyi (1835–c. 1848) came to the throne when already a very old man. He reigned for thirteen peaceful and uneventful years. His successor, Olimi V Rwakabale (c. 1848–1852) had ruled for only four years when his brother, Kamurasi, proclaimed rebellion. Civil war broke out and Olimi was killed by Kamurasi. The victor seized the throne and held it precariously until his death in 1869.

Kamurasi had seized the throne by the sword and had to retain it by the sword. But he did not always succeed. At one period the rebellious Biito princes from Chope managed for a while to drive him out of his capital. Having devastated the place they voluntarily marched back to Chope country. They had no wish to sit on the ancient throne of Kitara. But they had made their point: as far as they were concerned, Kamurasi's power counted for nothing. Here was a perfect demonstration of the weakness of the central authority. Kamurasi managed to re-establish his authority, but he never succeeded in dominating the princes and the aristocracy.

The kingdom of Bunyoro-Kitara was unstable in the feudal manner if we use the definition of feudalism employed by Karugire in his article on Nkore as 'a form of government in which political authority is monopolised by a small group of military leaders but evenly distributed among members of that group' and in which 'the king, at best, can merely keep peace among the lords and usually is unable even to do this.' This 'feudal' instability appeared to be a prime cause for the decline of Kitara as against the more centralised and organised kingdoms of Buganda and Nkore. Kabalega grew up amid this political instability and he seemed to have grasped more than his predecessors the cause of his kingdoms' feebleness. According to one of his surviving sons, Aramanzani Muirumbi, Kabalega made up his mind to (i) reassert the authority of royal power; (ii) stamp out dissident and rebellious elements; (iii) centralise the kingdom; (iv) undertake a policy of national reconstruction and reconciliation; and (v) restore the fortunes of the once powerful and famous empire of Kitara by reconquering the rebellious provinces. In short, Kabalega had taken on the task of founding a strong, united, and centralised state, modelled perhaps on the Ganda pattern, as the first essential stop towards the making of a new empire of Kitara which was, indeed, his ultimate ideal. Anyone who prevented his realisation of this goal was an enemy and must be resisted.

The war of succession, 1869–1871

So long as he was not king his ideals would remain merely dreams. He must therefore establish himself on the throne. This proved difficult. In December 1869 Kamurasi died. Kabigumire at once seized the dead body. According to Kitara custom, the prince who buried his father's body and killed his opponent became king. Civil War was was inevitable, with Kabigumire and Kabalega as chief contestants.

It was an unusual succession war. Normally aristocratic support tended to be evenly balanced between the opposing candidates. This time it was different. Given Kabalega's views on centralisation and the subordination of the aristocracy it was not surprising that practically all the Biito and the other important people in the kingdom supported Kabigumire who emerged as the aristocratic candidate. Only two Biito, Kabagonza and Nyaika, supported Kabalega. Of the important chiefs only Nyakamatura Nyakatura, saza chief of Bugahya, is known to have supported him. The majority of the Abahuma pastoralists also opposed him. Initially his prospects of success appeared slim. But it soon became clear that Kabalega had the enthusiastic support of the royal guards of Kamurasi as well as that of the *Abairu* (common people) agriculturalists. He therefore emerged as the candidate of the common man. The Arab traders divided their support between the two opponents. So the stage was set for a bitter contest.

By 1870 Kabalega had emerged victorious. Many of the aristocracy belatedly transferred their support to him. But Kabalega was aware that he had not won the war because of their help and did not owe his throne to them. By 1871 he was the undisputed ruler of his kingdom. Significantly, he chose the name of Cwa II. Omukama Cwa I Romomamahanga was one of the earliest Biito kings of Kitara, a great warrior who is remembered in Kinyoro history for his lengthy occupation of Ankole and Rwanda, from which he had attacked other areas, especially those beyond the western side of Lake Kivu.

Consolidation of power

Politics is power and the art of politics lies in acquiring power and keeping it. Kabalega proved to be a great politician. In the early years of his reign he set out to impose his new order and ideas. His aristocratic opponents had either to accept, flee or be destroyed. Japari, who had fought for the defeated brother, accepted, was praised by Kabalega for his military skill, and settled down comfortably in the kingdom. During the Anglo-Ganda combination against Bunyoro-Kitara he proved his loyalty to Kabalega by fighting with outstanding valour.

On the other hand, those who refused to accept their reduced political role or continued to intrigue against Kabalega were either killed or escaped. Some important Biito princes, and two of Kabalega's sisters who had acted as spies for Kabigumire, were executed. Two princes, Ruyonga and Mpuhuka,

The personal arms and drums of Kabalega

fled and established a stronghold of opposition in Chope. Rebellions and threats of rebellions fostered by the aristocracy plagued the early years of Kabalega's reign and he developed a wide network of informers to keep a check upon potential rebels. People from Chope were particularly suspect and some of them took refuge in Lango where they founded new homes and where they still live. In Nyoro tradition Kabalega is known as Ekituli Kyangire Abemi, 'he who does not tolerate the rebellious'.

Military reforms

Nyoro sources are unanimous in asserting that Kabalega's greatest achievement was military. His first major task on assuming the throne was to reform and re-organise the army which had fought so well for him during the succession war. This new army he called the abarusura. It was a national, standing army which saw the monarch as its ultimate authority. Kabalega became both the Head of State and the Commander-in-Chief of all the armed forces as well. This may have a modern ring about it; but the abarusura as an institution was surprisingly modern in conception and organisation. It involved the transference of military leadership from the saza chiefs to a new group of men who were professional soldiers and who took orders only from the king.

This was a very important development. It meant an important change in the basis of political power in the land. The formation of the abarusura meant the decline of chiefly and aristocratic political influence which had previously depended mainly on their possession of military power.

This was a revolutionary departure in the long history of Kitara and possibly in the history of the interlacustrine region. In southern Africa new ideas of political and military centralisation had emerged under Shaka and spread into Central Africa during the Mfecane (wars of wandering) and even via the Ngoni into the modern Tanzanian area. But the interlacustrine region does not seem to have been affected by the Mfecane. Kabalega's abarusura appears to be the first standing army in that area.

Why should it be so? By the time Kabalega became king not only had the old Kitara empire practically disappeared but the central kingdom itself appeared to be falling to pieces. The reasons were largely internal rather than external. Kabalega was quick to see how useful a national standing army would be in safeguarding his position and in preventing further disintegration.

Thus political centralisation and the standing army were in the first place responses to internal circumstances, but numerous external forces also justified a standing army. There was the persistent Ganda threat. For many centuries the Ganda had profited from the internal quarrels in the Kitara empire. They had systematically extended their small kingdom (originally Buganda did not cover more than a twenty-five miles radius from Kampala) at the expense of their big brother to the north. Also, by the second half of the nineteenth century, the situation was worsened by the devastation caused by the Arab ivory and slave traders against whose plots Kamurasi had proved powerless. In addition, there was the threat from the European-backed khedival regime in Egypt which nursed ambitions of annexing Bunyoro Kitara. And lastly, only a powerful, national standing army, would realise Kabalega's dream of refounding the once-famous Abachwezi empire of Kitara. Clearly, the traditional military organisation of Kitara relying on the *obwesengeze* (provincial armies) had proved unsuitable for such a purpose. On the contrary it had been the mainstay of the secessionist movements which had torn the empire apart.

The abarusura were organised in ten main *ebitongole* (battalions) each of which contained between one and two thousand men. There were also five minor ebitongole of about four hundred each. These ebitongole were scattered over the country to guard strategic areas. Their main duties were essentially three: to crush the rebellious aristocratic elements in the society; to defend the kingdom from external aggression; and to extend the kingdom to its original boundaries. The abarusura were armed with guns procured from the Zanzibari Arabs and Khartoum traders in exchange for slaves and ivory. A sizable number of them were foreigners recruited from the surrounding districts but the majority of them were of local origin. While it is fairly certain that the abarusura evolved from Kamurasi's ceremonial guards and from the traditional organisation of the obwesengeze, it appears likely that its composition, organisation and adaptation to new types of weapons arose out of Kabalega's own military genius.

Centralisation of administration

In pre-Kabalega days the Kitara empire—or what was left of it—was organised on a loose confederal basis. The outlying provinces had then exhibited a remarkable taste for independence. Often they had been successful. The result was the gradual supplanting of the power of Kitara by that of the highly centralised state of Buganda. Very likely Kabalega was impressed by the Ganda achievement, which involved not only the reform of the military but also the re-organisation of the administrative system of the state. Kabalega wanted to achieve as much for Kitara, but he was almost certain to fail without a drastic curtailment of the power of the aristocracy. He succeeded because he did not owe his throne to the aristocracy, but to the Abairu and the soldiers. This was a revolutionary change in the basis of royal power in Kinyoro history.

The reign of Kabalega, indeed, may fairly be described as the era of the common man's monarchy. It was a new, exciting, revolutionary era which was cut short by British intervention. Kabalega must be seen as one of the most tragic casualties of British imperialism.

With the abarusura he stamped out sectionalism. He insisted that both the saza chiefs and the leaders of the abarusura should live near the palace, so that he could watch over their activities himself. Any chief who left the royal city on duty was obliged to leave a representative behind. The abarusura acted as his 'ears' not only within the palace but also throughout the country. Those aristocrats who persisted in seeking a restoration of the ancient status quo were either killed or forced into exile and replaced by a group of new men—commoners—who appreciated Kabalega's new conception of Kitara society.

Increasingly promotion became simply a question of ability rather than birth. Kabalega made it plain that he was now the undisputed source of all authority throughout his kingdom, and that the backbone of that power was the people represented, so to speak, by the abarusura. He could promote or demote anybody at will. His authority was felt in every corner of the kingdom. He also became the supreme judicial authority. Sometimes when he found it difficult to reach a settlement, he would order the two litigants to fight a duel, the decision favouring the victor. The death sentence became his sole prerogative. He reversed the practice among his predecessors of appointing the Biito to the main chiefships of the provinces. Most of his chiefs were common men raised in the social hierarchy because of their ability and loyalty, but their influence was strictly limited so that they were more like bureaucrats than traditional chiefs.

National reconciliation

Kabalega was deeply concerned with national unity and reconciliation. He urged his people to work together towards a common destiny. He used the Ganda threat to appeal for unity, as the following song sung by a *murusura* before Kabalega testifies:

> I own goats and the Ganda
> Are planning to come over and seize them;
> The Ganda are vowing to help
> Each other and fight.
> When the Ganda come over,
> We should aid each other;
>
> We should love each other.
> I, the Omurusura of Omukama,
> By your Highness, I will have
> To do something—I swear
> I will beat them off.
> I vow to die with his Highness.

Many similar songs were devoted to the same theme.

Indeed, Kabalega was a remarkable nation-builder. By his military and administrative reforms he had lost the support of some people. He had also offended many interests. But only two groups of people were particularly upset by the new order. The first was the Biito and the saza chiefs who may be said to have constituted the aristocracy. The other was the *Abahuma* (pastoralists) who formed the equivalent of a middle group between the Biito and the Abairu (the lower group who formed the fighting population). But Kabalega was aware that the weaknesses of both these groups had been exposed by the succession war. They were lamentably small in numbers. They were not essentially fighters. They had maintained their hegemony over the kingdom only with the support of the Abairu. The first reaction of most of the pastoralists was to leave politics alone and return to their first love, cattle. And the aggressive inclinations of what was left of the aristocracy were suppressed by the vigour with which Kabalega treated rebellions.

For the first time in known Kitara history, the common man came into his own. But Kabalega was less concerned with destroying the old aristocracy than with bringing it into submission, and the common people were his instrument. He sought to make his government broadly based, and included members of the old aristocracy where and when he felt assured of their loyalty. He appointed Prince Kabagonza, his most trusted Biito, as the *Okwiri* (head of all the Biito) and he gave Prince Nyaika a couple of villages, but not a saza, to rule.

Intermarriages between the groups were apparently encouraged. This was not a new development. It seems, however, to have been accelerated in the nineteenth century. Usually the Biito men married Huma women because traditionally they were the prettiest. Kabalega himself seemed to have consciously or unconsciously set the fashion when he married a Muiru lady. She was called Achanda (now affectionately remembered by her family as Elizabeth) and came from the Kitwanga village of Chope (now Kibanda County). Achanda's family had refused to support Mupina's rebellion and had migrated southwards. Kabalega met her at Bugahya (Hoima) and made her his queen. He rewarded her parents with presents including servants. Altogether Kabalega had about 150 children. His wives came from all groups and, according to oral evidence, were all beautiful. The result of this development was that in Bunyoro differences on the basis of race do not exist.

Whether or not Kabalega was completely successful in his efforts at national reconciliation is difficult to say. Certainly there were no rebellions during the period of his effective power. Internally the country enjoyed peace and stability. This balance was upset by the Anglo-Ganda combination against Bunyoro-Kitara in the 1890s. Kabalega's great power and influence gave his people that self-confidence and pride in themselves which they had not known for some generations past. He was to them a focal point and symbol of national unity. They were all king's men.

Reconstruction

The succession war had devastated the country. Many people had lost their homes. Disease and famine were rampant. Kabalega did his best to lessen the sufferings of his people. Chiefs were commanded to grow more food—*oruharo*: food grown at the kings' command—for the relief of areas under their control. Sometimes he ordered chiefs to collect their men for the cultivation of his own farms and offered them cattle in return although he was under no obligation to pay for such services. The proceeds of his farms were used towards the maintenance of the king's household. After successful raids he would distribute some of the booty among his people.

During periods of national famine he would set a target for food production. Each citizen was required to produce within a specific period a bushel of millet (the national food). He would also supplement the stock of available foodstuffs by ordering millet from Bugangaizi, Kyaka, Ankole, and Lango. These would then be handed over to the chiefs for distribution among their people. He introduced a standard measure and severely punished traders convicted of selling at black market prices. All were obliged to use the Omukama's standard measure. Everyone was encouraged to work hard, for Kabalega hated laziness. He instructed his chiefs and his abarusura to show no mercy to rogues and bandits who lived off other peoples' labours. He encouraged the practice of building granaries under the ground, thereby storing food away from the reach of the enemy. The relics of these granaries still exist in some Nyoro homesteads. He also built quarantine enclosures to combat smallpox epidemics. Doctors were brought in from the north to treat the affected and inoculate others. Those who were cured acted as nurses for the sick.

Territorial expansion

According to Banyoro the second greatest achievement of Kabalega was his efforts to expand the kingdom he had inherited from his father. By 1869, as we have seen, the Kitara empire was practically non-existent. This was the result of a series of secession movements engineered primarily by the Biito provincial governors. Another major cause of the weakness of the Kitara empire was the frequency of inter-Biito struggles. All the earlier rulers of Kitara had fought among themselves, but the Biito excelled them all.

Once firmly established on the throne, Kabalega embarked on his programme of territorial expansion. His aim was the reconquest of those states which had cut themselves off from the main Biito line. He pacified Bugungu and Chope and re-integrated them into his kingdom. By 1876 he had succeeded, after several failures, in reconquering Tooro. But complete pacification proved difficult. Pockets of resistance against his rule continued until the British intervention in 1891. His soldiers were nevertheless in effective occupation of the province. Bulega, Busongora, Bukonjo, Bwamba, Bubira and Mboga were all reconquered and administered by Kabalega's representatives. A strong detachment of the abarusura occupied the Katwe salt mines.

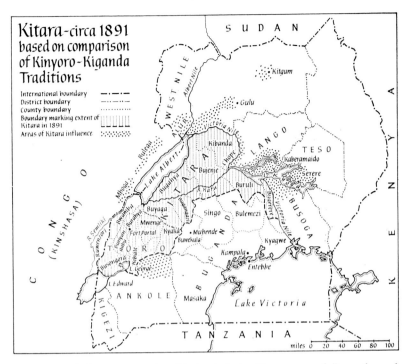

Kitara-circa 1891
based on comparison
of Kinyoro-Kiganda
Traditions

International boundary
District boundary
County boundary
Boundary marking extent of
Kitara in 1891
Areas of Kitara influence

Kabalega's influence was also felt in Ankole, Karagwe and Rwanda and although these kingdoms were independent, they were subjected to periodic raids by the abarusura.

To the north Kabalega exercised authority in certain areas of Lango, although it was an authority based more on informal influence than on conquest. He extorted tribute from the Alur who had supported him during the succession war. His influence also extended to Teso and Acholi.

Acholi had a peculiar relationship with Bunyoro-Kirara. Nyoro tradition claims that Acholi was a province of Bunyoro-Kitara. It was then called Ganyi, and the saza chief was 'Awich son of Ochamo of the Mubito clan'. This may be an exaggeration. There is little doubt, however, that some groups among the Acholi traditionally showed their recognition of the judicial authority of the Abakama of Bunyoro-Kitara by appointing them arbitrators in their disputes. This practice continued during the reign of Kabalega. As a student of Acholi traditions put it; 'The rulers of Bunyoro and Payera had a special status with regard to other rulers of Acholiland'. Payera was the leading chiefdom in Acholi, and it traditionally enjoyed the blessing and support of Bunyoro-Kitara. Stuhlmann noted that in 1891 the abarusura were found supervising the trade in ivory in Acholiland.

In the 1890s Kabalega invaded those principalities of Busoga which were paying tribute to Buganda. Earlier, in 1886, he had decisively beaten the Ganda at the battle of Rwengabi, which he followed up by interfering in the

Ganda succession dispute in 1890. His invading army was, however, repulsed with severe losses. Nevertheless, Kabalega was estimated to be holding some 20,000 Ganda subjects in slavery in the 1890s.

A man of the people

By 1890 Kabalega was at the height of his power. He had reconquered some of the provinces lost by his predecessors and posed a serious threat to both Buganda and Nkore. His fame, like that of the Bachwezi before him, had spread far and wide. His ideal of founding a new Kitara empire seemed a practical possibility. With some justification he saw himself as the 'arbitrator amongst the tribes of the lake district'.

The following year tragedy struck him from an unexpected quarter. Lugard invaded Tooro and surrounding districts, driving before him Kabalega's soldiers. The Tooro monarchy was restored and Kitara influence in Tooro snuffed out. Confused and surprised, Kabalega attempted to negotiate with Lugard. He was insulted and his efforts were rebuffed. In 1893 the British withdrew the Tooro garrisons. Almost immediately Kabalega attacked Tooro and drove away Kasagama, the man placed on the throne of Tooro by Lugard. Within the same year the British authorities decided on the total subjugation of Bunyoro-Kitara, a decision which ended Kabalega's hopes of making a new Kitara. By 1894 he had been chased out of his capital by Anglo-Ganda troops. He was resourceful enough to initiate

Kabalega (with bandaged arms) after his capture in 1899

a long drawn out guerrilla war, but was finally captured in the swamps of a Lango village in 1899.

Kabalega was banished to the Seychelles Islands where he remained until 1923, but throughout his exile many Nyoro continued to regard him as their Omukama. In the Seychelles he was guarded by a British police officer and local constables. He learned to read and write English and was baptised 'John'. Baptism, a European name, and literacy were the weapons and ritual by which the new invaders sought to make their opponents accept colonial subjection. Kabalega, like many other contemporary African monarchs, passed through the ritual. He died in 1923 at about seventy-three years of age at Jinja while on his way back to Bunyoro as 'Mr. John Kabalega—private citizen'. His death paralysed Bunyoro, and every activity came to a standstill; laughter was considered a national insult. By his own wish, Kabalega was buried at the royal village of Mparo where an imposing grass structure protects his grave. The ritual had not been entirely effective since he had requested that no European type roofing should ever be used to cover his corpse.

The story of Kabalega is a great tragedy. The prevailing belief among Nyoro that the Baganda were the cause of all their misfortunes, though understandable, is nevertheless not quite true. European imperialism in the nineteenth century, and not the Baganda, explains the tragedy of Kabalega and the Nyoro as well. Kabalega's dream of making a new Kitara was plainly overtaken by historical forces. He was a man born out of his time. Had he lived in the eighteenth century, for example, he might have achieved a natural historical eminence among the British and all Ugandans.

The royal tomb of Kabalega—no European-style roofing for his grave

Still he must be remembered as one of the great Africans. Certainly Nyoro regard him as their greatest Omukama. In moments of exuberant elation they assert that he was the greatest king in nineteenth-century Africa. Their feeling is understandable. To them he was a man of the people, a man who loved his country and his people, and a man who challenged for six years the might of Anglo-Ganda power.

An informant, son of a murusura, summarised these feelings:

He (Kabalega) ruled the country. He gave it peace. He installed chiefs. He created a powerful army. He vanquished the rebellious and purged whole areas of rebellious elements. He conquered many countries. People praised him. People played for him *entimbo, kondere* (flutes) and *entate merwa* (royal drums). And he killed many of the Biito who were against him. Those who submitted he left in peace and gave them areas to rule. The rebellious ones ran away because they found his power irresistible. He wielded great influence and commanded obedience. And his dignity, authority, power, let us say, were greater than any other king before him. He will be remembered for ever.

Notes

Bunyoro-Kitara—from about the fifteenth to the nineteenth century the large empire of which modern Bunyoro was a part was called Kitara. Once the empire fell apart the small heartland became known as Bunyoro supposedly derived from a Ganda nickname. The Nyoro, however, tend to refer to their homeland as Bunyoro-Kitara. Today Bunyoro is a district of the Republic of Uganda. The people of Bunyoro-Kitara are called *Banyoro* (plural), *Munyoro* (singular), or *Nyoro* (short form). *Huma* is the short form for *Abahuma* (plural) and *Omuhuma* (singular), the pastoralists. *Biito* is the short form for *Ababiito* (plural) and *Omubiito* (singular), the royal family. *Abairu* (plural) and *Omuiru* (singular), the agriculturalists. The language is called *Runyoro*. The adjective is *kinyoro* e.g. kinyoro history. *Omukama* (plural *Abakama*)—the king of Bunyoro-Kitara.

Moshesh and the survival of the Basuto Nation—The Second Phase

J. D. Omer-Cooper

The Great Trek faced Moshesh with new problems even more serious than those he had encountered in the first phase of his career. Up to that time his task had been to bring together the remnants of tribes that had been broken in the Mfecane, to weld them into a nation and preserve them from the attacks of Bantu and Griqua enemies. After the Trek his main concern was to preserve the nation he had created from the unremitting pressure of land-hungry white settlers pressing upon his borders. In facing this problem he was beset with many difficulties. The whites were in possession of superior armaments and Moshesh realised very clearly that he could not hope to hold out for long against the combined force of all the whites in South Africa. His only hope was to play one white group off against another. The British Government at the Cape was influenced, to some extent at least, by missionary and philanthropic attitudes and it did not have the immediate interest in the Basuto farming lands that was possessed by the Trek Boer. Mosh-

Moshesh 1860

esh, therefore, persistently tried to win the protection of the British Government without sacrificing the interests of his people in the process.

In addition to the fact that in the long run the whites were militarily stronger than his own people Moshesh was faced with grave internal problems. The task of creating internal unity in his kingdom was far from complete and in handling negotiations with his white neighbours he always had to keep an eye on the state of public opinion among the many different peoples who made up his kingdom. If he strained the loyalty of any group too far it might break away and start a process that would lead to the rapid disintegration of the new-born nation. On the borders of his kingdom he was still threatened by his old enemies, the Tlokwa, who had once besieged him on Butha Buthe. Under the leadership of their daring chief, Sikonyela, they were always waiting to take advantage of any sign of Basuto weakness. Also on his borders was the Rolong tribe of Moroka. They had come from the area of the present Transvaal with a missionary belonging to the Wesleyan Missionary Society. Moshesh gave them leave to settle on his land at Thaba Nchu, but once settled they repudiated his authority and, with the support of the Wesleyan missionaries, claimed complete independence. They were always ready to side with any move against Moshesh.

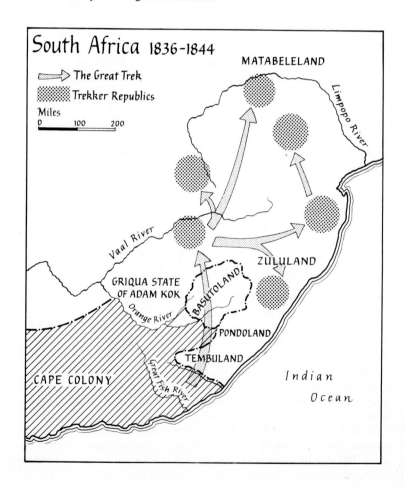

South Africa 1836-1844

MATABELELAND

⟹ The Great Trek

Trekker Republics

Miles
0   100   200

Limpopo River

Vaal River

GRIQUA STATE
OF ADAM KOK

Orange River

BASUTOLAND

ZULULAND

PONDOLAND

TEMBULAND

CAPE COLONY

Great Fish River

Indian

Ocean

To counterbalance these weaknesses the Basuto king had certain advantages. His mountain stronghold of Thaba Bosiu was strong enough to withstand an attack even from troops armed with the most up-to-date weapons of the day. His followers had not adopted the Zulu fighting methods which would have made them perfect targets for firearms, but they had taught themselves to manoeuvre on horseback and make use of guns. Though not so well armed as the whites, they could fight them with their own methods. In the missionaries of the Paris Evangelical Society, Moshesh had invaluable advisers who helped him to understand the intricacies of white politics and to prepare his diplomatic letters. They could also help to rouse philanthropic opinion in Europe in his support. Above all, Moshesh had his own genius for leadership and his talent for diplomacy that had already seen him through many difficult situations.

Even before the Great Trek small numbers of whites had come into Moshesh's kingdom. They had been well received and lived peacefully with the people. In the first years of the Trek, however, they began to arrive in large numbers and asked permission to graze their cattle for a time on Basuto lands until they were ready to move on further into the interior. Moshesh readily gave them his permission, but time passed and instead of the farmers moving on, their numbers increased. What is more, they began to treat the land on which they had been allowed to graze their cattle as their private property. They began to build houses and buy and sell their farms. Moshesh sent a circular letter pointing out that the land belonged to himself and his people and that the farmers should not treat it as their private property, but it was ignored and some of the settlers openly defied the authority of the chief. To deal with this problem Moshesh looked for help to the British Government and in May 1842 he asked the French missionary, Casalis, to write to the Governor at the Cape to enquire whether the British Government would be prepared to give official recognition to his people and enter into a treaty with him.

Basuto and British

In 1843 Moshesh signed a treaty with Governor Napier in which the Basuto chief was given official recognition and promised an annual subsidy of £75 either in money or arms and ammunition in return for maintaining order in his area of jurisdiction, promising to support the colonial authorities when called upon and to receive any agent whom the British Government might send to reside at his court. This treaty, however, did little to satisfy Moshesh for apart from issuing a proclamation warning the Trek Boers not to molest the tribes of the interior or seize their lands, the Governor left the chief to protect himself.

The Napier Treaty thus served little purpose and two years later Governor Maitland proposed a more realistic arrangement. The presence on Basuto soil of white settlers too powerful for Moshesh either to expel or control was recognised. The chief was asked to set aside part of his land for occupation by the settlers. This land would still legally belong to him but he would agree to allow it to be administered for him by a British Resident who would maintain order among the whites. No white settler would be allowed to live outside limits of the area specially set aside. Moshesh agreed willingly to this proposal and marked out a part of his territory in accordance with the scheme. But the farmers had already established themselves beyond this point and refused to move. The British Resident did not have the force at his disposal to make the settlers comply with the arrangement and it proved of little more value than the previous treaty.

In 1848 the newly-appointed and energetic Governor of the Cape, Sir Harry Smith, decided that the disturbed and chaotic conditions in the area of contact between the Boers and the Basuto must inevitably give rise to serious conflict which would affect the security of the Cape Colony. He felt that the only solution was to bring all the peoples of the area under British authority and to proclaim the annexation of the entire territory between the Orange and Vaal Rivers (including the lands of Moshesh, the area occupied by the Boers and the lands of the Griqua chief, Adam Kok) as the Orange River Sovereignty. Although this annexation meant that Moshesh and his people were to lose their independence he welcomed it because he believed it would mean effective protection against the encroachments of the farmers. He was soon to be bitterly disappointed. The British Government was not prepared to spend money on its new territory on the scale that would be necessary if the Resident in the Sovereignty was to be able to control the white farmers. Many of these farmers were hostile to the British Government and broke into rebellion when they heard the news of the annexation. Their forces were dispersed by Sir Harry Smith and the British Resident, whose name was Warden, was reinstated in his position but he was left in a situation in which he could only hope to govern if he could win the support of the very settlers who had so recently shown their hostility.

Warden's policy

In these circumstances it was inevitable that Warden would tend to support the farmers in their claims to the lands of the Basuto. Warden did indeed set up a commission to investigate the question of a frontier between the Basuto and the Boers without any Basuto representative. Not unnaturally, it defined a frontier very favourable to the white farmers. Almost all the white farms were included in the area to be set aside for the settlers but a large number of Basuto settlements were cut off from their people. The proceedings of the commission alarmed the Basuto who feared rightly enough that their land was to be taken away from them. Tension between them and the farmers increased and Moshesh wrote to the British Resident complaining about the whole procedure. 'One act I complain of,' he said, 'is the fixing of limits to people under me without any reference to me,' but on the other hand, he stated publicly 'that I have nothing to say in the matter.' He pointed out that in the annexation proclamation it had been stated that the purpose of the

British government was not to take away the rights of the people but to protect them from the aggression of the settlers. The new line, he said, 'would cut off the *half* of the habitable country, and some thousands of Basutos would be driven from their homes, . . . to give place to a very small proportion in number of British subjects.'

But Warden did not confine himself to defining a line between the Basuto and the Boers. Knowing the hostility of the Basuto to the idea of losing their land he began to side with the other chiefs against Moshesh. Boundaries were defined for the Tlokwa of Sikonyela and the Rolong of Moroka in such a way as to favour them at the expense of the Basuto. The original proposals for a boundary between the Basuto and the whites were modified slightly but still meant taking a great deal of land from the Basuto. Warden went so far as to encourage the minor chiefs to raid the Basuto and openly stated that he would only intervene to check them once Moshesh had agreed to the boundary. At last Moshesh agreed to sign but it was done unwillingly and with a sense of injustice, and soon afterwards fighting broke out between his people and their Bantu neighbours.

Warden had gradually become convinced that the strength of the Basuto was the chief obstacle to a general settlement of the affairs of the Sovereignty along the lines he desired and so he decided to take the opportunity to break Moshesh's power. He invaded the Basuto territory with a small force and a large body of Rolong allies. But Warden had completely miscalculated the

The Boer Trekkers

strength of the Basuto and greatly exaggerated the power of the minor chiefs whom he hoped to use to control Moshesh. The combined British and Rolong forces were completely defeated at Viervoet and Warden had to retreat hurriedly to Bloemfontein. Moshesh then had the Sovereignty at his mercy. Warden appealed for reinforcements to the Colony but all the available troops were involved in a war which had broken out on the colonial frontier. The only help which Warden received was a contingent of Zulus who were sent from Natal but they were gravely lacking in discipline and worse than useless. Moshesh, however, refrained from taking advantage of the situation to take vengeance on his enemies. Warden was not attacked at Bloemfontein and although some reprisals were made against the Rolong and those of the Boer farmers who had taken part in the invasion of Basuto territory, the majority of the white farmers were left in peace.

A soft answer . . .

The outbreak of war in the Sovereignty and on the eastern frontier of the Cape almost simultaneously had a great effect on the development of British policy. The British Government decided that instead of intervening in the areas where Boer trekkers and Bantu were living alongside one another, it would leave the different peoples to fight it out with one another. In accordance with this new policy the Boers in the Transvaal were recognised as independent by the Sand River Convention and preparations were made for withdrawing from the Orange River Sovereignty.

Before doing this, however, the new Governor of the Cape, Sir George Cathcart, decided to wipe out the memory of the British defeat by a show of force against the Basuto. He led a strong column to the borders of Moshesh's territory and demanded that the chief should come to see him. When Moshesh arrived he found himself faced with an ultimatum. He must agree to the boundaries drawn up by Warden and he must pay a fine of 10,000 cattle within three days to be used as compensation for the losses of those who had assisted Warden in the previous campaign. In face of this threatening attitude Moshesh preserved a calm dignity and a continuing desire for peace. He pointed out that it would be difficult for him to collect such a large number of cattle so quickly and pleaded for more time but Cathcart refused to allow any extension. Moshesh begged the Governor not to talk of war and not to push his people too hard for, he said, 'however anxious I may be to avoid it, you know that a dog when beaten will show his teeth'. At last, as Cathcart still refused to change his mind, Moshesh left saying, 'I will go at once and do my best, and perhaps God will help me.'

On the appointed day one of Moshesh's sons came to the British camp with 3,500 cattle, but Cathcart was not satisfied and his forces marched towards Thaba Bosiu. On their way they had to cross the Berea mountain and while doing so they came upon and captured a large herd of 4,000 cattle. But as they were occupied with the cattle, the Basuto launched their attack and after severe fighting the troops had to retreat to their camp taking the cattle with

them. Moshesh then took advantage of this partial victory to score a diplomatic triumph. He sent a messenger to Cathcart with a letter saying that as he had chastised the Basuto and taken many cattle, Moshesh hoped he would be satisfied and not punish his people any further. When he received this peaceful and humble letter Cathcart decided to take the offer of peace against the advice of many of his officers who wanted to send for reinforcements and carry on the fight to the finish. The British troops thus marched away leaving the Basuto victorious.

Sikonyela

In spite of this second victory over British forces Moshesh still remained moderate and peaceful. The white farmers were not seriously molested but Moshesh did take the opportunity to bring the long quarrel with the Tlokwa of Sikonyela to an end. Sikonyela's people took advantage of every occasion when Moshesh's attention was directed elsewhere to raid his people. Now that he was in an exceptionally strong position he made preparations for the final struggle. The Basuto forces surrounded the Tlokwa strongholds under cover of darkness and in the early light of dawn, they swarmed up the mountain sides climbing over one another's shoulders until they suddenly appeared on the top and caught their enemies unawares. The Tlokwa were decisively crushed and the remnants of the tribe were absorbed in the Basuto kingdom. Sikonyela himself with a small band of followers made his escape and fled to Bloemfontein. Moshesh generously offered to receive him and allow him to continue to rule his people, provided that he accepted the paramountcy of the Basuto king. However, he refused and the British Government allowed him to settle with his followers in the Herschel District of the Cape Colony.

Basuto and Boer

After Cathcart's inconclusive expedition, the British became even more determined to abandon all further responsibility for the Orange River Sovereignty. Many of the farmers were opposed to the departure of the British for they feared further troubles with Moshesh but independence was virtually forced upon them and, in 1854, the British Government entered into the Bloemfontein Convention. This document was very similar to the Sand River Convention; it recognised the independence of the Boers in the area between the Orange and the Vaal Rivers. It promised that the British would not interfere in their affairs or with their relations with the Bantu tribes. In the convention the British openly sided with the Boers against the Bantu by promising that the white farmers would have free access to the gunpowder market in the Cape colony but that the Bantu would not be allowed to buy arms and ammunition. Although Moshesh's experience of the British Government had been far from favourable, he was sorry to see it go. He realised that the land-hungry farmers were his most dangerous enemy and in spite of his recent victories he remained fully aware that, in the long run, the whites could count on much greater military force than he. Hoffman, the first President of the newly formed Republic of the Orange Free State, was an old friend of Moshesh, and so relations between the Orange Free State and the Basutos began on a very friendly footing. The President entertained Moshesh and two of his sons to dinner and in turn was received and entertained at Thaba Bosiu. But there was a strong section of the Boers who were opposed to this conciliatory policy. They took advantage of a rumour that Hoffman had given a small keg of gunpowder to Moshesh, in return for what had been fired in salutes during the presidential visit, to depose him forcibly.

The new President, Boshof, was not anxious to precipitate a quarrel with the Basuto but the frontier problem inevitably led to war. When the British abandoned the Sovereignty they had told Moshesh that the Warden line was cancelled, but the Free State insisted that this line, which the Basuto had always regarded as quite unjust, was the legal frontier. Many of the farmers had indeed hoped to see the line extended still further into Basuto territory. Tension mounted along the frontier and there were numerous reports of cattle thefts and of farmers being forced to abandon their farms. However, as the British agent in the area reported:

'The great object which these frontier Boers have in view and at heart and what they are trying to get their Government to insist upon is at bottom *the new line*. This cattle matter serves to introduce the subject and to talk about as a great grievance but the grand point to be gained is the land. The Basutos are equally resolved that they will not be driven back or lose the lands they occupy. . . . These people have no other country to fall back upon, and they fancy at present that it will be better to die defending it than to die of want or be dispersed afterwards.'

The Free State–Basuto Wars

Eventually the Free State decided to force matters to a conclusion. Moshesh was faced with an ultimatum demanding that he recognise the Warden line and pay heavy compensation for alleged thefts. The Free State Commandos advanced towards Thaba Bosiu but the Basuto made no serious attempt to stop them. They contented themselves with defending their mountain strong-holds and sent their own raiding parties deep into the Free State. When the Boers reached Moshesh's mountain they found the main strength of the Basuto drawn up against them. To storm the mountain in the face of such opposition was impossible and at the same time news came in that their farms were burning behind their backs. Suddenly disheartened, they broke up the commando in panic, each man riding off to defend his farm and family.   The President was faced with a desperate situation and appealed to Sir George Grey, then Governor of the Cape, to arbitrate peace between him and the Basuto. Though Moshesh had won the war, as he pointed out, before he had really started fighting seriously, he showed himself as moderate and reason-able as ever. For the sake of peace he accepted the Governor's arbitration. Sir George Grey defined a new frontier between the Boers and the Basuto which gave Moshesh a little more than the Warden line. It was still far from meeting the claims or the needs of the Basuto, however, and Moshesh accepted it unwillingly out of his respect for the colonial government. The frontier problem remained a source of continual tension until war broke out in 1864.

The cause of the second Free State-Basuto war was basically the same as the first. The frontier left the Basuto with too little land for their growing popula-tion and the Boers sought to squeeze the Basuto who were left on their side of the border off the land. Neither side possessed the means to keep its sub-jects in the border areas under close control, and in the atmosphere of ten-sion and bitterness, there were people on both sides who would be happy enough to provoke a conflict—Basuto who hoped to recapture their lost grazing lands—Boers who hoped that the Basuto would be defeated and the rest of their good lands given out in farms.

As matters came to a head, the Free State published a declaration of war on June 9, 1865, reciting the grievances of the farmers against the Basuto and calling on the Boers to rise 'to arms in the name of God for the defence of your homesteads and property, and for the suppression of the arrogance and violence of the Basutos'. Moshesh in turn published his own declaration. In it he declared:

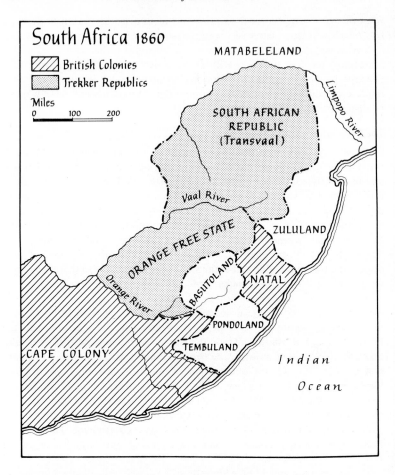

'I am sure all impartial persons will see that, although I am a true lover of peace, it would be wrong for me to allow the Free State to trample on my people . . . for all persons know that my great sin is that I possess a good and fertile country.'

By the time that this second war between the Basuto and the Free State broke out the balance of military power had shifted considerably. Moshesh was by then an old man and no longer able to give close personal direction to the conduct of the war. His sons were jealous of one another and did not co-operate fully even in the face of the desperate national peril. The white population of the Free State, on the other hand, had increased considerably. They were firmly united under the leadership of their outstanding President, J. H. Brandt. What is more, the Free Staters could rely on the goodwill and even active support of their fellow Boers in the Transvaal and had guaranteed access to ammunition supplies under the Bloemfontein Convention, while the

Basuto were prevented by the terms of the convention from any legal access to gunpowder.

The Free State commandos advanced into Basutoland and forced their way through to Thaba Bosiu. At the same time Basuto raiding parties penetrated the Free State and achieved a number of successes, though they lacked the fire power to face substantial Free State forces in the open field. After besieging Thaba Bosiu for some time the Boers made a serious attempt to storm the mountain fortress. The Basuto defended themselves desperately however, and two of the Boer leaders were killed just as their forces were about to force their way on to the summit. This spread panic through the ranks and brought about a disorderly retreat. Thereafter the siege was maintained with declining vigour until it was decided to call off the attempt at a direct assault on the Basuto capital and resort to a war of attrition. For this purpose the Boer forces, divided into a number of smaller highly mobile commandos, attacked the Basuto from several different directions.

The Treaty of Thaba Bosiu

Faced with this multiple attack the Basuto were forced back on purely defensive tactics and were no longer able to counter-attack into Free State territory. As stronghold after stronghold was stormed and the precious cattle were driven off, the dissensions within Basutoland were strengthened. One of Moshesh's sons, Molapo, abandoned the struggle and surrendered to the Free State, giving them free access to the extensive Leribe district in northern Basutoland. This made the Basuto position desperate and Moshesh decided to buy time by apparently yielding to the Boer demands. In the Treaty of Thaba Bosiu he agreed to cede the whole area occupied by the Boer commandos, amounting to virtually all the cultivable land of his kingdom, to the Free State. The weary commandos then dispersed and the Free State proceeded to allot portions of the conquered territory to its citizens. But the Basuto never intended to surrender their lands. As soon as the commandos dispersed they reoccupied them and began planting their crops. Once these were gathered they would be in a position to fight again. The Free Staters thus found themselves unable to occupy the ceded territory and so the commandos were reassembled and the war began again.

Once more the Boers followed the policy of gradually wearing the Basuto down, storming their mountain strongholds, capturing cattle and grain and destroying any crops on the open land. Even before he signed the Treaty of Thaba Bosiu, however, Moshesh had been writing to Governor Wodehouse at the Cape pleading for his intervention and for his kingdom to be taken under the British Government.

Moshesh's darkest hour

By the time the war broke out a second time circumstances had become more favourable for this request. At the time of the Treaty of Thaba Bosiu the Boers made the mistake of expelling the French missionaries from their stations on the grounds that they gave material aid to their enemies. This persecution produced a wave of philanthropic feeling in favour of the Basuto. The terms of the Treaty of Thaba Bosiu revealed the full severity of the Free State's intentions against the Basuto. If they were carried out it was clear that the Basuto would be unable to continue to exist as a coherent nation. They would be driven to desperation and dispersed to spread chaos and confusion amongst the tribes along the eastern frontier of the Cape. There were thus strong reasons why the British should intervene to preserve peace on their own frontiers. Governor Wodehouse saw these very clearly and begged for permission to be allowed to answer Moshesh's plea and place his kingdom under British protection.

At first the idea was strongly rejected by the Colonial Secretary on the grounds of expense but as philanthropic opinion became more concerned at the fate of the Basuto, and the Governor redoubled his arguments, the mood changed. The colony of Natal expressed a willingness to undertake the government of Basutoland, and Moshesh, in despair, was prepared to agree to any arrangement that would give him British protection. The Colonial Secretary then gave Wodehouse permission to annex Basutoland if arrangements could be made to place it under Natal.

The Basuto nation survives

By this time the position of the Basuto was really desperate. Thaba Bosiu still stood but almost all the other mountain strongholds where the Basuto kept their cattle and grain supplies had fallen to the Boers. The Free State forces were able to send long columns of wagons filled with captured grain out of the country and the Basuto people were on the brink of mass starvation. Repeated defeats and the political divisions of the country had undermined morale and the kingdom was on the verge of total collapse. In these desperate circumstances Moshesh received a secret letter from Wodehouse telling him that he had been given permission to extend British authority over the Basuto and urging him to hold out at all costs so that there would be a nation left to save. Heartened in their hour of despair, the Basuto rallied for a desperate defence of their remaining strongholds and Thaba Bosiu remained unconquered. Then as the process of making arrangements with Natal promised to take too long to save the Basuto, Wodehouse went beyond his instructions and, on the 12 March, 1868, simply issued a Proclamation declaring 'that from and after the publication hereof the said tribe of the Basutos shall be, and shall be taken to be, for all intents and purposes British subjects; and the territory of the said tribe shall be and shall be taken to be British territory.'

At the same time he sent units of the Cape police into Basutoland to warn the Free State forces to stop their attacks against the Basuto. Moshesh, old and ailing, could breathe again. His people would be saved from being broken up and dispersed. But long negotiations lay ahead before the situation was finally stabilised. The Proclamation declared the territory of Moshesh to be British territory but the question as to what constituted the land of Moshesh had still to be defined. The Free State was furious at the British intervention and claimed a right to all the land ceded to them in the Treaty of Thaba Bosiu. Wodehouse claimed that the renewal of war had abrogated the Treaty and tried to win back for the Basuto all the land within the old much-disputed frontier.

In the end a compromise was reached. The Basuto lost a great deal of their best and desperately needed land. In future they would be forced to supplement their resources by going out to work in the white-owned areas of South Africa but they did retain enough to keep their identity as a separate people.

The question as to how Basutoland was to be governed also raised problems. Wodehouse had originally been given permission to annex Basutoland to Natal and Moshesh had agreed in his hour of despair. But once British protection was granted, Moshesh pleaded not to be placed under the Natal government, and Wodehouse supported him, for both knew that the Natal settlers also had their eye on the rich lands of Basutoland. Finally, in accordance with Moshesh's wish, Basutoland became a direct dependency of the British crown. By this time the old chief was sinking fast, but he lived on just long enough for the negotiations to be concluded and in 1870 he died peacefully, secure in the knowledge that the nation he had created would survive.

Today the mountain of Thaba Bosiu where for so long Moshesh ruled his people and held his numerous and diverse enemies at bay, is deserted except for the spirit of the great chief and his successors. The mountain top which still bears the ruins of the buildings of Moshesh's time is kept sacred as a royal burial ground. The former Basuto nation is now independent (1966), under the new name Lesotho, but the people whom he moulded into a nation and preserved through appalling dangers still think of themselves as the children of Moshesh.

Apolo Kagwa: Katikkiro of Buganda

C. C. Wrigley

The child who later became Sir Apolo Kagwa, one of the chief architects of
the Uganda Protectorate, was born in Buganda in 1869, about the middle of
the reign of King Mutesa I. He was a member of the Grasshopper clan, which
had enjoyed a period of political prosperity during the reign of their 'son'
Kamanya, Mutesa's grandfather. Kagwa's own great-grandfather, a certain
Bunya, had held one of the great offices of the kingdom, as had several of his
relatives. Politics in Buganda, however, was a dangerous profession. Bunya's
career had ended in his execution, and for some time the family had been in
eclipse. However, this did not debar Kagwa's father from the privilege of
sending his young son to serve as a 'page' at Mutesa's court on Rubaga hill,
close to modern Kampala, which was the usual preliminary to a career in the
service of the state.

A young man at court

Life in the court of the quick-tempered Mutesa, who wielded more arbitrary
and absolute power than was usual among African rulers, was neither safe

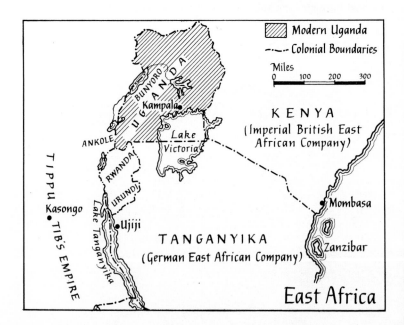

nor comfortable. But for an able and spirited boy it had many attractions. For some three generations Buganda had been the predominant power in the fertile region between the great lakes of east central Africa. Half a million people in a compact territory had been welded by an elaborate administrative system into a formidable military machine, which brought in a constant stream of tribute—women, livestock, ivory. The royal capital was the centre of a considerable empire, with a lively urban atmosphere unknown elsewhere in this part of the world. Here came the Arab merchants from Zanzibar, for Buganda was the commercial hub of the lakes region, and with them came news as well as consumer goods from a wider world.

The Arabs were not the only visitors. About the time of Kagwa's arrival at court, the first missionaries also took up their abode there—English Protestants in 1877, French Catholics two years later. Like many other of the 'pages', Kagwa was attracted to the society of the mysterious strangers and impressed—it is hard to say how deeply—by their message. The ground had already been prepared for conversion by the propagation of Islam and also by the rise of royal power. Buganda, unlike most African societies, was already a secular state, and the influence of the indigenous religion was on the wane. No doubt the commercial character of the capital encouraged scepticism about traditional customs and a welcoming attitude towards new ideas. At all events here, as nowhere else in East Africa, the missionaries scored a notable success before the establishment of European rule. Among their early converts was the young Kagwa, who gave his adherence to the Protestant religion at some time before 1885, receiving the baptismal name Apolo.

Meanwhile he was rising rapidly in the royal service, where his energy and intelligence were already making their mark. Major changes were taking place in the political system at this time, associated especially with the coming of modern firearms, which had become important in the 1870s. Hitherto the army of Buganda had been a general levy of peasant spearmen, mustered by the provincial chiefs. Now the emphasis was on picked corps of riflemen, who were recruited in the main from the palace youths. The result was a marked tendency towards tyranny, which became more prominent when the old king was succeeded by his vicious and unstable son, Mwanga, in 1884. With this went a rise in the power and status of the young men about the palace, who had the guns in their hands and were not slow to use them, against the king's subjects more often than against his enemies. In the memoirs which he wrote in his respectable middle age Kagwa does not conceal that at this period he was one of the gang of youths who went round the country with the king at their head, looting at their pleasure. Nevertheless, the position of those of the royal thugs who were Christians (or for that matter Muslims) was not secure. The European scramble for Africa was beginning, and the king began to doubt the loyalty of those who so closely associated themselves with the white men. Tension was aggravated by the fact that Mwanga was a pervert, and expected his 'boys' to indulge him. For the Christians, natural aversion was reinforced by religious conviction. For this and other reasons, Mwanga decided on a purge, and in 1886 some forty of the young converts suffered death by burning. Kagwa, though he boldly avowed himself as a 'reader', got off with a severe beating, and within a year he was appointed captain of the Gwanika, one of three newly formed companies of privileged royal guards.

The Christian revolution

In fact, the executions of 1886 gave only a very temporary check to the rise of the new class of 'king's men', in whom were combined the two elements— new weapons and new beliefs—which were disturbing Ganda society at this time. But a more serious reaction was preparing. The older chiefs and courtiers, in particular the *Katikkiro*, or head of the royal administration, were perturbed by the growing power of these upstart and unruly youths, and in 1888 they persuaded the king to eliminate them, as being a danger to the state. The plan, however, miscarried. Instead, the Christians and Muslims temporarily united, turned their guns on the palace and the king was forced to flee across the Lake. One of his brothers was installed as the puppet of the victorious rebels.

It was not as difficult to overthrow a government, as construct a new one. The complex system which had maintained unbroken internal peace in Buganda for three generations, was now shattered; for it had rested on unquestioning allegiance to the monarch, and that allegiance had been rudely broken. Within weeks, fighting broke out between the Christians and the Muslims, and the Christians in turn found themselves driven into exile. The majority, led by Kagwa and the Catholic leader Nyonyintono, withdrew westwards to the neighbouring state of Ankole, whose king welcomed this addition of fighting men. For this expulsion of a dissident faction there was more than one precedent in earlier Ganda history, but now there was a major difference: the exiles were determined to recapture power and able to do so. Aided by a freelance Irish arms trader, a certain Charles Stokes, they mounted a campaign which, after several reverses, ended in success. In October 1889 the Christians re-entered the capital. To preserve a semblance of legitimacy, they brought King Mwanga back with them, but the effective power of the state was now in their hands. Among them Kagwa was pre-eminent. For the acknowledged leader of the Christian party, Nyonyintono, had been killed in battle, and Kagwa, as the next senior man, was able to claim the office of Katikkiro. His position, however, was by no means secure, for as a Protestant he belonged to the weaker of the two factions into which the Christians were themselves divided. The Christian victory led to the second stage of the curious episode known as the religious wars of Buganda.

A less sectarian age finds it hard to sympathise with the emotions which led European missionaries to incite strife among Africans in the name of sixteenth-century theological disputes. However, it should also be said that, although some Baganda became adept in theological debate (able, for instance, to appreciate the significance of different Luganda representations of the word 'is' in the formula 'this is my body'), for most of them, and certainly for Kagwa, 'Catholic' and 'Protestant' were little more than convenient labels in the struggle for power which normally develops among successful revolutionaries. If religion had not provided a line of cleavage, some other principle of division would probably have been found.

Kagwa and Lugard

Meanwhile the last act in the drama of the scramble for East Africa, which had begun with the seizure of parts of Tanganyika by the Germans in 1884, was fast approaching, and the independence of Buganda, generally regarded as the key to the rich and populous Lake regions, was in grave danger. The internal politics of Buganda thus became involved in the international struggle. The Protestant leaders, conscious of their weakness, looked to Britain for support, and became known as the 'English' party. The Catholics were naturally the 'French' party, but as France was not at this time competing for power in this part of Africa it was to the Germans that they looked for a counterbalance to the British threat. However, in June 1890 this matter was settled by European diplomacy; the Anglo-German Agreement of that month confirmed the understanding arrived at in 1887, that Buganda lay within the British 'sphere'. A few weeks later the Imperial British East Africa Company, which represented British interests in the region and had by now established its base at Mombasa, despatched a small force under the young Captain Lugard to make good the British claim. Lugard arrived at Kampala (as the area of the royal capital was later called) in December, and at once demanded that the king and his chiefs should sign a treaty of protection. Kagwa and his followers were, of course, willing; Lugard's mission was in a sense the response to a plea which their envoy had made to the British consul in Zanzibar at the beginning of the year. The Catholic leaders at first refused, but on the advice of their priests, gave way, and a treaty was signed on 26 December, 1890. It must be emphasised that Lugard's force was far too small and poorly armed to have confronted the united army of Buganda; only its internal divisions enabled him to insert the wedge of imperial power.

One reason for the Catholic surrender was undoubtedly the continuing threat from the Muslim Baganda forces, which had been driven out of the country but were still formidable. Soon after the signature of the treaty Lugard and Kagwa marched out together to deal with this menace. The Baganda Christians, with Lugard's contingent in a supporting role, won a decisive victory over the Muslims near the border of the kingdom. This, it may be said, was Kagwa's only important personal victory in the field. Powerfully built and fearless, he was a fine warrior but an indifferent general, his tactics being limited to the frontal assault, which against most opponents ended in disaster. It was in politics rather than in war that his talents found their most effective expression.

Lugard's compromise

After the defeat of the Muslmis the uneasy alliance of the Christian factions
fell apart, and there followed a period of growing tension. For some time
Lugard endeavoured to keep the peace, but in December 1891, having failed
to reconcile the Christian parties to one another and both to his presence, he
decided on a show-down, which had become more urgent in his eyes in that
the company which he served was on the verge of bankruptcy and the future
of British power in the region was in doubt. Moreover, King Mwanga, after
much wavering, had thrown his influence on the side of the Catholics, as the
party more likely to preserve the independence of his throne. Guns were now
issued to the Protestant forces, and fighting broke out in the capital. Here
Kagwa's impetuous tactics would have ended in defeat had it not been for
Lugard's machine-gun, which broke the Catholic ranks and enabled the
Katikkiro's men to drive them in rout. The Protestants now believed that
their political triumph was complete, but to their chagrin (and that of their
missionary friends) they found that Lugard, whose interest in religious disputes was zero, was insisting on a compromise. The arrangements which he
now forced through, after some modification by his immediate successor,
formed the basis of the Buganda political system throughout the colonial
period. Chiefships were allocated on a religious basis, ten of the twenty
'counties' going to the Protestants, nine to the Catholics and one to the
Muslims. Kagwa was confirmed in the office of Katikkiro, but had to accept
a Catholic, Mugwanya, as his most senior colleague, in the newly created post
of *Omulamuzi* (Chief Justice). The central government, however, was completed by a third post of *Omuwanika* (Treasurer), which was to be held by a
Protestant. By these astute devices, the final edge of power was reserved for
those who were comitted to the British 'alliance', yet the others were given
concessions sufficient to reconcile them to the new regime.

The moment of truth

In 1893 the British Government at last decided to accept formal responsibility
for Buganda, and a protectorate was proclaimed in the following year. It is
doubtful whether this change meant much to Kagwa and his friends, who
clearly believed that they would continue to rule the kingdom with British
support. More important to them was the victory which the combined
British and Baganda forces won in 1894 over the ancient rival of Buganda,
the kingdom of Bunyoro, a victory which brought them large accessions of
territory. It was in 1896 that the moment of truth came for the Christian
leaders who had thrown in their lot with the British. For Mwanga at last
grew weary of the humiliating position in which he had been placed, escaped
from the capital and raised the standard of revolt. The chiefs had now to make
an agonising decision, and Kagwa himself has graphically described the
night-long conclave in which they resolved their problem: to support their
king against their British protectors, or the British against their king. It is
true that they had fought against the king before, but the present situation was

fundamentally different. For what was at stake was not the person of the king but the survival of the kingship itself, and the kingship was a vital symbol of a continuing autonomy; without it, as they saw, they would be mere agents of British rule. Nevertheless, for the great majority there was no choice: they were too deeply committed to the British connexion to withdraw from it now. Kagwa and Mugwanya rode to the ensuing battle on their newly acquired horses, but it was clear that the military role of the Baganda was now no more than that of auxiliaries to the greatly strengthened British forces. Nevertheless, after Mwanga's defeat and deposition, the British Commissioner agreed to let his infant son carry on the kingship and to let him be formally chosen by the council of chiefs.

The Buganda Agreement, 1900

British power now seemed to be firmly established, but in 1898 it was shaken to its foundations by a general mutiny of the Sudanese mercenary troops on whom it rested. In this crisis the Baganda chiefs again remained 'loyal'. Their military contribution was not very great, for against trained troops they had little chance, and it was Indian reinforcements that finally restored the situation. But they had fought bravely—Kagwa had himself led two charges against entrenched positions, which were repulsed with heavy loss—and a genuine feeling of comradeship had developed between them and the desperate British officials, a feeling which probably had some influence on the political developments which followed. In 1899 Sir Harry Johnston arrived in Kampala to effect a permanent settlement of the affairs of Buganda, and after lengthy negotiations a new treaty, the Buganda Agreement of 1900, was duly signed. In the main, this gave both parties what they wanted. On the one hand, the Baganda agreed to be disarmed and to pay taxes to the Protectorate Government, whose power was thus rendered unassailable. On the other hand, the continuance of the kingship was assured, and a considerable measure of autonomy was granted to its government. More important to the Baganda negotiators, the Christian chiefs, the revolutionaries of 1888–9, were confirmed in their position as the ruling class of Buganda. This was symbolised by the very unusual arrangements which were made over the distribution of land. Johnston's scheme was in essence very simple: half the land should go to the chiefs, half to the Crown. The unusual feature was that the chiefs' share was to go to individuals in the form of estates which would be surveyed and held in outright ownership with documentary title, the customary system of land tenure, in which the chiefs merely held rights of control over the areas to which they had been temporarily appointed by the king, being completely superseded. In practice, the immediate effect on the condition of the peasants was not great; they continued to cultivate the land, paying dues and rendering services to the chiefs as they had done for generations past. In the long run, however, the new dispositions had a profound influence on the development of Ganda society, in ways which cannot be entered into here.

T.L.—5*

The negotiations

Apart from the king and his immediate relatives, Kagwa received the largest single allotment: thirty square miles. There was also an appendix to the Agreement, which caused eyebrows to be raised both then and later. It stipulated that some hundreds of cattle should be presented by the British Government to Kagwa and the other principal signatories. This clause, however, should not be misunderstood. It was, of course, a 'dash' in the true sense of the term—not a bribe but a token that the bargaining had been freely conducted and had ended in good-will. There is a sense in which Kagwa may be said to have sold his country, but he did not sell it for three hundred cows. Indeed, the whole transaction was of an entirely different character from that of the usual 'treaties' of the period in East and Central Africa, in which petty chiefs signed away their people's lands and sovereignties for some trivial present. The negotations which preceded the Buganda Agreement were genuine negotiations, in which the Baganda had quite powerful bargaining counters and played them with great skill. For, although the British were by now in full military control, they knew that they could not govern the country cheaply and smoothly without the willing collaboration of the Baganda chiefs, and to get this they had to make substantial concessions. The degree of autonomy that was finally conceded was probably a good deal greater than either Johnston or his superiors in London had really intended. Certainly a 'Nigerian' official, Sir William Gowers, who became Governor of Uganda in 1925, found the existing system of British rule in Buganda much too 'indirect' for his liking. And the land settlement had given some of the Baganda a security, dignity and independence which were not available to any other of the East African peoples at this time. It is true that these benefits were confined, in the first instance, to the three or four thousand people who made up the ruling oligarchy. But in this there was nothing new; it was a long time since the interests of the common people had counted for much in Buganda. And in the long run they too benefited from the obstacles which the land settlement placed in the path of alien settlers and from the special status which the Buganda kingdom enjoyed in its relations with the colonial power.

Western and traditional culture

Moreover, although Kagwa's religious convictions were probably not very profound, and his conformity to parts of the new moral code (such as the rule of monogamy) is believed to have been only nominal, there can be no doubt of the genuineness of his enthusiasm for the new worlds of experience which had opened up before the Baganda during his youth. By the turn of the century he was living in a two-storey house complete with electric bells, typewriters and secretaries. All this, though it had no parallel elsewhere in East Africa at the time, might be dismissed as superficial imitation, like the tea-parties at which missionaries and officials were solemnly entertained. But there was more to it than that. Kagwa was an eager patron of the missionaries' educational efforts and of the early experiments in commercial agriculture. He was also a writer of books. The first edition of his *Book of the Kings of Buganda*, a record of the oral traditions of the kingdom together with a much fuller account of the events of his own time, appeared, in Luganda, in 1901, and was, by a wide margin, the first written essay in ethno-history to be attempted by a native of East Africa. Other volumes, on *The Customs*, *The Clans* and *The Legends* of the Baganda, followed at intervals during the next two decades. These works have no great literary merit. Kagwa's style was flat and ungraceful, and he did not possess much gift for vivid narration. But they are remarkable for their calmness and objectivity. He did not always tell the whole truth but he told no lies. He did not gloss over the defeats of the Baganda, or his own, and he abstained entirely from rant and cant; indeed, he rarely permitted himself any personal comment at all. This is not to say that his writings had no ulterior purpose. They had a very clear purpose, stated by Kagwa himself: to justify the exceptional degree of autonomy that was claimed by the Baganda, by showing that they had already displayed exceptional capacity for 'government'. In a more general sense, he was, in recording the events and customs of the past, attempting to preserve the continuity of Ganda society and the self-respect of the Baganda people, in a time of rapid and, in some respects, humiliating change. In this, he was setting the tone for the future conduct of the Baganda, who throughout the colonial period have been at one and the same time the most eager 'westernisers' among the east African peoples and among the most tenacious of the essentials of their traditional culture.

In the first decade of the twentieth century Kagwa was at the zenith of his

Katikkiro Apolo Kagwa and his carriage

career. Within Buganda, his position was unchallenged. He was not only katikkiro but also the senior of the three regents who governed the country during the minority of the young king, Daudi Chwa. The patronage of the Protestant half of the country was largely in his hands, and in addition he was a great private landowner, who was steadily adding to his original estates by prudent purchases. Among the British rulers of the Uganda Protectorate he enjoyed a considerable measure of respect, and rewards for his services continued to be heaped upon him. In 1902 he paid an official visit to Britain to attend the coronation of King Edward VII and was much feted in imperialist and missionary circles, returning to Buganda as Sir Apolo Kagwa, K.C.M.G. A later Governor was much put out to find that a 'native chief' stood at the same point in the hierarchy of British honours as himself, and suggested that the award of a 'K' must have been the result of a clerical error. At the time, however, Kagwa was accepted as a kind of honorary member of the colonial 'establishment'—a curious fate, in a way, for one who in his youth had been first a ruffian and then a successful revolutionary. In the photographs of the period his rough-hewn features wear a faintly uneasy look.

Kagwa's fall

But time slowly eroded his power, and the story of his later years is a rather sad anti-climax. No man could be so prominent for so long in political life without making enemies, and as time went on there were growing rumbles of resentment against Kagwa's rule. He quarrelled bitterly with one of his colleagues, who held the semi-ritual office of Mugema, over their respective roles in the coronation ceremonies which were held for King Chwa when he attained his majority in 1914; and the Mugema was the leader of a general outbreak of unrest, known as the Bataka movement, which swept over Buganda in 1922. The Bataka were the traditional 'land-chiefs', heads of clans and lesser kin-groups. For some time before the coming of the British these people had been losing ground to the military and administrative chiefs appointed by the king, and the revolutionary period between 1888 and 1900 had completed their eclipse. In the land settlement of 1900 their claims had been almost totally ignored.Now they were re-asserting them, and in the process they were rallying all the elements in Ganda society that were hostile to Kagwa and to the regime of which he was the head.

This would have mattered little, if Kagwa had still enjoyed the favour of the British authorities. But the new generation of British officials looked on the ruling class of Buganda in a new and less favourable light. They no longer saw them as Christian converts, comrades in arms, allies in the reform of Africa. They saw merely a group of stubborn, ageing men, who had been over-flattered by the missionaries and badly needed to be reduced to the ordinary status of African chiefs under colonial rule. In particular, the commanding figure of Sir Apolo Kagwa was becoming an anachronism in the days of settled administration. The Bataka movement they chose to regard as a protest of the peasants against the exactions of the landlord class which, as was now believed, had unjustly arrogated the rights of ownership in 1900. Plans of reform, both of land tenure and of the administrative system, began to be framed; and it was evident that they could not easily be carried through so long as Kagwa was in control of affairs.

To get rid of him was not, now, very difficult. A new generation of chiefs, trained during the colonial period, was waiting in the wings. Moreover, the young king was chafing against the power of a minister who had so long acted as the effective monarch, and was eager to assert his own authority. The end, when it came in 1926, was sadly trivial. A dispute arose between the king and his Katikkiro over the issue of beer permits in Kampala. The Provincial Commissioner sided with the king. Angry exchanges followed. Kagwa was accused of impertinence and obliged to resign the office which he had held for nearly thirty-seven years. He did not give up without a struggle, writing rather pathetic letters to the Colonial Secretary, in which he rehearsed his past services and honours, and, when these brought no response, setting out for London to present his case in person. But on the way through Kenya in 1927 he fell sick and died.

The occasion of his fall was trivial, but the fall itself was symbolic of the end of an era. In the 1920s there was no longer any room for African chiefs with knighthoods.

Kagwa's place in history

To a modern African nationalist, Sir Apolo Kagwa must appear a somewhat dubious figure. It would be easy to see him as a collaborator, who invited the colonialists into his country for the sake of personal and factional advantage. However, it would be unjust to condemn him in the light of ideas alien to his generation. In passing judgment on statesmen, historians customarily apply the criterion of success, and by this criterion Kagwa must rank high among African statesmen of his own or any other time. For himself, he achieved a tenure of power unparalleled by any earlier or later Katikkiro of Buganda and rare among non-hereditary rulers in any country. For his religion (or, more accurately, his party) he achieved at least as much. He helped to make Buganda Christian sooner and more thoroughly than any other part of East Africa—thus securing for it, apart from other considerations, a long lead in modern education. Against the odds, he made it, in a political sense, pre-dominantly Protestant. For his country? It is true that he assisted in the destruction of its independence. If, however, one accepts that by 1890 the independence of Buganda was already doomed, that even a united people could not have staved off the European conquest for more than a few years, then Kagwa must be given high credit for the realism which secured for his country exceptionally favourable terms of surrender. More than anyone else, he preserved the kingdom, and all that that meant for the Baganda people. He secured for it an extension of territory and a unique status in its relations with the imperial power. It is true that 'his country' was what would now be

Apolo Kagwa

called a tribe, and that in the 1950s the size and special status of Buganda would be a serious impediment to the construction of a Uganda state and nation. But to condemn him for not arriving at the concept of Uganda nationalism would be as unrealistic as to condemn Queen Elizabeth I or Cardinal Richelieu for not subscribing to twentieth-century doctrines of European unity. It should also be said that, though respectful towards the British, he was never servile. Unlike his immediate successors, he never adopted the manner of a sergeant in a white-officered army; indeed, he eventually fell precisely because he would not be treated like a sergeant.

It is not probable that Kagwa was an entirely likeable human being. Even allowing for the scowl commonly adopted by those unused to the camera, the photographs do not suggest amiability. Nor, although they always referred to him with respect, do the Anglican missionaries appear to have entertained for him the warm personal feelings which were aroused by some of their other early converts. Indeed, no one could have come to the top, and remained there, in the turbulent politics of late nineteenth-century Buganda without possessing a strong streak of ruthlessness and a capacity for successful intrigue. Yet, considering his long tenure of almost autocratic power, he is not unkindly remembered in Buganda, where his reputation is that of a generous man, who used his power, on the whole, with justice. And, when all is said, he was a big man, a man of dignity and presence, who compelled respect at a time when this was very rarely accorded to Africans of East Africa.

Notes

Apolo Kagwa—In modern Luganda 'Kaggwa' but spelled here as he spelled it. His baptismal name does not come from the Greek god, Apollo, but from Apollos, colleague and rival of St. Paul. In the history of the early church Apollos was a questionable figure and the name may suggest that the missionary who baptised Kagwa had some doubts about the character of his convert.

Buganda—the state; *Baganda*—the people of Buganda; *Luganda*—their language; *Ganda*—an adjective, e.g. Ganda society; *Uganda*—the British protectorate which included the kingdoms of Buganda, Bunyoro, and Ankole along with others.

Katikkiro—head of the administration, prime minister.

Reader—term used in the 1880s for converts to Christianity and Islam: the only Baganda who had learnt or were learning to read!

Abdel Kader and French Occupation of Algeria, 1830-1847

E. A. Ayandele

The territory of Algeria, over which the French ruled sternly for over one hundred years, has a rich and inspiring past. For centuries inhabited almost exclusively by the fiercely assertive people known as Berbers, the invasion of their territory in the seventh century by militant expansionist Arab jihadists marked a new era in their history. For the monotheistic creed of Islam soon displaced the traditional religion and became the state religion of the kingdoms of Bougie, Tlemcen, Tennez and Algiers, which were eventually to evolve into the modern state of Algeria. It is an established fact that in all places where it has become the state religion Islam has affected all aspects of the society's life, including politics, law, ethos and foreign policy. It is not

Abdel Kader's mountain stronghold

surprising, then, that by the fifteenth century Islam had already leavened the Algerian society. When therefore they were faced with the menacing activities of the infidel Christians of Spain, Portugal, France and the Italian states in the sixteenth century, the Berbers of Algeria invoked the help and protection of their co-religionists, the Ottoman Turks, against the infidel danger.

Algeria under the Turks

The Ottoman Turks, who already had an extensive empire in which Islam was strongly emphasised, stayed on in Algeria for centuries and established an administration which suited the Berbers in many ways. The military strength of the Turks in Algeria itself, about 7,000 soldiers, and the naval capacity of the Turks on the Mediterranean, which harassed the shipping of the Christian powers, safeguarded the territorial integrity of Algeria. Moreover the Turkish administration, aware of the passionate love of the Berbers

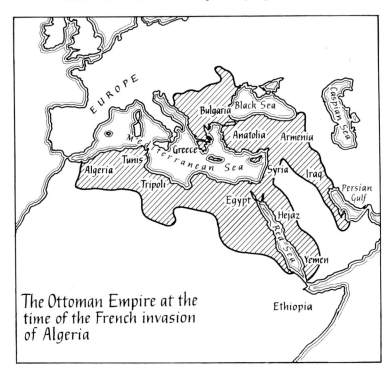

The Ottoman Empire at the time of the French invasion of Algeria

for independence, allowed the people to govern themselves so long as they paid their taxes. In the garrison towns the Turkish soldiers, known as janni-saries, maintained law and order and settled disputes among tradionally warring tribal groups. The Turkish administration was headed by the Dey, who was appointed by the Sultan of Constantinople from among the soldiers quartered in the country. He was expected to be advised by a *Diwan*, or council, composed of about thirty colonels. The Regency, as Algeria was described in the administrative arrangement of the Turkish Empire, was divided into three administrative provinces, viz. Western, Titan and Eastern, with headquarters respectively at Oran, Medea and Constantine. Of course there were the mountainous regions of Aures and Kabylia in the interior where the Turkish writ did not run.

But from the beginning of the nineteenth century Algeria, like all North African states, began to be threatened by European economic and imperial interests. European eyes were fixed particularly on Egypt and Algeria. In the former state the emergence and career of an Albanian adventurer, Muhammad Ali, and the way he consolidated his hold over Egypt postponed the occupation of that part of Mediterranean Africa by Europeans for over seventy years. The fate of Algeria was different. In about 1798, it is said, the British had unofficially drawn up a 'plan for the Conquest of Algiers' and even thought of putting the entire Sahara under the Union Jack. In 1808 Napoleon I drew up a plan for the occupation of Algiers. But it was not until 1830 that Algeria was actually invaded, by the French. Several factors were responsible for this singularly decisive event which marked the beginnings of effective European occupation of Mediterranean Africa. On the surface Franco-Algerian relations were cordial until the third decade of the nine-

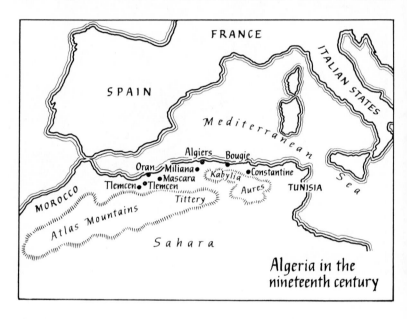

Algeria in the nineteenth century

teenth century. Indeed since the eighteenth century the French connection had been economically beneficial to Algeria, the latter producing grain and olive oil for France. The commercial relations of the two countries improved further during the Napoleonic wars when Algeria supplied provisions for the French armies of Egypt and Italy, and Louis XVIII, the restored Bourbon monarch of the French, concluded many commercial treaties with the Deys of Algeria.

Prelude to invasion

Franco-Algerian relations became strained to the breaking-point over the financial dealings of two Jews, Bacri and Busnach, and the insulting and over-bearing behaviour of Deval, the French consul. For centuries Jews had dominated the commercial life of the Magreb, and as from the end of the eighteenth century these two Jewish businessmen had attempted to mono-polise all the export trade of Algeria. The Dey, Hussain, was involved in their financial transactions in a manner which is not quite clear. But it is clear that he came to have the impression that he had been swindled and his alleged debt to the Jews had to be reduced by the Bourbon administration from twenty-four million to seven million francs. The appointment of Deval, a man of doubtful character, did not improve the state of affairs, for Deval had a reputation for shady dealings. In fact he was said to have been hand in glove with the Jewish financiers. It is important to note that several times Hussain had called upon the French Government to remove the consul, but the French persistently ignored his requests, while at the same time refusing to investigate charges against the consul. An apparently small incident became the pretext for the invasion of Algeria. Deval and Hussain had quarrelled over the supply of grain to France. On April 29, 1827, Hussain struck the consul with a fly-whisk after the latter had provoked him. According to the Dey, Deval told him in an insulting manner that the Dey could not expect the French Government to reply to his letters, and then added derogatory remarks about Islam.

This was the insult which the French alleged had been inflicted upon France, and which needed to be avenged. It was indeed a godsend to Charles X whose regime at home was most unpopular and who thought he could achieve popularity in France by a war against Algeria. The French attempted to cloak their economic and imperialistic interests in the Algerian affair by contending that the invasion was being undertaken in order to suppress piracy on the Mediterranean. It may be mentioned at this point that until now Europeans were themselves participating in piracy, and that until 1856 piracy was recognised by European Powers as a legitimate method of warfare. In 1830, in a rather dramatic fashion, the French sent thousands of soldiers to conquer Algeria.

Few allies for the Berbers

This was the situation that the Berbers of Algeria had to deal with. They looked upon the impending French attack as a predominantly religious one, a jihad. But theirs was a perilous situation. They could not measure their military strength with that of the infidel French who had better weapons. In the past the Berbers in such circumstances used to ask for the help and protection of fellow Muslim states. But in 1830 no Muslim state, except feeble Morocco, was willing to risk the fire and sword of the French by helping their Algerian co-religionists. The Ottoman Empire was weak and was already falling into parts. Only three years before, the Greeks had rebelled against Constantinople, with the encouragement of infidel European powers. And the Sultan had become the laughing-stock of the Europeans who nicknamed him the 'Sick Man of Europe'. The Hussainic Bey of Tunisia, Algeria's eastern neighbour, would rather co-operate with the French and annex the Constantine (eastern) area of Algeria, than join hands with the Algerian co-religionists in repelling the infidel invaders. Even Muhammad Ali, the strong and distinguished ruler of Egypt, was tempted to extend his empire westward as far as Algeria, with French encouragement.

It therefore looked as if the Berbers would be crushed by the French within a very short time and in a very easy manner. This was what the French invaders expected. It was in this state of distress and helplessness that Algeria produced a unique leader who organised the Berber resistance against the French in a manner and on a scale bewildering to the French, inspiring to the Berbers and heroic to many contemporary observers. It is not an exaggeration to say that nineteenth-century Africa produced few other figures of his stature. He is one of the few African personalities of the nineteenth century whose qualities and career have attracted the attention of foreign biographers. His name was Abdel Kader.

Abdel Kader

Born in May 1807 in the province of Oran, Abdel Kader developed an appetite for learning at the age of five. At fourteen he became a Hafiz, that is, one who knew the Koran by heart. In the course of his life he was to become a religious leader, a statesman, a scholar, an author, an administrator and a diplomat all rolled into one. In the period of the French invasion of Algeria, when Berber nationalist feelings and sense of common identity rose to unexampled heights, Abdel Kader became their leader by popular acclamation and was made Sultan in 1832. The Sultan used the occasion of the French danger to weld together normally factious tribal groups. The tribal groups who submitted to his authority included the Beni Yakub, the Beni Abbas, the Beni Amer, the Beni Mejaher and the Beni Hashem. Many of these and others Abdel Kader forcefully brought into the orbit of his authority. And although not all the tribal groups in modern Algeria submitted to his rule at all times, and although many withdrew their loyalty whenever the French aggression receded, yet perhaps no one before him administered centrally an area as large as that administered by Abdel Kader.

A Berber state

If anyone ever founded a state then, in a sense, Abdel Kader founded the modern Algerian state. For not only did he inspire the Algerians with the fact that they constituted a people, a nation, distinct from others, but he established an administration which gave Algeria the semblance of a state. He divided the country into eight *Khalifaliks*, the most important of which were those of Tlemcen, Mascara, Miliana and Medea. Tekedemt, a town sixty miles south-west of Oran, was made the capital. Every tribal group was held responsible for the peace and good order of its locality, under a khalifa appointed directly by himself. Each khalifa was given a number of soldiers who were to help in the maintenance of law and order. Every khalifa was expected to send him weekly reports on the state of affairs in his district.

Abdel Kader made the Koran the basis of his administration and he himself has been described by all his biographers as a genuinely pious man, who observed the ceremonies and rituals of the Muslim faith. He never demanded anything outside the Koranic taxes of *ashur* (one-tenth of agricultural produce) and *zakah* (two and a half per cent of one's property to be given to the poor by all faithful believers). In the schools which he established throughout the territory the subjects taught were mainly the principles of Islam, reading, writing and arithmetic. Those who wanted higher education were encouraged to enter into the *zawiyas* (similar to the monasteries of Medieval Europe) and mosques. The laws by which Abdel Kader ruled his state were Islamic laws. He sent salaried *qadis* to all districts for administration of justice and he punished crimes severely. Himself an ascetic and hater of luxuries, he forbade the use of gold and silver ornaments, proscribed alcohol and tobacco and attempted to put an end to prostitution. As he moved from place to place he constituted himself the sole dispenser of justice. He indicated his punishment with a gesture. If he raised his hand the victim was carried back to prison; if he held it out horizontally, the victim was executed; if he pointed to the ground the victim was bastinadoed. He presided over a tribunal of *ulemas* which was the final court of appeal, but sometimes he referred doubtful cases to Egypt and Morocco.

Berber victories

Abdel Kader had little time to administer. He had to fight most of the time. Although in terms of weapons and men Abdel Kader's forces were inferior to those of the French, yet the Berbers enjoyed the advantages of local knowledge and geography. Kader's tactics eventually humiliated the French in the 'thirties. In many instances they were starved into submission by the Berbers who obeyed the Sultan's instructions that they should sell no provisions to the French, who depended mainly on local supply. The Algerian forces also used English and French muskets, purchased from Morocco and Tunisia. But the Sultan also made his own ammunition at Tlemcen, Mascara, Miliana, Medea and Tekedemt. And at the seat of government of each of his khalifas he placed tailors, armourers and saddlers, who made the clothing for his troops, repaired their arms and kept up their horse equipment. Swift French incursions into the interior were generally followed by swift retreats, largely because of lack of provisions which, on Kader's orders, the Berbers buried. Kader also employed the tactics of luring the French into dangerous mountain passes and the trenches which he had dug. Moreover, so long as the lines of his communications with Tunisia and Morocco were not disturbed by the French, Abdel Kader remained militarily strong.

Much against their will the French had twice to concede victory to the Sultan in 1834 and in 1837. In the former year General Desmichels, the French commander, decided to negotiate with Kader, without prior consultation with Paris. The Desmichels Treaty indicated, in a sense, the extremities into which the French had been driven by Berber resistance. Kader had compelled the French to sue for peace, and he had dictated his terms. By this treaty Abdel Kader was to pay no tribute and his territory was not limited. The French general acknowledged his independence by recognising the Sultan's power to appoint and receive consuls. The French were to load at one port alone, and to submit to his tariff. Kader felt he had obtained a mandate to organise the trade of Algeria on a state monopoly basis. Certainly he had scored a diplomatic triumph.

But the Desmichels Treaty was not a complete victory for the Sultan and the Berbers. By recognising French rights to the maritime area of the territory it gave tacit approval to French presence on Algerian soil. Some of the more fanatical Berbers became disappointed at a treaty which they regarded as a gross betrayal of the sacred cause of the jihad. In the Sultan's judgment, however, by negotiating with the infidels, he was only being realistic and he extracted from them the maximum possible concessions. Like Muhammad Ali of Egypt in his foreign policy and like Bismarck in the way he united Germany in stages, Abdel Kader knew when, where, and how to stop. He was aware that French imperalism had come to stay, and that the French had superior arms and that if they decided to launch a full-scale attack the Berbers would not be able to resist them. In Kader's view, it was better to salvage as much as he could of Algeria's sovereignty and territorial integrity. In a war such as the Berbers were engaged in, ultimate and complete victory was out of the question. Indeed in the circumstances in which he found himself the Sultan believed that he had gained enormously by the treaty. He had obtained concessions for Islam and its culture; he needed a breathing space to organise the tribes who had submitted to his rule and force those who would not have his authority into submission. Moreover, there were already appearing centrifugal forces among the tribal groups who found unpalatable his stringent application of Islamic laws.

The French Government regarded the Desmichels Treaty as a great humiliation and instantly recalled its unauthorised architect. His successors, particularly General Bugeaud, sought either to reduce the power given to the Sultan by the Desmichels Treaty or neutralise it. The Sultan was able to stand up to the French generals. Through the French newspapers, which he read, he was able to measure the barometer of public opinion in France. He was aware that the absence of sensational military successes by the French army in the country did not make the invasion popular in France. The Sultan employed spies and agents to organise propaganda in his favour among influential people in France. These agents attempted to persuade the French to believe that it would be in France's interest to befriend rather than alienate such a revered person. These agents, it is said, extolled Abdel Kader's merits and enlarged upon his talents for administration. The situation which General Bugeaud met in Algeria in 1836 made him abandon his attempt to resort to arms. He therefore agreed to make peace with the Sultan as a humiliating necessity. The Berber leaders in a general meeting decided to grant a further concession to the French. The latter were given the plain of Algiers.

The Treaty of Tafna

On May 30, 1837, the controversial Treaty of Tafna was signed. According to one version of the treaty, to which Abdel Kader *did not* affix his seal, the

Sultan acknowledged the sovereignty of France. But according to the Arabic text, which he did sign, Abdel Kader said only that he acknowledged that there was a French king, and that he was powerful. The difference in the textual wording of this clause in the French and Arabic versions was a potential cause for war, and reminds us of a similar difference in the Amharic and Italian texts of the Treaty of Ucciali between Ethiopia and Italy in 1889, one of the causes of the Adowa war. The French and Arabic texts were agreed on the wording of the remaining clauses of the treaty. The frontiers of France in Algeria were delimited, consisting mainly of the plains of Algiers. Abdel Kader was recognised as the Sultan, to administer the provinces of Oran and Tittery and part of the province of Algiers not occupied by the French. The Sultan was not to exercise any authority over the Muslims who resided on the territory reserved to France, but they should be free to go and reside in the territory under the Sultan's jurisdiction; the Arabs living in French territory were to enjoy the free exercise of their religion; they might build mosques, and follow their religious discipline in every particular, under the authority of their spiritual chiefs; the Sultan was to give the French army 30,000 measures of corn, 30,000 measures of barley, 5,000 heads of oxen; the Sultan should be empowered to buy powder, sulphur, and the arms he required in France; commerce was to be free between the Arabs and the French; the farms and properties which the French had acquired, or might acquire, on the Arab territory would be guaranteed them; the Sultan engaged not to give up any part of the coast to any foreign power, without the authorisation of France; the commerce of Algeria should be carried on only in French ports and France should maintain agents near the Sultan, and in the towns under his jurisdiction, to act as intermediaries for French subjects, in any commercial disputes they might have with the Arabs. The Sultan would have the same privilege in French towns and seaports.

It is clear that the Treaty of Tafna severely modified that of Desmichels. The independence of Algeria was already compromised politically and commerically. The French, in effect, became a state within a state. Algeria's independence in foreign affairs was bartered away. Nevertheless the French believed that too much had been granted to Abdel Kader in this treaty. General Bugeaud had been strictly enjoined by Paris to confine the Sultan to the province of Oran only; on no account, he was instructed, must he cede to the Sultan the province of Tittery, and he must insist on his paying tribute to France. But the treaty confined the French substantially to the coast with very circumscribed adjacent territories, while all the fortresses and strongholds in the interior were left in the hands of their adversary.

It is not surprising, then, that within two years of the Tafna agreement differences over the text and interpretation of the treaty by Algeria and France led to resumption of war. Apart from the dispute over the sovereignty clause there was the boundary question. Marshal Valoe, the man who had assumed the functions of Governor-General in Algiers in November 1837, was asked to discuss the details of the treaty with the Sultan. In 1839 Abdel Kader occupied a territory which the French also claimed. This country, lying to the south-east of the province of Algiers, was one of the greatest utility to the French because the garrison of Constantine drew its provisions from it, and they could not help feeling that Abdel Kader could now at any moment stop the supply. The treaty was clear over the ownership of the territory; it belonged to Abdel Kader. The French Marshal declared that he wanted the treaty revised; Kader refused to budge. And as European powers were to do in other parts of Africa in the nineteenth century, whenever it suited their interests, the French began to violate the treaty they had solemnly pledged to observe. Contrary to the treaty, the French prevented Muslims in their territory who wanted to settle in Abdel Kader's territory from doing so. Then Kader's agent, through whom he obtained ammunition and other supplies from France, was suddenly arrested by the French, put into chains and sent to France. Also the French withdrew recognition from Kader's consul at Algiers, an Italian called Garavan, and they attempted to instruct the Sultan whom he was to appoint. The French deliberately violated Abdel Kader's territory. The Sultan saw no alternative to declaring war in November 1839.

The turn of the tide

The French decided to take decisive action. A military offensive was launched, granaries hidden underneath the ground were scouted and corn was milled by machines carried about by the troops. A systematic dislodging of Abdel Kader's infantry was undertaken. The Sultan's communications with Morocco and Tunisia were interrupted and the rulers of both territories were warned against giving any more support, moral or physical, to the Algerian Berbers. Sensing the importance of the *tariqas* the French satisfied the cupidity of the most important of them all, the Tijaniya, the head of which openly offered moral and material support to the French against Abdel Kader.

By 1843 the backbone of the Berber resistance was already broken. Many of his khalifas were either captured or dead; many of the Berber tribes not only surrendered to the French, but actually fought on the side of the infidels against their Sultan. Abdel Kader's state lost cohesion. As the English poet, W. M. Thackeray, put it, 'with traitors around him, his star upon the wane', the Sultan fled to Morocco whose Sultan was persuaded by the French to set a price on his head. It is fair to add that Sultan Abdul Rahman of Morocco did the French bidding only reluctantly, after the French had defeated the Moroccan army at the battle of Isly. It was an irony that the Muslim forces of Morocco had to fight against Sultan Abdel Kader, in obedience to infidel France. This was a bitter experience for Abdel Kader. By 1847 he had noticed that he could no longer rouse the Berbers to continue the Holy War. He was alone, singularly alone, with only a small band of faithful followers. He was at the end of his tether. Rather than surrender himself to Morocco he decided to hand himself over to the French. This he did on December 23, 1847, on the condition that he be treated generously and landed in a Muslim country. The French gave these guarantees, but in their usual way, they did not honour their pledge. The Sultan was taken to France and put in solitary confinement. He never saw Algeria again before his death in Damascus in 1883.

Bitter fruits of defeat

With the exit of Abdel Kader from the Algerian struggle Algeria entered perhaps the bleakest period in its history. For the resistance they had offered to the French the Berbers were heavily punished. They were forced to pay all the expenses the French incurred in the invasion of their country, and the French are said to have derived a profit of not less than seven million francs on the operation. It is interesting to note that many Frenchmen acknowledged their barbarity. 'We have burnt a great deal and have destroyed a great deal,' declared General Bugeaud. The French, who began the colonisation of Algeria without delay, deprived the Berbers of their best lands; the code of Napoleon was introduced in the hope that it would ultimately displace traditional Islamic laws; Berber culture was expected to give way to French customs and institutions. For the French the only good Berber was the Frenchified Berber; the Berbers were given no political rights; the concept of the Algerian state and the ideology of Algerian nationality, on behalf of which Abdel Kader had fought, were discountenanced and condemned by the French rulers in Algeria. It was not until after the First World War that the Berbers were able to gather their strength gradually and begin to fight again for the ideals of Abdel Kader. The French ultimately yielded to force and granted independence to Algeria in 1962. The President of independent Algeria today is building on the foundation laid by Sultan Abdel Kader.

Notes

jihad—holy war waged by Muslims against unbelievers

monotheistic creed—a religion based on the doctrine that there is only one God

ethos—characteristic spirit of a community or people

infidel—an unbeliever, from the Muslim viewpoint

the porte—the Sultan of Constantinople

qadis—Muslim judges who decide all criminal and civil cases according to Muslim law

bastinadoed—beaten on the soles of the feet

ulemas—doctors of Islamic law and theology

consul—agent of a state in a foreign country whose duties were mainly to protect the subjects and interests of the state he represented

centrifugal forces—forces which tend to divide a people into factions and undermine the central administration of the people

Tariqas—religious brotherhoods

Lobengula: Achievement and Tragedy

Ian Henderson

The only photograph taken of Lobengula, the last king of the Ndebele
—and its authenticity is doubtful—shows a beetle-browed, heavily-built
man apparently wearing monkey skins round his waist and a roll of cloth

Lobengula (supposed to be the only known photograph)

slung over his shoulder. He frowns at the camera as he smokes his pipe.
Beside him is seated an unidentified European apparently dressed for an
audience, with collar and tie and broad-brimmed hat. The photograph
tells us very little, and illustrates how limited our knowledge is even of
Lobengula's physical appearance.

Descriptions of Lobengula by witnesses tend to be contradictory, and depend on the extent of their prejudices. E. A. Maund in 1885 described the king as a 'gross fat man' with a 'cruel restless eye'. On the other hand,

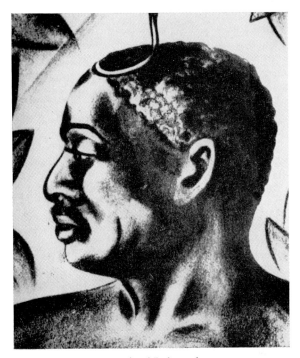

Portrait of Lobengula

the French explorer Declé considered him 'the most imposing monarch he had ever seen, except the Tzar Alexander'. J. Cooper Chadwick described him thus in the late 1880s:

> 'Lobengula stands over six feet in height, but is so enormously fat that it makes him look smaller, though his proud bearing and stately walk give him all the appearance of a savage king. His features are coarse, and exhibit great cunning and cruelty; but when he smiles the expression completely changes, and makes his face appear pleasant and good-tempered.'

Photographs of the European empire-builders, in contrast, abound. Moustachioed, bearded, staring into the far distance, they evidently saw themselves as cast in a heroic mould. With bandoliers and weapons displayed, they were a formidable group, utterly determined and completely convinced of the righteousness and desirability of British rule in Africa. In 1877, seven years after Lobengula had succeeded to the Matabele kingship, Cecil John Rhodes in Kimberley wrote:

'I contend that we are the first race in the world, and that the more of the world we inhabit, the better it is for the human race. I contend that every acre added to our territory provides for the birth of more of the English race, who otherwise would not be brought into existence . . .'

These were the forces which confronted each other in Central Africa in the 1880s and 90s. All the advantages of modern technology and communications lay with the Europeans. Significantly also for the historian, all the written and graphic evidence comes from European sources. We see Lobengula through the eyes of Baines, Moffat or Dr. Jameson; European motives are interpreted by Europeans. The illiterate Lobengula left no written relics except his mark (an irregular cross) on several highly important historical documents, themselves drawn up by Europeans.

To grasp Lobengula's achievement and his ultimate tragedy we must first understand the nature of the Ndebele state. For this in turn we must go back to the greatest cataclysm to hit Southern Africa before the Europeans came—the breaking off from the Zulu Empire of the Kumalo clan, and Shaka's consolidation of the Zulu Empire in the south.

Ndebele origins

Early in the nineteenth century in South-East Africa there was a scarcity of land which had led to warfare among the Bantu-speaking peoples of the area. More especially, between the Drakensberg Mountains and the Indian Ocean, the Nguni-speaking peoples fought each other for supremacy. The needs of warfare brought about two revolutionary changes in social structure and in battle tactics: the age-regiment and the tactics of the short stabbing spear.

The gathering together of young men into separate settlements orientated towards war was the logical response of some of the Northern Nguni to the needs of the situation. The military strength of the people was thereby highly concentrated and ready to be used effectively, and cut across the old Bantu clan groupings, where an infinite number of opportunities had presented themselves for grumblings and dissent, and consequently for disunity in war. The age-regiments were given cohesion by the king, and by him alone: they ate his meat and were given cattle by him to tend. They could not marry until they had blooded their spears on an enemy. Even when married, the older men were still organised on a regimental basis as a second line of defence.

The new battle tactics were similarly a contrast to the traditional Bantu methods. Instead of throwing their assegai in the usual way, thereby leaving themselves unarmed, the Nguni retained a short stabbing spear which was used in the same way as a sword. This meant that they kept their battle line intact and could charge with devastating effect. All this required nerve and discipline in equal proportions, and it is not surprising that the Zulu Empire, which emerged under Shaka as the dominant force in South-East Africa by the 1820s, emphasised these virtues in its ethics and in its social system. It was a tight-knit, autocratic state-system, the kind that most societies find best suited to a state of semi-permanent war.

Mzilikazi

In 1821 Mzilikazi, chief of the Kumalo clan, quarrelled with Shaka, his overlord, seemingly over the giving up of some booty cattle, which Mzilikazi refused to do. We shall probably never know the other reasons

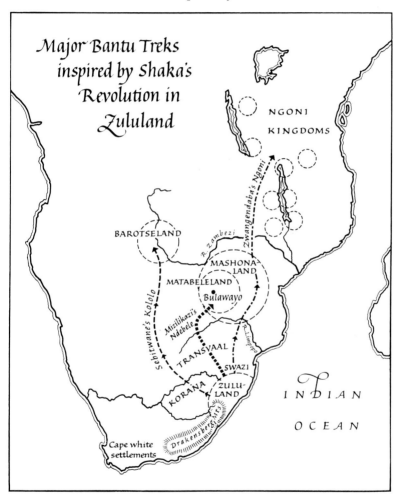

Major Bantu treks inspired by Shaka's revolution in Zululand, showing some of the states which emerged as a result. Mzilikazi led the Ndebele from Zululand in 1821 and reached their new home in 1838. Zwangendaba and his Ngoni left in 1818, reaching East Africa in 1845. Sebitwane and his Kololo left in 1823 and conquered Barotseland in 1838. The Ndebele who considered Mashonaland their empire and the Shona their subjects, settled in Matabeleland. Here Zwangendaba destroyed the old Rozvi empire before proceeding on to East Africa for the break. The result was that Mzilikazi and the Kumalo fled north-wards from Shaka's wrath, settling in the present Transvaal, where they became known to the Sotho living there as Ama-ndebele (meaning 'people of the long shields', or possibly simply 'aliens').

The Ndebele were a formidable force in the land of the unorganised Sotho. With their revolutionary battle tactics and their cattle-raiding economy, they brought destruction to a wide area between 1825 and 1837. But then external threats persuaded the Ndebele to move further into the interior: attacks were launched on them in the 1830s by the Korana, by the Zulu, and by the Boers. Chastened by the fire-power of these last two groups, Mzilikazi led his people northwards to what is now the western part of Rhodesia, there setting up yet another home among the scattered remnants of the Kalanga people of the old Rozvi Empire, which had been pulverised by Zwangendaba in another Nguni trek between 1831 and 1835. This was to be the last home of the Ndebele. Mzilikazi died at Ingama Kraal, near the present Bulawayo, in 1868.

The Ndebele state set up in the present Rhodesia had a largely Zulu-type structure. The young men were still organised into regiments, though in-creasingly these regiments became identified with particular geographical areas, apparently a modification of the Zulu structure. The king's indunas and wives were scattered through every province, and formed a focus for loyalty to the king. A military nation needs to have its morale constantly renewed, and its loyalties clearly demonstrated. This was done in the annual Great Dance and in the rain-making ceremonies presided over by the king, both of which gave the king great prestige and set apart the Ndebele as a nation different in kind from the people surrounding them. The direct links between the king and the regiments remained, and were a vital part of the cohesion of the nation. It was a nation poised for war, for raiding, and for constant aggressive activity on the part of the Matjaha —the young warriors—who could not marry until they had killed an enemy. It was a nation which depended a great deal, not only on the institution of kingship, but on the personality of the king. For this reason, the choice of a successor to Mzilikazi was an important one.

Son of Mzilikazi

The death of Mzilikazi brought about a succession crisis among the Ndebele which lasted nine years. In a 'normal' succession the kingship would go to the first son to be born to the king's chief wife after he had become king. But the heir-apparent on this reckoning, Nkulumane, had, according to Ndebele tradition, been sent out of the kingdom in order to prevent factions growing round the heir. Accounts agree that he was sent south, but in 1868 he was nowhere to be found, and there was a growing presumption that he was dead. Who then was to succeed to the vital office of king? Could the chaos and secessions often associated with Bantu succession disputes be avoided?

Most prominent among the candidates for the kingship was Lobengula, son of Mzilikazi by a Swazi princess, and possibly Mzilikazi's own choice as successor. But Lobengula was cautious, and did not thrust himself forward. He allowed the induna Nombate to lobby on his behalf. At a Great Council (*izikulu*) in 1869 witnesses testified that Nkulumane was dead, and it seems to have been agreed—with important dissensions— that Lobengula should be king.

What did the choice of Lobengula mean for the Ndebele in 1869? To understand its implications, we must remember that the succession crisis coincided with the first great influx of Europeans to Matabeleland, some of whom were hunters, but most of whom had come in search of the gold which had been discovered by Hartley in 1865 near the present-day Rhodesian town named after him. The nature of European interest in the Ndebele dominions was far different in scope from the earlier contacts between Mzilikazi and the missionary Robert Moffat.

At the beginning of his reign Lobengula employed this European factor with some skill and delicacy. His position between 1868 and 1877 was by

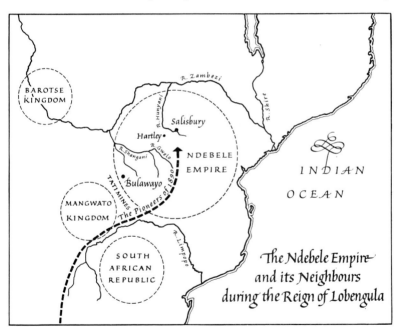

The Ndebele Empire and its Neighbours during the Reign of Lobengula

no means a safe one. He had to contend with threats from various sources: from Ndebele groups who, for their own reasons, maintained that Nkulumane was still alive and therefore the rightful king; from groups of white men who sought to manipulate Ndebele politics for their own advantage; and more distantly from Sir Theophilus Shepstone, Governor of Natal, who attempted to influence events from 600 miles away. During this nine-year succession crisis Lobengula showed a remarkable skill in keeping the Ndebele state together in spite of internal and external stresses.

Opposition to Lobengula within the Ndebele state came from the Zwangendaba regiment under its leader, Mbigo. The reasons for this are not clear: it is probable that Nkulumane had been a member of the regiment; it is also possible that Mbigo had a stake in the succession dispute through a sister who is said to have married Mzilikazi and had a son by him.

The immediate danger to Lobengula in 1870 came from the possibility that the Zwangendaba regiment would combine with the Europeans in Matabeleland, and thereby bring in more incalculable forces from the South. Lobengula quickly forestalled this by granting the first-ever mining concession to Thomas Baines of the Durban Gold Mining Company. The company was granted permission to mine between the Gwelo and Hunyani Rivers—a large tract of the coveted northern fields, populated by the Shona subjects of Lobengula. Later the London and Limpopo Company of Sir Thomas Swinburne was granted the Tati Concession to mine in a disputed area between Lobengula's kingdom and the Mangwato kingdom to the south.

What had induced Lobengula to do this? The reason lies in the intricate machinations of the previous few weeks. An Ndebele delegation found the supposed Nkulumane working as a stable-hand under the name of Khanda in Natal. The most curious part of this episode is that 'Khanda' worked for Sir Theophilus Shepstone, the Natal Governor who sought to manipulate the African politics of Southern Africa for the benefit of Natal. Evidently 'Khanda' was Shepstone's candidate for the succession, and much depended on the attitude of Baines and Swinburne in Matabeleland. Would they support 'Khanda' or Lobengula?

At this point came the concession, which riveted the Europeans firmly to Lobengula. Baines and Swinburne seem to have come to some sort of agreement with Lobengula whereby they would not help the cause of 'Khanda', while Lobengula on his side broke with Ndebele tradition by giving the generous and unprecedented concession of 1870.

Feeling secure in his alliance, Lobengula now wrote truculently to Macheng of the Mangwato, warning him to stop molesting Ndebele travellers and to stop taxing the Tati miners, since he (Lobengula) was now 'the friend and ally of the white man'. Shortly after that, he crushed the Zwangendaba regiment decisively.

Here we see Lobengula's later policy in embryo. He was beset by internal problems, and a coup d'état by some of the disaffected regiments was always possible. He was also plagued by Europeans wanting to dig for gold, who might pull strings leading to the Cape, or the Transvaal, or Natal. He therefore made concessions to the Europeans, though not enough to endanger his sovereignty, nor enough to bring about an anti-foreign reaction in the nation. With the external threat at an end, he was then able to deal with the internal one. It worked in 1870. It failed disastrously in

1890. However, the succession crisis shows Lobengula's considerable knowledge and political skill, even if in the long run the consolidation of Ndebele power led inexorably to the later, fatal clash with Europeans.

The Scramble

Southern Africa in the 1880s became a more dangerous place, especially for a nation like the Ndebele, who stood astride the only viable route to the interior. That interior was now to become the scene of a fierce contest among Boer, Briton, German and Portuguese. By the late eighties it was no longer enough for European powers to try to control the interior by corresponding with chiefs, under the polite fiction that they were heads of states equal in strength and prestige to European powers. From 'informal control' European powers were now moving to 'formal control'. The discovery of gold in the South African Republic (now the Transvaal) in the 1880s made several European powers dream of the riches beyond the Limpopo. The Europeans who were to confront Lobengula in the last five years of his reign were infinitely more impatient, and driven by more powerful forces than the missionaries, hunters, and small-scale gold-prospecting companies who had come before, and whom Lobengula had been able to weave successfully into his pattern of politics.

The Boers of the South African Republic made the first move. Pieter Grobler, representative of President Kruger, persuaded Lobengula to sign a treaty in July 1887, which was a far-reaching non-aggression pact between the Ndebele and the South African Republic, binding Lobengula to send military help to the Boers when required, and to admit within the Ndebele kingdom all who had passes from the President of the South African Republic. Like all the documents 'signed' by Lobengula, there are grave doubts about the validity of the Grobler Treaty. There seems to have been a very large gap between what was said and what was written down. Lobengula afterwards insisted that it was merely the revival of an old, non-committal treaty of friendship signed in 1852 between Mzilikazi and the Boers.

The British were stung into action. If Lobengula allied himself with the Boers, the road to the north, with its supposed mineral wealth, would be closed to British expansion. What the British wanted was a guarantee by Lobengula that he would make no concessions of land without the prior agreement of the British. This was the guarantee which Lobengula gave in the Moffat Treaty with the British in 1888. Thus he repudiated the Grobler Treaty and brought Matabeleland into the British 'sphere of influence'.

Then, on October 30, 1888, came the most important document of all—the Rudd Concession. This was no treaty between sovereign states, as the Moffat Treaty had been, but a concession to a commercial company the British South Africa Company, controlled by Cecil John Rhodes at the Cape, and backed by his vast wealth derived from the diamond mines of Kimberley. The company did not seek mere declarations of friendship, but a concession to mine for gold. Why did Lobengula sign this document, so different from the Moffat Treaty of a year before?

The answer lies in the pressure on Lobengula which we first saw in his succession crisis of twenty years before. There was an unprecedented influx of white men of all kinds after the Moffat Treaty had been signed, not only prospectors and traders but others of more dubious repute. Different groups urged him to sign concessions in their favour, hoping that this would be a passport to quick and unlimited riches. Lobengula was aware that he could not fend off the Europeans indefinitely. He was also aware that the Matjaha were straining at the leash to be permitted to massacre all whites. 'Their argument was,' Moffat is quoted as saying, '. . . . that although there are only about thirty white men here now, who, as they said, would be a mere breakfast for them, thousands may come hereafter unless the few are killed, so as to frighten the others; and they also clamoured to be led against the white man's towns.'

Lobengula could not restrain his 'Red Guards' indefinitely. But he could try to get what he could from an impossible situation. He signed the Rudd Concession, and hoped by so doing that he would kill two birds with one stone: by admitting one group to his kingdom he could thereby exclude all others; and by signing the limited terms—as he thought—of the Concession, he could prevent, or at least postpone, the full impact of European control, for his knowledge of events south of the Limpopo was such as to make him familiar with the pattern of white conquest.

Thus the Rudd Concession opens, 'Whereas I have been much molested of late by divers persons seeking and desiring to obtain grants and concessions of land mining rights in my territories . . .', and goes on to authorise the company 'to take all lawful steps to exclude (such persons)'. Lobengula assigned to the company 'complete and exclusive charge of all metals and minerals situated and contained in his kingdoms, principalities and dominions', and conceded to them, in a significantly vague phrase, 'all things they may deem necessary to win and procure the same'.

What were 'all things necessary to win and procure' the minerals in Lobengula's dominions? Did it mean that Lobengula had sanctioned white settlement in his kingdom? Lobengula was no fool. He knew that such a far-reaching interpretation of his concession would set the Ndebele against him. His own interpretation at the time seems to have been that the whites would come, dig for gold, then go away again. This had happened at the Tati gold-field. This was the interpretation encouraged by the company men during their conversation with Lobengula. According to the Rev. C. D. Helm of the London Missionary Society,

'The grantees explained to the Chief that what was deemed necessary to get out the gold was to erect dwellings for their overseers, to bring in and erect machinery and use wood and water. They promised that they would not bring more than ten white men to work in his country, that they would not dig anywhere near towns, etc., and that' they and their

Detail of the Rudd Concession showing Rudd's signature and Lobengula's cross

people would abide by the laws of the country and in fact be his people.
But these promises were never put in the concession.'

Helm was present at all the negotiations prior to the concession, and as a
supporter of British power in Matabeleland, he can be expected to give a
British slant to the evidence. Yet he mentioned the phrase 'no more than
ten white men', and revealed the significant difference between what was
said during the negotiations and what was written into the concession. It is
hard to see this discrepancy as a mere 'misunderstanding', or as an example
of how Lobengula's 'savage' mind was 'unable to grasp' the subtle provisions of the concession. The evidence shows that there was a clear deception on the part of the British, and that Lobengula was a victim of that
deception.

Lobengula soon learnt that the South African newspapers interpreted
the Rudd Concession very widely, assuming that it opened the way to
large-scale mining operations and white settlement. To counteract this,
Lobengula had a newspaper advertisement inserted to the effect that the
concession was suspended until further notice. (This advertisement, despite
doubts by some historians, was probably genuine). He also sent two indunas
to Queen Victoria to try to control events at the London end. At this stage,
the British Government had not committed itself to the British South
Africa Company, and Queen Victoria, in the shape of the Colonial Secretary Lord Knutsford, cautioned Lobengula; saying that the white men had

no official status, and that this included Rhodes. 'A King gives a stranger an ox, not his whole herd of cattle', said the message.

But events moved too quickly for Lobengula. Rhodes pulled the strings in London and Cape Town, and the British South Africa Company obtained government backing in the form of a Royal Charter at the end of October, 1889. The Charter was based on the Rudd Concession, and was

Concession seekers at Lobengula's Court, Bulawayo

granted three days before another letter was received from Lobengula to Queen Victoria, repudiating the concession. 'If the Queen hears I have given away the whole country,' he said, 'it is not so.'

The charter did not give the company any rights in Matabeleland and Mashonaland other than those 'granted' by Lobengula, but it gave the company an official monopoly from Britain, and rights to set up an administration. White rule moved a little closer, and Lobengula slept more uneasily.

The British South Africa Company was now poised for its occupation of part at least of Lobengula's dominions. Whether that occupation was to be peaceful or bloody, and whether it would include Matabeleland proper as well as Mashonaland, depended on Lobengula. At this point he made his last tactical concession to the white men: he reinstated the Rudd Concession, though he remained stubbornly silent about whether this sanctioned the occupation of Mashonaland by the company.

News of this move reached London on December 21, 1889. Two weeks previously, a secret agreement had been reached between Rhodes and two soldiers of fortune, Frank Johnson and Maurice Heany, whereby Johnson and Heany, after a trumped-up incident, would 'carry by sudden assaults all the principal strongholds of the Matabele nation' with a force of 500 Europeans, and 'so to break up the power of the Amandebele as to render their raids on surrounding tribes impossible . . .'

This plan, so similar to the harebrained Jameson Raid of 1896, was only dropped when news came of Lobengula's change of front, and another was substituted, namely to send an armed 'road-making party' to make a wagon road to Mount Hampden, near the present Salisbury. The party, whatever its name, would be in effect an occupation force, and would skirt Matabeleland proper and pass through Mashonaland, where Lobengula's power only extended to seasonal raids. Thus the Pioneer Column entered Lobengula's dominions in July and reached Fort Salisbury in September 1890. White Rhodesians used to celebrate the latter date annually as 'Occupation Day', but recently this has been tempered to 'Pioneer Day'. Whatever the name, it was the beginning of white Rhodesia as a nation, and the beginning of the end of the Ndebele nation. The two could not co-exist for long.

Lobengula, adopting the only course open to him short of national suicide, played for time. He sent the Pioneers a message:

'Has the king killed any white men that an impi is collecting on his border? Or have the white men lost anything they are looking for?'

But the situation at Bulawayo was tense. According to one witness,

'Day after day the different impis came pouring in to the king demanding the white man's blood in the country, and for leave to attack the army which was coming up to eat them. Meetings of the excited warriors were held, and it became a question whether Lobengula would be able to restrain them or not. At one stormy meeting held in Bulawayo the old men, who sided with the king, stood up and said the young soldiers must fight them first before attacking the few whites, who were the king's visitors. The king's position was now an unenviable one, the whole nation rising against him, and it required his utmost tact and judgement to deal with them without losing his dignity or showing want of courage . . .'

That the Europeans reached Fort Salisbury without incident was, in a way, a tribute to Lobengula's political skill. The Matjaha, despite their eagerness, were held in check. But there were limits beyond which Lobengula could not go without inviting a rebellion against him within the nation. This, in 1890–93, was Lobengula's great dilemma: how many 'incidents' between Europeans and Ndebele could be allowed to happen without Lobengula's prestige suffering? Above all, did the Ndebele retain the right to raid where they had always raided—among the Shona? If that custom was menaced, then truly Lobengula had betrayed the nation.

Thus, when some of an Ndebele raiding party were shot by Pioneers in July 1893 near Fort Victoria, Lobengula made preparations for war, and recalled an impi sent to Barotseland. To make further concessions would have been to lose the loyalty of the Matjaha completely, for the latter were already 'trigger-happy', and willing to create incidents in the hope of the fight that they had long desired.

For their part, the settlers, led by Jameson, armed themselves for war and sought the earliest opportunity to decide who was to rule the subject Shona—Lobengula or the whites.

Further brushes followed, and at the end of October 1893 the company's men advanced into Ndebele territory with two eight-pounder guns, five Maxims, and other machine guns. The Ndebele War was soon over, with the white man's weapons having a deadly effect on the morale of the Ndebele regiments. The crack Imbezu Regiment was decimated, together with the Mhlahlanhlela. The others depended on Lobengula for a lead, but Lobengula knew, as he had known all along, that ultimately the man with the Maxim wins against the man with the assegai. In despair, he fled northwards, had a severe attack of gout, and died near the Zambezi River at the end of January 1894.

The Ndebele nation lay in ruins. In a sense this had been inevitable from the first. Matabeleland lay on the direct route from the South to the goldfields of the far interior. Unlike the Mangwato of Khama, who submitted peacefully to a British Protectorate, the Ndebele were a coherent state, determined to hang on to their sovereignty. Cattle raiding and the kidnapping of women and children from neighbouring tribes was a vital part of the Ndebele economy and state system, and it could never exist side by side with white settlement, with its emphasis on peace and tranquillity for development, and on a plentiful supply of labour from the tribal areas. Lobengula symbolised this fierce obstinacy, just as Rhodes symbolised the ruthless determination of international capital to exploit the interior of Africa. The clash, when it came, was a loud and resounding one because of this coincidence of circumstances. Rhodes wielding the armed might and financial power of the Cape, and ultimately of Britain; Lobengula, ruling a fighting nation which happened to occupy an area rich in gold and other minerals, and favoured with good soil and a climate, in the phrase of the time, 'suitable for white settlement'.

But though the clash was inevitable, and Lobengula saw this ('You are driving me into the lion's mouth,' he told his young warriors), he nevertheless acted above all as a rational man who wanted to spare his nation the rigours of conquest, and who to this end manipulated the different white groups with all the sagacity at his command. Unfortunately, he could not control events, because the whites would, in the last analysis, stand together against the black man. He summed up his plight to the missionary Helm in a famous simile:

'Did you ever see a chameleon catch a fly? The chameleon gets behind the fly and remains motionless for some time, then he advances very slowly and gently, first putting forward one leg and then another. At last, when well within reach, he darts his tongue and the fly disappears. England is the chameleon and I am that fly.'

Ndebele warrior

But though the structure of the nation was smashed after the Ndebele War and the later rebellion, respect for the royal house of Kumalo remained. Lobengula's sons, Nyamanda, Njube and Nguboyena, all in their separate ways, provided a focus for the lost cause of Ndebele nationalism in the twentieth century. In particular, Nyamanda, Lobengula's eldest son, led the campaign for an Ndebele National Home, and a revival of the Ndebele kingship, in the years after the First World War. 'There can be no doubt,' says Terence Ranger, 'that the surviving institutions and memories of the traditional political structure of the Matabele provided a base for "modern" politics which was lacking in Mashonaland.'

Lobengula was a rational man caught up in a situation which he was unable to handle with the resources available to him. Like any rational man—and unlike many of the empire-builders—he preferred conciliation to war, but war was the only way of providing a solution to the question of who should control Matabeleland and Mashonaland. The leaders of the settlers were not interested in compromise, and a gradual takeover was impossible where Matjaha and settlers were anxious to leap at each other's throats.

It might be argued that Lewanika of Barotseland collaborated with the British, and that as a result Barotseland survived as a separate protectorate with a kind of Home Rule until comparatively recent times; could not Lobengula have achieved the same sort of settlement? The answer is that the Europeans would be satisfied with nothing less than the conquest and parcelling-out of Matabeleland, an area far more desirable than Barotseland was ever to be. The Victoria Agreement at the beginning of the war gave each white volunteer the right to a 6,000-acre farm, 20 gold claims in Matabeleland, and a share of half of Lobengula's cattle. The chameleon had at last gobbled up the fly.

Notes

Bantu-speaking peoples—The majority of the people of South, Central and East Africa who speak related languages and are therefore presumed to come from a common stock. In South Africa the Bantu are divided into two major language groups, the Sotho and Nguni.

Coup d'état—A sudden change of government by force. In a modern military coup it is the army which effects this change.

Jameson Raid of 1896—Cecil Rhodes and the British colonial secretary, Chamberlain, encouraged English gold miners on the Rand to rebel against President Kruger to bring the South African republic into the British Empire. Rhodes' agent, Jameson, led a British force across the border to the aid of the rebels. The plan failed. Jameson and his raiders were captured by Kruger's forces. See Van der Poel, J., *The Jameson Raid*, Oxford, 1951.

Khama—Chief of the Mangwato, who form a part of modern Botswana; Khama accepted a British protectorate in 1885; see 'Khama the Good' in Gollock, G., *Sons of Africa*, New York, 1928, pp. 90—106.

Korana—People of mixed Boer and Hottentot descent who had trekked out of the Cape and settled in the Orange River valley.

Kruger, Paul—Boer President of the South African Republic 1883–1900; died 1904. For a good yet inexpensive reference on South Africa, see Keppel-Jones, A., *South Africa: A Short History*, Hutchinson, 1963.

Kumalo—A Nguni-speaking clan; Mzilikazi was the clan chief. Formed the original core of the Ndebele before the assimilation of great numbers on the trek north. Mzilikazi founded the Kumalo dynasty or royal house of Kumalo.

Lewanika—King of the Barotse Kingdom 1878–1916, see Stokes & Brown (eds.), *The Zambesian Past*, Manchester, 1966, pp. 261–301 and Mackintosh, C., *Lewanika: Paramount Chief of the Barotse*, London, 1942.

Ndebele—also Matabele. The former is more linguistically correct and is therefore used in this article to refer to the people. Matabeleland is used in reference to the area directly ruled by Lobengula. Matabeleland and Mashonaland are the two major administrative divisions of present-day Rhodesia.

Nguni-speaking peoples—One of the major language groups of the Bantu language family. Nguni speakers include the Zulu, Swazi, Ndebele and Ngoni of East Africa. Nguni and Ngoni are different spellings of the same word but it has become customary to use 'Nguni' for the Nguni-speaking peoples as a whole while the form 'Ngoni' is used when referring specifically to those Nguni which Zwangendaba led into East Africa.

Rhodes, Cecil—An English immigrant into South Africa who became a millionaire through diamond mining. See Lockhart, J. and Woodhouse, C., *Rhodes*, Hodder and Stoughton, 1963.

Sotho—Pronounced Sooto. Includes Basuto and Kololo.

Zwangendaba—The name of one of the Ndebele regiments. It should not be confused with Zwangendaba, the Ngoni leader of the trek to East Africa.

Koko: Amanyanabo of Nembe

E. J. Alagoa

The climax of the career of Koko, Amanyanabo (King) of Nembe was his attack on the Akassa depot of the Royal Niger Company on January 29, 1895. The attack on the headquarters of the company in the delta, and Koko's subsequent stand against the forces of the Niger Coast Protectorate, also marked a turning point in the history of the Nembe kingdom. It was,

Koko: Amanyanabo of Nembe, 1889–98

in addition, only one of a series of similar manifestations of resistance by the peoples of Nigeria to increasing British commercial and political control in the last decades of the nineteenth and the beginning of the twentieth centuries.

The best known of the early casualties of the new wave of British expansion in Nigeria was King Jaja of Opobo, who was exiled in 1887 for his opposition to British penetration of his interior markets. In 1892, the Ijebus were overcome by superior military power in their fight to retain control of trade routes through their land. The list of casualties increased with the years, and in 1894, Nana Olomu, ruler of the Itsekiri on the Benin River was ousted from his stronghold in Ebrohimi. After Koko had staged his attack in 1895, Oba Ovonramwen of Benin was defeated and exiled in 1897, and his son-in-law and leader of the opposition to British advance, Ologboshere, was captured and executed in 1899. In the same year (1897) that Oba Ovonramwen lost his independence, the Royal Niger Company had extinguished the remaining claims to independence of the rulers of Nupe and Ilorin by direct military attack. In 1898, the year of Koko's death, Ibanichuka, king of Okrika, was exiled for showing lack of respect for the authority of the Niger Coast Protectorate.

There was one common element in all of these cases where Britain overcame Nigerian rulers by force. In every case there had been a disagreement over the interpretation of the nature of the relationship with Britain. Each of the rulers and their people believed themselves still possessed of sovereignty and freedom to set down the terms of trade or other association with the British. The conflicts resulted because Britain had the strength and desire to read various clauses in earlier treaties of 'protection' in a manner depriving these rulers of their freedom of choice. The wars, therefore, represented the final struggle of Nigerian peoples to maintain their independence.

British expansion in late nineteenth-century Nigeria

Britain began to take official interest in the internal affairs of Nigerian and other West African peoples after she had accepted the responsibility for enforcing the abolition of the slave trade after 1807. The problem was tackled at first as a naval one. That is, suitable stations were found on the coast from which the British navy could operate to prevent ships exporting slaves. On the Nigerian coast, the island of Fernando Po was used for these early operations. The slaves taken from ships were landed at Freetown in Sierra Leone by the British; the French used Libreville in Gabon, and the Americans, Monrovia in Liberia.

In 1849, John Beecroft was appointed Consul at Fernando Po to watch over British interests on the Nigerian coast in the 'legitimate trade' in palm oil and other products, which was thought of as a profitable alternative to the slave trade. A second Consul was later stationed at Lagos, so that the Consul at Fernando Po looked after British interests in the Niger Delta, the Cross River region, and the Cameroon coast alone.

As a result of the rising interest of other European powers (especially France and Germany) in Africa, the British Consul, Edward Hyde Hewett, signed a number of treaties in the Niger Delta in 1884, to be presented at the Berlin West African Conference in order to claim a British 'sphere of influence' in this part of West Africa. Accordingly, in 1885, Britain declared a protectorate over the eastern and central coast of Nigeria from 'a point on the shore of the Bight of Benin about 10 miles north-west of the Benin River to Rio del Rey on the Gulf of Guinea'. This portion of the coast was named the Oil Rivers Protectorate, because of the palm oil exported from it.

Meanwhile in 1879 George Goldie had united a number of British firms trading in the Niger Delta into the United African Company (later the National African Company). Some of the treaties used to press British claims at the Berlin Conference had been presented by that company. By a charter of July 10, 1886, the British Government gave control of a portion of the territory of the Oil Rivers Protectorate to the National African Company, under its new name of the Royal Niger Company. The territory was defined as lying between the rivers Forcados and Nun, and extending to an undefined extent northwards along and beyond the Niger and Benue.

At the time of these conflicts in the last decades of the nineteenth century, the southern portion of Nigeria was divided up into three British areas of control, namely, the Colony and Protectorate of Lagos, the Oil Rivers Protectorate, and the Niger Territories allotted to the Royal Niger Company. In May 1893, the Oil Rivers Protectorate was named the Niger Coast Protectorate with Claude Macdonald as Imperial Commissioner and Consul General.

The conflicts cited above were, therefore, between the various Nigerian rulers and different British authorities. Thus Harry Johnston deported Jaja of Opobo in 1887 by authority of the Oil Rivers Protectorate; Nana Olomu (1894), King Koko (1895), Oba Ovonramwen (1897) and Ibanichuka (1898) treated with the Niger Coast Protectorate Government; and the Ijebu were conquered by the government of the Colony and Protectorate of Lagos. The Royal Niger Company made the campaigns against Nupe and Ilorin in 1897, since it claimed authority over territory embracing all of northern Nigeria. Koko was, indeed, forced to fight because, although his kingdom of Nembe lay within the Niger Coast Protectorate, all of his traditional markets or trading stations in the hinterland were within the area marked out for the Royal Niger Company. Thus, having attacked one British authority, the Royal Niger Company, that claimed monopoly over trading areas Koko believed to belong to his people, he faced punishment by another, the Niger Coast Protectorate, which claimed direct authority over him and his people.

Genesis of the confrontation

Nembe was one of a number of trading kingdoms in the Niger Delta, among the best known of which were Bonny and its nineteenth-century off-

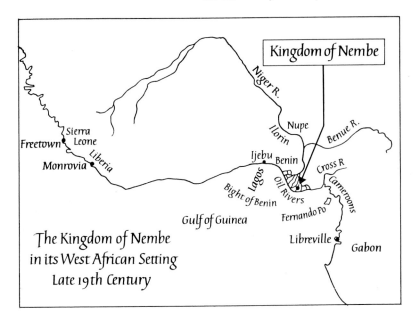

Kingdom of Nembe

Sierra
Freetown Leone
Monrovia Liberia

Niger R.

Nupe
Ilorin   Benue R.

Ijebu Benin
Lagos   Cross R
Bight of Benin Oil Rivers   Camerooons
Gulf of Guinea   Fernando Po
Libreville
Gabon

The Kingdom of Nembe
in its West African Setting
Late 19th Century

shoot Opobo, as well as Kalabari, Okrika, and Calabar. The lists of
dynastic kings and genealogies of these kingdoms indicate that they were
already monarchical states by the beginning of the sixteenth century at the
latest. Early accounts of European activities on the West African Coast,
such as those of Duarte Pacheco Pereira (circa 1500) and John Barbot
(1699–1705) indicate that some of the rulers of these kingdoms were
already engaged in exchanging produce from the lands beyond the delta for
European manufactured goods.

Trade relationships with the Europeans grew with the increasing use of
African slave labour in American plantations. When Britain announced
her intention to switch from trade in slaves to trade in palm oil, the delta
rulers were surprised, but willing to agree. They signed treaties renouncing
the slave trade and entering into the terms for the regulation of 'legitimate
trade'.

The chiefs at Nembe signed a treaty for the abolition of the slave trade in
1834. Another treaty of 1856 set out the terms on which 'legitimate trade'
was to be conducted on the Brass River. Those British who were in charge
of the cargoes were to pay fees called *comey* to the Amanyanabo of Nembe
on entry to the river, and to respect local customs. The local authorities,
on their part, were to protect the traders from arbitrary exactions, and to
see that debts were collected. It may be seen that in spite of the presence of
a British Consul at Fernando Po at this time, the rulers on the Oil Rivers
exercised control over the British traders in the area.

The manner of the trade at this time was for the British trader to give
credits called 'trust' to local chiefs on arrival at the coast. These chiefs then

went into the interior where the palm oil was produced, and brought it down to the coast. The super-cargo (the man in charge of the cargo) got his palm oil, and the trading chief his profits. In this way, the kings and chiefs of the Niger Delta kingdoms exercised control over the trade as middlemen, and also levied comey fees. Nembe's control of her hinterland markets was not seriously challenged until after 1879 when Goldie formed his National African Company out of a number of small firms.

The National African Company operated up the Nun River next to the Brass River, and attempted to bar both the Nembe traders and all other British firms stationed on the Brass River from the hinterland markets which could only be reached through the Nun. It was this threat from a British firm that made the Nembe chiefs reluctant to sign a treaty with Consul Edward Hewett in 1884. Hewett persuaded them to sign for only six months. Later, the Consul promised help against the National African Company's attempts to exclude Nembe traders from markets, in order to renew in 1885 the treaty of 1884, prior to the British declaration of the Oil Rivers Protectorate.

Nembe's acceptance of these treaties of 'protection', accordingly, meant simply agreement for the British Government to help control the excesses of some of its nationals in the area. The Protectorates, when declared, only meant the stationing of Consuls on the rivers to whom both the rulers and the British super-cargoes could take their grievances. It may be added that normal trade disputes were settled by Courts of Equity composed of super-cargoes and chiefs. Thus in the Nembe area at this time there was a Court of Equity on the Brass River to settle commercial disputes. It was the Niger Company at Akassa, only some ten miles away on the Nun River, that was a danger to the survival of the Nembe Kingdom. Between 1886, when the National African Company received its Royal Charter and became the Royal Niger Company, and 1895 when Koko led his attack on Akassa, various approaches were made to the representatives of the British Government—the officials of the Oil Rivers and Niger Coast Protectorate. It was when things were obviously getting worse, and the government authorities were unable or unwilling to curb the company that Koko led his people to war.

Koko's leadership

Oral tradition remembers Frederick William Koko as a young man compared with other chiefs when he became king in 1889. He would, therefore, have been between thirty and forty years old. This means that he was born during the years of the palm oil trade and grew up in the atmosphere of the struggle of his people to maintain their middlemen position against British attempts to establish direct contact with the producers. Moreover, Koko had served in the trading canoes of his uncle Chief Igbeta, who, after the death of King Ockiya in 1879, became regent and conducted all the negotiations with the British concerning the National African Company (Royal Niger Company after 1886). Chief Igbeta was elected by the chiefs and the high priest to be king, but declined the honour. Koko's appointment as king after Igbeta's death in 1888, over the heads of older and more experienced chiefs, is traditionally explained by the recommendation and special grooming of Chief Igbeta. It is, however, likely that he had even at this early date shown something of his intrepid temper, and the younger elements in the town may have favoured him as leader in this time of impending conflict.

The other chiefs were leaders because they succeeded to the leadership of Houses, which were both military, commercial, and kinship units in the state. Koko was picked to be king without the benefit of prior leadership of any such group. This gave him the advantage of appearing as a truly

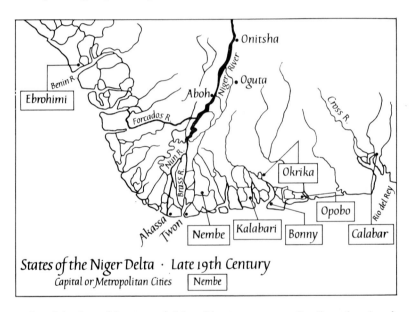

States of the Niger Delta · Late 19th Century
Capital or Metropolitan Cities — Nembe

national leader without special loyalties to a group. On the other hand, Koko was a little handicapped in the matter of equipping his own war canoe, since he was not the head of a House whose members he could commandeer. His contingent for the Akassa war had, therefore, to be made up by contributions from members of the group of Houses descended from Kulo, founder of the lineage to which Koko's mother belonged.

There is at least one piece of evidence that Koko set out from the beginning of his reign to win the support of the traditionalist elements in the society. He had been a Christian and church leader, but renounced Christianity in order to be free to carry out all the prescribed traditional rites of kingship. This act has been interpreted in the European accounts as a further sign of Koko's disenchantment with the British as a result of the Royal Niger Company's pressure on Nembe.

The Christian church was established in Nembe only in 1864, and when economic conditions became desperate, the people naturally returned to the worship of the gods under whom they had previously prospered. The decreasing numbers of churchgoers and declining physical condition of the churches reported by Macdonald in 1895 was the result of the difficult times, and not because Christianity was European. Some of the most influential chiefs remained Christian, and King Koko himself played host to a Roman Catholic priest a few days before the attack on Akassa.

Koko would seem to have decided on war as the only solution when he became king in 1889. He was chosen as a crisis leader. In that same year Macdonald had been sent to investigate conditions on the Oil Rivers. The leaders of Nembe and the British traders on the Brass River complained bitterly about the monopoly of the Royal Niger Company on the Niger. Injustices resulted from the boundary between the Royal Niger Company and the Niger Coast Protectorate, which cut Nembe off from her markets. The boundary was defined as 'a straight line commencing with a point midway the Nun mouth and the mouth of the Brass Rivers and terminating at the town of Idu.' The Royal Niger Company was thus given all the northern delta oil-producing lands north-west of Nembe, the Oguta lakes area to the north, and all the open river routes to Aboh.

This separation of Nembe from its old markets was particularly important because between 1889 and 1895 the Royal Niger Company gradually tightened its squeeze on the Brass River trade. Duties on trade in the Niger Territories were so high that no profits could be made by Nembe traders or by other British firms. That meant that the Brass River overseas trade was virtually halted, and the comey or trade duties to the Amanyanabo, as well as the profits due to the trading chiefs, lessened. The mass of the people was hit by the decline of trade and prosperity, but especially by the Royal Niger Company's activities even against canoes which traded in its territories for foodstuffs. Traders in palm produce were said by the company to be smugglers and the canoes were fired on or seized; but it was the stoppage of food canoes which was felt most keenly. Company officials boasted that the Nembe would be forced to eat dust.

Koko mobilises for war

Koko's difficulties in preparing for war included the internal problems of getting agreement from all his subordinate chiefs in Nembe, as well as from others in the neighbouring towns, while there was in addition the need to keep these matters from the ears of the Vice-Consul on the Brass River at Twon, and from the Royal Niger Company officials at Akassa.

The metropolis of Nembe is divided into two halves, Ogbolomabiri and Bassambiri, by a narrow creek. The Amanyanabo of Bassambiri, Ebifa, is said to have opposed resort to force. Koko, accordingly, waited, and continued with the policy of protest to the officials of the Niger Coast Protectorate until Ebifa's death in 1894. Koko then took into his confidence a selected number of influential chiefs at the metropolis who were of his way of thinking. The general public was told that the king had decided to seek a route to the interior markets that would by-pass the Niger Territories. All able-bodied men were asked to get ready to deepen a narrow and shallow creek for this purpose. Such an operation meant full-scale preparations for war, since the peoples living on this creek might conceivably refuse to permit the changes planned. It was after the force had left home that the king announced Akassa as the destination and not the creek.

According to the traditions of Okpoma, King Koko personally went to consult with the king and chiefs of that town. Koko would appear to have used a combination of persuasion and threats to obtain their alliance. King

Koko's war canoe on the way to Akassa

Obu of Okpoma reportedly refused at first on the grounds that Koko had previously shown hostility to Okpoma, and that Okpoma took little part in the overseas trade and had no direct quarrel with the British. Koko threatened to block all food supplies to Okpoma.

Officials of the Royal Niger Company alleged, after the 1895 attack on Akassa, that Koko had coerced some Ijo people in its territories to revolt. This is not supported by the evidence. At the inquiry conducted by John Kirk after the attack, the company called a single witness, Chief Nangi of Ekowe. He said Koko had sent him a bottle of rum three days after the attack on Akassa, and asked him to kill all company employees at Ekowe. The company admitted having burnt five other towns. Oral tradition confirms that most of these towns had fired on company boats but not because of intimidation by Nembe. In 1964 one elderly king, who had been a young man in 1895, said that his people fought the company because the Nembe were their 'brothers'.

There is evidence that Koko also sought allies in other parts of the delta. He wrote to the rulers of Bonny and Kalabari. The Niger Coast Protectorate officials obtained the letter to Bonny, and it contained no threats, but an appeal 'as brethren' to fight a common enemy. The chiefs received the letter after the attack on Akassa, and so did not act.

The war fought by Koko was different from the other conflicts between African kings and the British in that Koko was executing a planned attack, and not merely resisting. The problems of organising a large force over a fairly wide area in secrecy were many. Koko is estimated to have led out a force of thirty to forty war canoes carrying upwards of 1,500 warriors. The company's depot at Akassa was surprised and destroyed. The European officials escaped, but many Kru and other African employees were killed or captured.

It was in the subsequent counter-attack on Nembe by the combined forces of the Niger Coast Protectorate and the Royal Niger Company that Koko's spirit of unyielding resistance showed itself. King Koko could only be persuaded to leave Nembe when all hopes of successfully defending it had disappeared. And once in self-imposed exile in the remote village of Etiema, he refused to treat with the British. The British officials interpreted his refusal to meet them as a sign that he wished to appear to his people as a sacred priest-king. The truth was that Koko was unwilling to be the Amanyanabo to hand over his kingdom to the British. He also remembered that Jaja of Opobo had been carried away from his home in 1887 by trusting Johnston, a British consul.

The restless shark

Koko's attack on Akassa was significant for the fortunes of the Royal Niger Company. It gave point to criticism in Britain of the company's monopoly. A royal commissioner, John Kirk, was appointed to investigate. It led finally to the abrogation of the company's charter, and to the constitution of the southern part of the company's territories, together with the Niger Coast Protectorate, into the Protectorate of Southern Nigeria in 1899. The northern section of the Niger Territories became the Protectorate of Northern Nigeria. But between 1895 and 1899, since Koko had neither withdrawn his hostility to the company nor surrendered, the company was restricted in its activities. Large forces had to be kept in the delta. Accordingly, British military operations in other parts of Southern Nigeria in this period entailed the mobilisation of larger forces than were required for the particular operation.

Koko gained in stature in the estimation of his delta neighbours. Macdonald had said that the burning of parts of Nembe constituted humiliation for Koko and his people, since the metropolis had been thought to be impregnable. Koko did, in fact, consider it a humiliation, but his neighbours were more impressed with the fact that he had had the boldness to

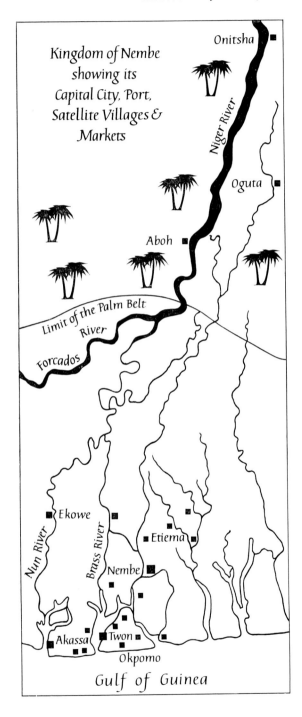

Kingdom of Nembe
showing its
Capital City, Port,
Satellite Villages &
Markets

Onitsha

Niger River

Oguta

Aboh

Limit of the Palm Belt

River

Forcados

Ekowe

Nun River

Brass River

Etiema

Nembe

Akassa Twon

Okpomo

Gulf of Guinea

attack the British; they were also impressed by the fact that he refused to give himself up. The cause of his death in 1898 at Etiema is not fully known, but he is believed to have committed suicide rather than be taken alive.

To his own people too, Koko has left an image of a dashing military leader wedded to the traditions and independence of his people. One of his drum names was *Ofirima Leke Leke,* 'The restless shark'.

'Whiteman war never finishes'

After the war with the British, Koko was worried by the manner in which they kept searching for him and putting a price on his head. He composed the following drum name:

BIKINI IKOLOGO BERE DUBA DUBA	Whiteman is tough
BIKINI IKOLOGO BERE FA GHA FA	
GHA	Whiteman war never finishes
BIKINI IKOLOGO BERE DUBA DUBA	Whiteman war is always big

It is this realisation, that he had attacked a people possessing overwhelming force who never fought wars in a small way, which has made the name Frederick William Koko a symbol of the tough fighting leader willing to give his life in defence of the interests of his people and kingdom. He typifies numbers of patriotic Nigerians who died in the last decades of the nineteenth century defending the sovereignty of the small portions of Nigeria they knew as their nation.

Oba Ovonramwen and the Fall of Benin

Philip Igbafe

Idugbowa, who as son of Oba Adolo ascended the Benin throne as Oba Ovonramwen in about 1888, and who swallowed the bitter pill of conquest and deportation in 1897, spending the rest of his life in exile till his death in 1914, has probably been more sinned against than he ever sinned. This is probably because his place in Benin history has not, with only one exception, been critically examined nor has any objective appraisal been made of the relative importance of the factors which during his reign

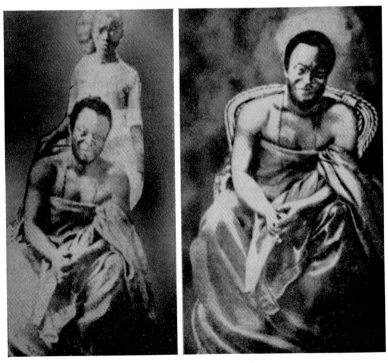

(Left) A contemporary photograph of Ovonramwen
(Right) A Bini artist's impression

brought Benin and the British to grips in the closing years of the nineteenth century. Oba Ovonramwen has been unkindly treated by historians because it was during his reign that the Europeans finally succeeded in breaking into the Benin kingdom and gained political and economic control of the hinterland. Ovonramwen has also been much maligned because the massacre of the European party in January 1897 has been blamed on him, and participants in the Benin City expedition painted lurid pictures of the traditional usages to which he was still clinging. These lurid pictures have fastened on to Benin the stamp of savagery and barbarous customs. Names like the 'City of Blood' and the 'City of Skulls' have endured with remarkable tenacity and persistence, and surviving accounts have largely served to stress the humanitarian aspect of the overthrow of Ovonramwen.

The consolidation of his power

Oba Ovonramwen succeeded to a much depleted inheritance because attacks by neighbouring powers on the peripheral peoples of the empire had diminished the size of the Oba's dominions and the size of his income. In spite of this Ovonramwen still retained sufficient power to be able to keep his subject peoples firmly under control. He maintained court in the tradition of his ancestors and sought to preserve the stature and dignity associated with the ancient rulers of Benin.

Soon after his accession in 1888, Ovonramwen addressed himself to the problem of maintaining internal stability by suppressing centres of disaffection and bringing to justice all persons found guilty of conspiracy against his accession. Many prominent chiefs like Obaraye, Obazelu and Eribo were executed in this first purge to rid the city of factions and dissident elements. Chief Uwangwe's special position as the Oba's favourite and as head of the senior palace association of *Iwebo* led to other palace chiefs of the association conspiring against him and finally murdering him in 1895 because they felt he had inspired Ovonramwen's bold stroke against the chiefs. This political murder led to an enquiry and a second purge resulted in the execution of Erasoyen, Obaduagbon and others who were either accomplices or directly responsible for the murder. The execution of many nobles in Benin indicated that Ovonramwen was determined to rule as a king, was determined to be respected, and was intolerant of saboteurs and rebels.

The Oba also sent the traditional chalk to outlying areas under his authority and none preferred hostility to peace. The liquidation of opposition in Benin City probably had the indirect effect of keeping subordinate areas quiet for some time after Ovonramwen's accession. The only recorded disaffection in the early years of Ovonramwen's reign was from Akure where the Deji in about 1889 attempted to make ceremonial state swords without reference to and sanction from Benin. The Oba sent one of his warriors to Akure with an army to seize the forbidden swords, which he easily did.

When Agbor revolted against Benin control in 1896 Ovonramwen began collecting soldiers from various areas of his empire to build up a formidable army with which to overawe Agbor. To this end a camp was established at Obadan, according to Benin traditions, and ten thousand soldiers

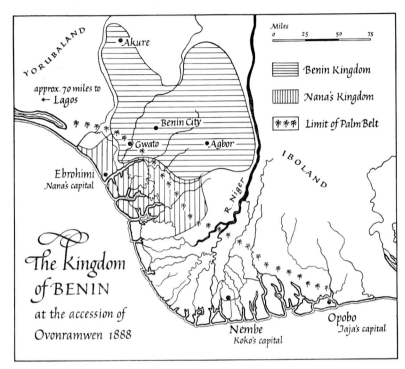

Miles
0   25   50   75

Benin Kingdom

Nana's Kingdom

Limit of Palm Belt

Y O R U B A L A N D

• Akure

approx. 70 miles to
← Lagos

Benin City

Gwato   • Agbor

Ebrohimi
Nana's capital

The Kingdom
of BENIN

at the accession of

Ovonramwen 1888

R. Niger

I B O L A N D

Opobo
Jaja's capital

Nembe
Koko's capital

gathered there for the Agbor campaign. However, the crushing of the people of Agbor had still not been carried out when the preparations were overtaken by the events of the massacre of the Europeans and the subsequent expedition of conquest.

It must be seen therefore that Oba Ovonramwen had a clear conception of his powers and a rigid determination to rule in the tradition of his ancestors. In ordinary circumstances he was not the man to surrender his independence willingly or to sign away his freedom to exercise his traditional powers.

Ovonramwen's commercial policy

In one other direction—that of commerce—Oba Ovonramwen consistently pursued the policy of his ancestors. It was the tragedy of Ovonramwen's position that although robbed by the treaty with Gallwey of the erstwhile traditional commercial monopoly of the kings of Benin (to be discussed later) he still tried to carry on the practices of his forbears, thus running against the commercial interests of the British whose opposition had been strengthened by that treaty. Even after the treaty, Ovonramwen continued to extract presents from the Itsekiri middlemen and to close the trade with them if the presents were withheld. It was his practice to keep up the royal monopoly in some products, such as palm kernels, on which he could still place some embargo. The Acting Consul-General of the Niger Coast Protectorate, J. R. Phillips, reported in November 1896 that Ovonramwen

> 'has permanently placed a "juju" on kernels, the most profitable product of the country . . . he has closed the markets and he has only occasionally consented to open them on receipt of presents from Jekri chiefs.'

In April the same year, the Oba had stopped all trade with the middlemen, and the Itsekiri chiefs, on the advice of Consul-General Moor, sent him a present worth forty pounds which was contemptuously refused as insufficient. It was only accepted after it had been doubled.

Under Ovonramwen, the traditional method of dealing with the middlemen was pursued. There were constant quarrels between the Itsekiri traders and the Benin and Urhobo oil producers over the issue of credit facilities and arrangements. The Oba gave as his reason for the constant closure of markets the incessant complaints by his people that the Itsekiri traders were cheating them. The Oba's agents often taxed these middlemen heavily and they ran the risk of having their goods confiscated if they refused to pay. Had the Acting Consul-General not intervened, the Itsekiri traders would have acceded to the Oba's demands for one thousand corrugated iron sheets for the roofing of his palace as a condition for opening the closed markets in 1896. The British did not, of course, understand the Oba's attitude to the closure of markets.

When in 1896 a Lagos trader, on the orders of Consul-General Moor and with gifts worth about thirty pounds went to persuade Ovonramwen to start a rubber industry because rubber was so plentiful in the Benin forests, the Oba ignored the request.

Apart from showing that Oba Ovonramwen had the trade of Benin with the middlemen well in hand in the tradition of his forbears, his restrictions on trade and demands for presents show him clearly as one who did not accept any limitations to his commercial authority. The Oba still permitted the activities of the trading associations of which he was the patron and the virility of these trading associations was not lost till well after the conquest of Benin by the British. Under Ovonramwen, Benin's pattern of trade still remained as it had been for centuries. Trade in some products was organised under royal monopoly and was carried on with the Itsekiri middlemen who, as well as trading under the aegis of associations made up largely of the higher palace nobility, had direct contact with the Europeans. The Oba was still in the habit of closing trade at will to the middlemen and this made trading difficult for the Europeans on the coast. The clash between the Bini and the British centred upon the issue of who—the British Consul or the Oba—would control the trade of Benin.

The pneumatic tyre and Benin

Oba Ovonramwen was pursuing a rigidly controlled economic policy at a time when the pressure of industrial and economic needs in Europe heightened by commercial rivalries, colonial agitation and international competition along the Bights of Benin and Biafra were making it necessary for Britain to make a push from the coast into the interior and to adopt a bold forward policy. It was the era of increased competition for colonial acquisitions and Germany and France were speeding up their struggle for new territories. In these circumstances African potentates like Oba Ovon- ramwen who refused to surrender their power to British officials were doomed by the economic imperialism of late Victorian England to be swept into war.

It was during this period that an event which was to have momentous consequences for Benin occurred in Britain. This was the invention of the pneumatic tyre by the Scottish surgeon and inventor, J. B. Dunlop. He constructed a pneumatic tyre for his child in 1887 and after being tested, it was patented on December 7, 1888—the year of Ovonramwen's accession. The production of the pneumatic tyre on a commercial scale, first for the use of bicycles and later for cars, in turn stimulated the demand for crude rubber and the desire to penetrate tropical forests, like that of Benin, which abounded in large quantities of rubber-producing trees. This increased the British urge to get into contact with the Oba of Benin and so gain access to areas and forests under his control. People like Chamberlain, the Colonial Secretary in Lord Salisbury's Government, began speaking of colonies as 'undeveloped estates' and sent out despatches to governors requesting information on the products available in their colonies. These goings-on at the Colonial Office were bound to influence the men at the Foreign Office who were in charge of the Niger Coast Protectorate.

The early consular activities which were mainly confined to the coast began to take on the more aggressive appearance of forcible penetration inland in the 1880s. Consuls Hewett, Blair and Annesley attempted to visit Benin in 1884, 1885 and 1890 respectively. It is no wonder then that as Vice-Consul on the Benin River in 1891, Gallwey prepared to visit Benin in 1892 after spending the previous year making exploratory journeys along the creeks, the Benin River tributaries and into the interior Urhobo markets.

Gallwey seeks fame

Vice-Consul Gallwey decided to visit Benin in 1892 possibly to make the Oba understand the extent of British interests, and his visit was signifi- cant in more ways than one. It was the first official visit since Burton's of 1862 and was a harbinger of the events which finally brought Ovonramwen to defeat and deportation. Secondly, Gallwey apparently succeeded where Hewett, Blair and Annesley had failed. Thirdly, Gallwey pushed through a treaty whose opening article claims that it was signed at the request of the king of Benin and that the Government of Her Britannic Majesty was merely complying with Ovonramwen's wishes! By this treaty the Oba signed away his freedom and independence and granted freedom of trade to all foreigners within his territories.

The kindest thing that can be said about Gallwey is that he was naïve, the most honest is that he was deceitful. The Oba of Benin did not request the treaty and neither he nor his chiefs would have signed it had its clauses been faithfully explained to them. For the Oba to have willingly signed away his freedom and independence and for him to have granted freedom of trade to all foreigners within his territories against the practice which he had inherited is inconceivable. In Bini eyes it would have amounted to a reckless abdication of his responsibilities. The treaty was a huge success for Gallwey and the cause which he represented. By the treaty, he had provided Britain with the legal grounds for subsequently holding Oba Ovonramwen accountable for practices which were adjudged obstructionist and hostile to British commerce and the policy of penetration into the interior of the country.

The treaty did not mention anything about human sacrifices or bloody customs, except in so far as these may, by some wonderful stretch of the imagination, have been vaguely implied in the last part of article five which mentions the Oba's agreement to cooperate with British officials in the interest of 'order, good government, and general progress of civilisation'. Despite the bogus treaty Benin's economic policy remained as it had been. Gradually the British began to shift their emphasis from their own commercial ambitions to the fetish practices of the Oba about which the treaty had been silent. This shift was partly due to the greater emotional appeal of such things as human sacrifice over commercial exploitation and partly to discredit the Oba who stood in the way of exploitation. The Consul-General, Macdonald, wrote about the rich products of the Benin forests, access to which was blocked by the Oba's 'fetish rule'. Moor, his successor, also hated the form of government in Benin because of its effects on British trade. From 1892 onwards, consular officials began making persistent reports of the 'unsatisfactory state of affairs in the king of Benin's dominions', and there was talk as early as 1895 of the need for a punitive expedition.

The demand for blood

While consuls were making persistent efforts to make the Oba live up to the treaty of 1892, the traders were egging them on to take firmer action against him. Traders such as James Pinnock, the Miller Brothers, Bey and Zimmer and representatives of the Imperial African Association persistently complained against Ovonramwen's stoppage of trade. Moor's despatches, at the instance of the traders, began to take on a belligerent note saying that force would be necessary if peaceful means failed to make Oba Ovonramwen amenable. By the middle of 1896 the constant attempts by consular officials to get in touch with Oba Ovonramwen, the vociferous clamour of the traders for consular action against the adamant Benin ruler, the Foreign Office demands for reports on steps being taken in the Protectorate to go into the interior, and the advocacy of the use of force by successive consul-generals, all pointed to an imminent clash.

It was at this juncture that James Phillips took over the duties of Acting Commissioner and Consul-General of the Niger Coast Protectorate. After reviewing the whole situation on the Benin river and listening to aggrieved Itsekiri traders on developments leading to the stoppage of trade in the middle of 1896, Phillips came to the conclusion that force must be used against Ovonramwen. The Foreign Office ultimately vetoed the decision to send an armed expedition in 1896 owing to lack of sufficient troops but Phillips did not wait for this decision. He hurriedly set out for Benin, completely disregarding the remonstrances of the Itsekiri traders, the advice of Chief Dogho, the Oba's refusal to see him and the traditions and susceptibilities of the Benin people.

Trespassers and spies

Why against all advice did Phillips set out for Benin? Firstly, the Oba's defiance was lowering the prestige of the protectorate government. Secondly, Phillips feared the Foreign Office would refuse to use force and he decided to go on a spying mission as he was convinced that force must ultimately be employed. Thirdly, he desired to advance his career and thought he would receive commendation if he could persuade the Oba to adopt a policy of free trade. Lastly, Phillips was arrogant and had a low opinion of the martial qualities of the people of Benin. Thus on January 2, 1897, Phillips and his armed party set out on a spying mission, violated the sovereignty of the kingdom of Benin by crossing its frontiers without permission and arrogantly ignored repeated warnings, even pleadings, by the Oba's messengers.

No nation with any pride could accept such provocation. Since Phillips was determined to ignore the rules of behaviour which govern the relations between civilised nations, he and most of his pary were wiped out on January 4 on the Gwato-Benin road by a troop of Bini soldiers. A few African porters and two Europeans escaped. Since the bloody reputation of the Bini was later to be exaggerated it may be necessary to say that one of the escaped Europeans reported a certain reluctance on the part of some of the soldiers to carry out their duty.

By this time the kingdom of Benin was in a state of high tension. British pressure on the kingdom had been mounting since the Gallwey treaty of 1892 and after the British had attacked and exiled Nana in 1894 the Bini had constantly expected the 'whiteman's war'. They did not believe that Phillip's party was unarmed as it was pretending to be and they suspected that the boxes carried by the party contained things 'with which to catch the king'. They were right, since Phillips issued revolvers to members of the party but ordered that they were to be kept hidden. It is unthinkable that the Bini did not know this and the secrecy of the action suggests a plan of deception. As the Oba's excited messengers returned to Benin to report the steady advance of Phillips and his men the atmosphere in the capital must have been building up to an explosive point when the news came of the death of Phillips.

Blood and fire

The relief was short for almost immediately the British began preparations for the invasion of the kingdom. A month later the British mounted a three-pronged attack—through Ologobo creek, the Jamieson river and Gwato Creek—which aimed not only to destroy Benin but also to create an impression of British might and to strike fear into peoples for hundreds of miles around. Benin City fell to the invaders on February 17, 1897. On that day the proud kingdom of Benin lost its independence, its

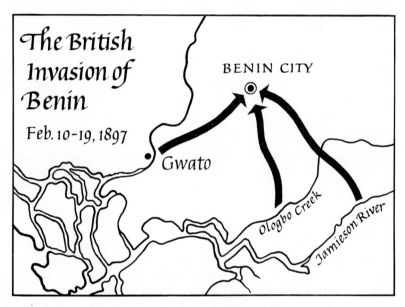

sovereignty, its Oba, its control of trade and its ancient pride. Benin was humbled in a manner experienced by few others in the area later known as Nigeria.

Benin, 'the City of Blood', got its reputation from the eye-witness accounts produced by individuals in the conquering army of 1897. In Benin slaves were sacrificed when there appeared a need to appease the gods to avert national danger. Sacrifices might take place in periods of famine, excessive drought or rain and on the anniversary of the Oba's father's death or at the death of the reigning Oba. Many rites required the sacrifice of animals; only a handful of nobles and the Oba were permitted to make human sacrifice. Under normal conditions the freeborn were buried and the corpses of slaves were placed in unoccupied bush. Thus neither was all the blood in Benin human, nor were all the skeletons those of sacrificial victims. Certainly there was no truth in Commander Bacon's assertion that 'every person who was able indulged in a human sacrifice...'

Sacrifices were made to appease the gods when there was a threat of national calamity. In February 1897 the kingdom of Benin was facing the greatest national disaster of its history. There are few calamities more degrading to a nation than defeat and foreign subjugation. Because of the overwhelming military superiority of the invaders only the gods could save Benin but despite the sacrifices, the gods would neither be appeased nor lend their assistance.

The city fell to looters and trophy-hunters. The ivory at the Oba's palace was eagerly seized. Nearly 2,500 of the now famous Benin bronzes plus other valuable works of art such as the magnificent carved doors of the palace were carried back to Europe for sale, so that today almost every museum in the world possesses art treasures from Benin. Once they had stripped it of its treasures the invaders set the city ablaze.

The trial of Ovonramwen

After months in hiding, Ovonramwen appeared in Benin City on August 6, 1897. The trial of the Oba and chiefs began on September 1st under the newly-formed Council of Chiefs presided over by Ralph Moor, with Captains Roupell and Carter in attendance. Moor claimed that the trial for the murder of Phillips and his companion should be under African law and custom. There was no Bini law or custom which made white foreigners chiefs but Moor asked the council to give the perpetrators of the massacre the traditional punishment for those who had killed chiefs. The trial was a sham because as the despatches show the chiefs had been presumed guilty long before the trial. Even before asking the Benin chiefs for their verdict, Moor summed up by saying that the chiefs were murderers and should be killed without arms as they had killed the unarmed(?) white men. The evidence pointed to the Oba's innocence. Perhaps the witnesses tried to save the Oba but it would appear that the events leading to the massacre show that just before the British invasion the influence of the Oba was declining and the power of the chiefs was increasing. Of the six chiefs held responsible for the massacre of Phillips—Ologboshere, Obadesagbon, Obayuwana, Usu and Iguobasoyemi—only three were publicly executed. The others committed suicide.

Ovonramwen was deposed, deported and exiled forever on September 13, 1897. From his home of exile in Calabar, he attempted to maintain touch with his people but was checked by the British officers. All efforts to get him returned to Benin failed, even after Nana's return from exile in 1906. Ovonramwen became seriously ill on January 9, 1914 and died on the 13th in Calabar.

Ovonramwen fell, not because of the human sacrifices in his kingdom but because of factors which were mainly economic. His fall was the inevitable result of a clash implicit in his policy of attempting to confine the

Altar to Ovonramwen

Europeans to the coast at a time when they were determined to go into the hinterland. Ovonramwen fell for the same reasons as other great African rulers of the late nineteenth century who resisted the determined thrust of the white man who was resolved to take over the political and economic control of the African interior—Jaja of Opobo in 1887, Nana the Itsekiri in 1894, Koko of Nembe in 1895 and Prempeh of Ashanti in 1896. The Oba fell in defence of his inherited traditions.

Consequences

The capture of Benin opened the way for British military occupation and the subsequent conquest of adjoining areas. Benin became merged into a wider political unit under British administration, the Niger Coast Protectorate, then into the protectorate of Southern Nigeria and finally into the colony and protectorate of Nigeria. Economically the fall of Benin opened up its forests to British exploitation. Trade expanded, although the largest part of the new wealth fell into foreign not Bini hands. Subjection paved the way for what the British liked to call 'civilising influences' but there was no stampede—as in some areas of Africa—for the white man's gadgets, his gods, his schools or his top hat and khaki shorts. With the throne vacant the nation no longer existed as an entity. After Ovonramwen's death the British came to realise that if they were to secure even the grudging co-operation of the Bini they must restore the monarchy. Thus the fall of Ovonramwen did not mean the collapse of the monarchy which still today commands respect and affection. Despite the prolonged imperial effort to hold up nineteenth-century Benin and its Obas—especially Ovonramwen—as an example of the failure of African leadership, the people of Benin still look back with pride upon their achievements in the era which ended with Ovonramwen in 1897.

Note

The Oba's court in Benin. The illustration on page 176 shows an artist's impression of a possible court scene during the reign of Oba Ovonramwen.

The Oba is seated on a slightly raised platform and on either side of him stand two senior chiefs. Also on the platform is a water jug in the shape of a ram, and near the ram, but not on the platform, are two decorated urns.

In front of the Oba is a boy carrying the state sword.

To the right of the platform are the Oba's servants and behind them stands a palm oil lamp which may be as much as 20 feet high.

To the right of the picture, standing level with the state sword bearer is a horn blower, and in front of him are the old warriors. These men are holding shields, and each one should be accompanied by a small boy carrying the warrior's kola-nut box. In this illustration there is only room for one of these small boys to be shown.

In front of the old warriors stand the young warriors.

On the left of the picture are the dancers and the drummers.

The Oba's court in Benin. An artist's reconstruction following the style of Benin Art. (See the note on this illustration on page 175.)

Further Reading

ABDALLAH BIN HEMEDI L'AJJEMY, *Habari za Wakilindi*, English translation edited by J. W. T. Allen and published as *The Kilindi* by the East African Literature Bureau, 1963.

ABDEL QADIR in *Encyclopaedia of Islam*.

ALAGOA, E. J., *The Small Brass City-State*, Wisconsin and Ibadan, 1964.

——*The Akassa Raid 1865*, Ibadan, 1960

ANENE J., and BROWN, G., *African History Handbook for Teachers and Students*, Ibadan University Press and Nelsons, 1965.

BARBOUR, N. (Ed.), *A Survey of North West Africa*, O.U.P., 1959.

BEATTIE, J., *Bunyoro: An African Kingdom*, New York, 1960.

BINNS, C. J., *The Last Zulu King, Life and Death of Cetshwayo*, Longman, 1963.

BLUNT, W., *Desert Hawk*, London, 1947.

BROWN, R., 'The Ndebele Succession Crisis' in *Historians in Tropical Africa*, Salisbury, 1962.

BROWN R., and STOKES, E., *The Zambesian Past*, Manchester, 1966.

CHURCHILL, COLONEL, *The Life of Abdel Kader*, London, 1867.

CROWDER, M., *The Story of Nigeria*, London, revised paperback, 1966.

COUPLAND, R., *East Africa and its Invaders*, Oxford, 1938.

DARK, P. J. C., *Benin Art*, Hamlyn, London, 1960.

DUNBAR, A. R., *Omukama Cwa II, Kabarega*, East Africa Literature Bureau, Nairobi, 1966.

——*A History of Bunyoro-Kitara*, East African Publishing House, 1969 (second edition).

EDELI, T. C., 'Oba Overami of Benin' in *Eminent Nigerians of the Nineteenth Century*, Cambridge, 1960.

EGHAREVBA, J. U., *A Short History of Benin*, Ibadan, 1960.

EKEMODE, G. O., *The Kilindi Kingdom of Vuga 1725–1890*, M.A. thesis, University of Ghana, 1966.

FLINT, J. E., *Sir George Goldie and the Making of Nigeria*, London, 1960.

GLUCKMAN, M., 'The Zulu Kingdom', in M. Fortes and E. Evans-Pritchard, *African Political Systems*, O.U.P., 1940 (Teachers' reference).

GOLLOCK, G., 'Sir Apolo Kagwa' in *Sons of Africa*, New York, 1928, pp. 107–121.

GRAY, J. M., 'Zanzibar and the Coast, 1840–1844, in R. A. OLIVER, and A. G. MATTHEW, *History of East Africa*, Vol. I, 1963.

——*The Gambia*, Oxford, 1940.

HOLE, H. M., *The Passing of the Black Kings*, Philip Allan, 1932.

IGBAFE, P., 'British Rule in Benin 1897–1920: Direct or Indirect?' *Journal of the Historical Society of Nigeria*, iii, 4, 1967.

IKIME, O., 'Nana Olomu: Governor of the Benin River', *Tarikh*, i, 2, 1966

INGHAM, K., *A History of East Africa*, Longman, 1963, pp. 143–159, 183–186, 305–308.

JONES A., and MONROE, E., *A Short History of Ethiopia*, Oxford, 1962.

KIWANUKA, M. S. M., 'The Empire of Bunyoro-Kitara: Myth or Reality,' *Makerere History Papers*, No. 1, Longman, 1968.

——*A History of Buganda from the Foundation of the Kingdom to 1900*, Longman, 1971.

LEGASSICK, M., 'Firearms, Horses and Samorian Army Organisation 1870–98', *Journal of African History*, vii, 1, 1966, pp. 95–115.

MARSH, Z., and KINGSWORTH, G. W., *An Introduction to the History of East Africa*, Cambridge, 1963, pp. 115–147.

MASON, P., *The Birth of a Dilemma*, Oxford, 1958.

NYAKATURA, J., *Kings of Bunyoro-Kitara*, translated by T. Muganwa and edited by G. N. Uzoigwe, Uganda Publishing House, 1970.

OGIERIAIKHI, E., *Oba Ovonramwen*, University of London Press, 1966.

OLIVER, R., *The Missionary Factor in East Africa*, Longman, 1952, pp. 128–149.

OMER-COOPER, J., 'The Mfecane and the Great Trek' in J. Anene and G. Brown, *African History Handbook for Teachers and Students*, Ibadan University Press and Nelsons, 1965.

——*The Zulu Aftermath*, Longman, 1966.

——*The Mfecane, a Nineteenth Century Revolution in Bantu Africa*, Longman, December 1965.

PANKHURST, R., 'Menelik and the Foundation of Addis Ababa,' *Journal of African History*, ii, 1, 1961.

——'The Independence of Ethiopia and Her Importation of Arms in the Nineteenth Century,' iv-v, *Présence Africaine*, English edition, June-Sept., 1960.

PERHAM, M., (ed), 'The Story of Ndansi Kumalo of The Matabele' in *Ten Africans*, Faber, sec. ed., 1963.

QUINN, C., *Traditionalism, Islam and European Expansion: The Gambia 1850–1890* (Unpublished Ph.D. Thesis, University of California, Los Angeles, 1967).

—— *Mandingo Kingdoms of the Senegambia*, Northwestern University Press, 1972.

RITTER, E. A., *Shaka Zulu, The Rise of the Zulu Empire*, Longman, 1955. (A simplified edition of this book is also available for junior classes.)

RIVLIN, H., *The Agricultural Policy of Muhammad Ali*, Cambridge, Mass., 1961.

ROSCOE, J., *The Bunyoro of Bakitara*, Cambridge, 1923.

SANDERSON, G., The Foreign Policy of Negus Menelik, 1896–8, *Journal of African History*, v, 1, 1964.

STEWART, D., 'Mehemet Ali, Pasha of Egypt', *History Today*, May 1958.

TIGNOR, R., *Modernisation and British Colonial Rule in Egypt, 1882–1914*, Princeton, 1966.

TIGNOR R., and COLLINS, R., *A History of Egypt and the Sudan*, Prentice-Hall, 1967.

TORDOFF, W., 'Relations Between Samory and King Prempeh I of Ashanti', *Ghana Notes and Queries*, No. 3, September-December 1961.

TYLDEN, G., *The Rise of the Basuto*, Cape Town and Johannesburg, 1950.

WALKER, E., 'Moshesh and Waterboer 1854–1870' in *A History of Southern Africa*, Longman, 1957, pp. 270–327.

WINANS, E. V., *Shambala: The Constitution of a Traditional State*, California, 1962.

WRIGHT, M., *Buganda in the Heroic Age*, O.U.P., 1971.